Campaigns on the Cutting Edge

Campaigns on the Cutting Edge

Second Edition

Edited by

Richard J. Semiatin
American University

Los Angeles | London | New Delhi
Singapore | Washington DC

Los Angeles | London | New Delhi
Singapore | Washington DC

For information:

CQ Press
An Imprint of SAGE Publications, Inc.
2455 Teller Road
Thousand Oaks, California 91320
E-mail: order@sagepub.com

SAGE Publications Ltd.
1 Oliver's Yard
55 City Road
London, EC1Y 1SP
United Kingdom

SAGE Publications India Pvt. Ltd.
B 1/I 1 Mohan Cooperative Industrial Area
Mathura Road, New Delhi 110 044
India

SAGE Publications Asia-Pacific Pte. Ltd.
3 Church Street
#10-04 Samsung Hub
Singapore 049483

Printed in the United States of America

Library of Congress Cataloging-in-Publication Data

Campaigns on the cutting edge / edited by Richard J. Semiatin.
—2nd ed.

p. cm.
ISBN 978-1-4522-0284-6 (alk. paper)

1. Political campaigns—United States—History—21st century.
2. Elections—United States—History—21st century. 3. United
States—Politics and government—21st century. I. Semiatin,
Richard J.

JK2281.C37 2012
324.70973—dc23 2011051835

This book is printed on acid-free paper.

Acquisitions Editor: Charisse Kiino
Production Editor: Brittany Bauhaus
Copy Editor: Melinda Masson
Typesetter: C&M Digitals (P) Ltd.
Proofreader: Inge Lockwood
Indexer: Wendy Allex
Cover Designer: Mike Pottman, M Design & Print
Marketing Manager: Christopher O'Brien

MIX
Paper from responsible sources
FSC
www.fsc.org **FSC® C014174**

12 13 14 15 16 10 9 8 7 6 5 4 3 2 1

To our families and friends,

to whom we owe so much

Contents

PREFACE   xi

CONTRIBUTORS   XIII

PART I: THE NEW POLITICAL CAMPAIGN   1

RICHARD J. SEMIATIN

1. Introduction – Campaigns on the Cutting Edge   3

Campaigns are becoming more individualized, and tailored to you, the
voter. They are also becoming more mobile to adapt to changes in the
political environment.

ROBERT G. BOATRIGHT

2. Fundraising – Continuity and Change   11

The standard practices of fundraising are still with us, and likely always
will be. Yet innovations in the use of social media and changes in the legal
treatment of campaign spending have made it necessary to rethink some
of the lessons of the 2008 election.

TAD DEVINE

3. Paid Media—In an Era of Rapid and Revolutionary Change   28

Political advertisers, however, must still reach that enormous segment
of voters who are less involved than activists. For the foreseeable future,
the most powerful way to reach those voters is through television
advertising. Television is still the king of media.

MICHAEL TURK

4. Social and New Media – An Evolving Future   48

Campaigns can spend less time and money trying to attract supporters
and more time working with supporters on centralized platforms to build
networks of people to carry their message. With open platforms connected
to millions of voters, the possibilities are almost endless.

CANDICE J. NELSON

5. Polling in the Twenty-First Century – Part Past, Part Future   65

*Five years ago landline phone surveys seemed to be headed to extinction,
yet remain the most prominent way surveys are conducted by political
campaigns. The problems of cell phone and Internet surveys that existed
five years ago still remain today, so their use in campaigns has not increased
as quickly as might have been predicted.*

RICHARD J. SEMIATIN

6. Voter Mobilization – Into the Future   81

*Understanding how to mobilize voters in the future means understanding
what each potential voter wants.*

**PART II: THE EVOLVING CAMPAIGN—ADAPTATION BY POLITICAL
INSTITUTIONS AND GROUPS**   101

TARI RENNER

7. Political Parties – Beyond Revitalization   103

*The national party organizations have dramatically increased their role
in candidate recruitment, fundraising, targeting of campaigns,
communication, and get-out-the-vote (GOTV) operations. They have adapted
to, and even thrived, in an era of changing campaign technologies.*

NINA THERESE KASNIUNAS AND MARK J. ROZELL

8. Interest Groups and the Future of Campaigns   121

*As we prepare for the 2012 elections, it is clear that interest groups
will have a larger and more pervasive influence on campaigns than
ever before.*

JOSEPH GRAF AND JEREMY D. MAYER

9. Campaign Press Coverage—Instantaneous   138

*The Internet has opened up American politics to a new set of players
without discarding the old power structure.*

PETER L. FRANCIA, WESLEY JOE, AND CLYDE WILCOX

10. Campaign Finance Reform in the Post–*Citizens United* Era   157

The Citizens United *court decision in 2010 has had the effect of allowing
corporations, unions, and associations to expressly advocate for the election
or defeat of a candidate. The decision has far-reaching consequences that
allow for greater spending in elections without disclosing the sources of
who contributes for these new activities.*

JEFFREY CROUCH

11. Redistricting – The Shift Toward South and West Continues 177

In 2012, the apportionment of congressional seats following the 2010 census will reflect the continuing shift of Americans from the Northeast and Midwest to the South and West that began in the late 1940s and early 1950s.

SUSAN A. MACMANUS

WITH RENEE DABBS AND MARY L. MOSS

12. Women and Campaigns – Growing Female Activism From the Grass Roots to the Top 193

Path-breaking women candidates such as Hillary Clinton and Sarah Palin have benefitted from the growing female political activism— voters, party activists, campaign strategists, and media consultants. But because of their gender, each has been subjected at times to an overemphasis on style rather than substance, much to their chagrin.

ATIYA KAI STOKES-BROWN

13. Minority Candidates and the Changing Landscape of Campaigns in the Twenty-First Century 211

The development and adoption of new technologies can facilitate the mainstreaming of minority candidates, enabling them to transcend their minority status and reducing the likelihood that their candidacies will be marginalized.

DICK SIMPSON

14. New Political Campaigns and Democracy 226

The nation needs an aware and informed electorate that will elect candidates who use new campaign techniques to increase democracy and to defeat those who would subvert it.

INDEX 241

Preface

Ever since the last edition of *Campaigns on the Cutting Edge*, the speed of politics has increased at an unprecedented rate. It's hard to believe that the hand-held smartphone has more power in it than a personal computer did just twenty years ago. In fact, the Internet is now a middle-age technology. The frontier described as new in the last edition is no longer new but it is an ever-expanding frontier as the virtual media used to reach voters make campaigning more mobile. No longer is video communication or online communication in a fixed place; rather, it is portable. And given the short attention span so many people have online, communicating messages more simply and effectively is a necessity. But still, the effectiveness and appeal of online media can be oversold. The millions of paid staff and volunteers who knocked on doors to get out the vote for the Obama campaign in 2008 and the tens of thousands on behalf of the Tea Party in 2010 demonstrate the remarkable resilience of personal campaigning. Personal outreach is still the most effective communications device for any campaign. In the end, people crave the human contact and interaction that politics has always been about.

The personal campaign politics that dominate the first presidential precinct caucus (Iowa) and presidential primary (New Hampshire) remain critical for Republicans—just ask former Massachusetts governor Mitt Romney who ran for the Republican nomination for president in 2008 and is doing so again in 2012. However, with the Internet and responsive media, major campaigns for national political office are virtually or actually alive 24 hours per day. The pressure on candidates, consultants, campaign organizations, political parties, interest groups, and the press is unceasing. The election cycle for presidential races is now two years and for major senate races, in many cases, 36 months. Books and articles have been written on the permanent campaign. Today, we have the *ever-present* campaign—that is both exciting and challenging to both the campaign consultant and the arm-chair political analyst.

The book you are about to read captures the transformation that is taking place in campaigns today and where they are headed in the future. The book's scope goes beyond the 2012 election and looks toward the next decade of campaign politics.

The authors are asked to make informed speculations on the next wave of political change so that the book remains as relevant in 2014 or 2016 as it is today. These authors are not only skilled political scientists, but also participants—including Tad Devine (media consultant and chief strategist for Al Gore), Michael Turk (Online director for Bush-Cheney 2004), Tari Renner (congressional candidate 2004) and Dick Simpson (congressional candidate 1992 and 1994). Most others have lived and worked in the cauldron of Washington, D.C., politics and policy or in states with national political significance. The book is written to give students, faculty, and political observers a keen sense of the reality of national political campaigns from an insider's perspective. In that light, the book is written without a lot of jargon.

We cannot account for all changes that may take place over the next five or ten years, but we look through the lens of contemporary politics to see what cutting-edge changes are on the horizon. The import of what those changes may mean is expressed eloquently in the book's conclusion on the implications for the democratic process.

I would like to thank my colleagues who have written chapters for this manuscript; and a special welcome to our new authors, Atiya Kai Stokes-Brown, Jeffrey Crouch, Susan MacManus, and Michael Turk. The contributors to this volume have written and edited scores of scholarly books. Thus, it was a great honor to work with such a group of thoughtful and active scholars.

I would like to thank reviewers of the first edition for their excellent suggestions for the second edition revisions: Ralph J. Begleiter, University of Delaware; Blaine Garvin, Gonzaga University; Ryan Lee Teten, University of Louisiana; Brian Vargus, Indiana University-Purdue University Indianapolis; and David L. Welch, Indiana University. I'd also like to thank the editors and staff at CQ for their help and support. I would like to thank Charisse Kiino for another wonderful job providing overall direction for the project and shepherding the manuscript. She spent a lot of time with me on the project and I appreciate it. Brenda Carter deserves many thanks for giving the go-ahead to the second edition. Nancy Loh, who serves as Charisse's right hand, was very helpful in providing help with many logistic aspects of the project. Elizabeth Kline and Brittany Bauhaus did a superior job managing the production process, and Melissa Masson did superb work copyediting the manuscript in the writers' voices.

And to repeat myself from the first edition, I would like to thank my good friend Max Cleland, who is one of the most kind-hearted, thoughtful, and inspirational people you will ever meet. A special thank you to my students, especially the wonderful ones, from whom I have learned from—just because someone is twenty, does not mean they cannot teach you. Finally, I want to thank my wonderful parents, siblings, nephews and nieces for putting up with me for the last half century. What a wonderful family I have and what an honor it is to be one of them. Now, I want to welcome the reader into the contemporary and future world of campaigns—it's exciting and provocative.

Contributors

About the Editor

Richard J. Semiatin, American University, Academic Director and Assistant Professor of Government, is a current faculty member of the Washington Semester Program where he has served for over 20 years. Semiatin specializes in campaigns and elections. He is also the author of *Campaigns in the 21st Century* (2005), five monographs on elections, one monograph on impeachment and trial, book chapters, and articles. He was selected by the Carnegie Foundation for the Advancement of Teaching to participate in its Political Engagement Project (PEP). He received his BA from Connecticut College and PhD from American University.

About the Contributors

Robert G. Boatright is an associate professor of political science at Clark University. He is the author of Interest Groups and Campaign Finance Reform in the United States and Canada (University of Michigan Press, 2011), and Expressive Politics: Issues Strategies of Congressional Challengers (Ohio State University Press, 2004). He has published articles on interest group activities in campaigns, campaign finance, and congressional elections, and he is currently finishing a book on congressional primary challenges.

Jeffrey Crouch is an assistant professor of American politics at American University. He is the Reviews and Book Editor for *Congress & the Presidency* journal, and his first book, *The Presidential Pardon Power,* was published by the University Press of Kansas in 2009. His research focuses primarily on the Constitution, the presidency, and the separation of powers.

Thomas A. (Tad) Devine is a Democratic media consultant who has produced political ads for candidates in the United States and around the world. He is president of Devine Mulvey, a media and strategic consulting firm in Washington, D.C. He has created media in twenty winning U.S. Senate and Gubernatorial campaigns. Tad has also worked on dozens of winning races for the U.S. House of Representatives and local elected officials. He has extensive experience at the highest levels of U.S. presidential campaigns and has worked on ten winning campaigns for president or prime minister outside the United States. Devine has taught courses on campaigns and media at Boston University, The George Washington University Graduate School of Political Management, and in 2011 as a Resident Fellow at The Institute of Politics at Harvard University's Kennedy School of Government. In October 2010, Tad Devine was recognized as one of "the most respected media consultants" in the nation by *USA Today.*

Peter L. Francia is associate professor of political science at East Carolina University. He is co-author (with John C. Green, Paul S. Herrnson, Lynda W. Powell, and Clyde Wilcox) of *The Financiers of Congressional Elections: Investors, Ideologues, and Intimates* (2003) and author of *The Future of Organized Labor in American Politics* (2006). His most recent work includes (with Burdett A. Loomis and Dara Z. Strolovitch) *Guide to Interest Groups and Lobbying in the United States* (2011) and (with Jody C. Baumgartner) *Conventional Wisdom and American Elections: Exploding Myths, Exploring Misconceptions,* 2nd ed. (2010).

Joseph Graf is an assistant professor in the School of Communication at American University. He has published extensively in the areas of political communication and online politics and his work is focused on the intersection of civic involvement and new media technology. Graf is the former research director for the Institute for Politics, Democracy and the Internet, which promotes Internet politics to improve civic engagement. He has been a visiting professor at The George Washington University, and began his career as a newspaper reporter in Wisconsin and Pennsylvania.

Wesley Joe is an adjunct assistant professor of government at Georgetown University in Washington, DC. He is formerly the Director of Research for the Campaign Finance Institute, a nonpartisan think tank that is affiliated with The George Washington University.

Nina Therese Kasniunas (PhD, Loyola University Chicago) is an assistant professor of political science at Goucher College. Her research focuses on interest groups and the legislative process as well as the pedagogy of political science. Publications include *Campaign Rules: A 50 State Guide to Campaigns and Elections* with Dan Shea and articles on using Supreme Court oral argument re-enactments in the classroom. Current research projects include examining the impact of active learning strategies on civic engagement and the influence of interest groups in congressional committees.

Susan A. MacManus, who received her MA from the University of Michigan and PhD from Florida State University, is a Distinguished University Professor at the University of South Florida in the Department of Government and International Affairs. For the last six election cycles, she has served as political analyst for WFLA NewsChannel 8 (Tampa NBC affiliate).Since 2008, she has been a featured columnist on sayfiereview.com—a widely-read Florida-based political website. MacManus is the co-author of *Politics in States and Communities,* 14th ed., with Thomas R. Dye (2012), Florida's Politics, 3rd ed., with Aubrey Jewett, Thomas R. Dye, and David J. Bonanza (2011), and Florida's Politics: Ten Media Markets, One Powerful State with Kevin Hill and Dario Moreno (2004). She is also the author of Young v. Old: Generational Combat in the 21st Century? (1996), and Targeting Senior Voters (2004), along with numerous articles on women and minorities in politics.

Jeremy D. Mayer is an associate professor; and director, Master of Public Policy Program in the School of Public Policy at George Mason University. Most recently he is the co-author of *Closed Minds? Politics and Ideology in American Universities* (Brookings, 2008), co-editor of *Media Power, Media Politics, 2nd ed.* (Rowman and Littlefield, 2008), co-author of *Deconstructing Reagan: A Critical Analysis of Conservative Mythology* (2006), and the author of *American Media Politics in Transition* (McGraw Hill, 2006).

Candice J. Nelson is an associate professor of Government and academic director of the Campaign Management Institute at American University. Her most recent books are *Grant Park: The Democratization of Presidential Elections, 1968–2008* (2011) and *Campaigns and Elections American Style,* (3rd edition, 2009), co-edited with James Thurber. Nelson is a former American Political Science Association Congressional Fellow. She received her Ph.D. from the University of California at Berkeley.

Tari Renner is a professor of political science at Illinois Wesleyan University. He served as department chair from 1994 to 2008. Renner served three terms as an elected member of the McLean County (Bloomington area) legislature. In 2004, he was the Democratic nominee for U.S. Congress in Illinois' Eleventh Congressional District. His research interests include American electoral behavior and local government structures. Renner received his Ph.D. from American University in 1985.

Mark J. Rozell is professor of public policy at George Mason University and the co-author of the book "Interest Groups in American Campaigns: The New Face of Electioneering" (3rd edition, Oxford University Press).

Dick Simpson has uniquely combined a distinguished academic career with public service in government. He began his academic career in 1967 at the University of Illinois at Chicago, where he has taught for more than forty years and where he currently serves as department head and professor of political science. Simpson was alderman for Chicago's 44th ward and leader of the opposition bloc from 1971 to 1979. He ran for Congress in 1992 and 1994 against Congressman Dan Rostenkowsi. Simpson has published [more than ninety] numerous professional journal articles, magazine articles, book chapters, documentary films, and book reviews. He is the author and coauthor of [sixteen] books on political action, elections, ethics, and politics, including *Inside Urban Politics* (2004); *Rogues, Rebels, and Rubber Stamps* (2001); [and] *Winning Elections* (1996), *and Twenty-First Century Chicago (2012)*.

Atiya Kai Stokes-Brown is assistant professor of poltiical science at Bucknell University. Her research and teaching interests are in the areas of race, ethnicity, and gender and the politics of representation and identity in the U.S. Her work has appeared in several academic journals and in various edited volumes. Her most recent work includes a book titled The Politics of Race in Latino Communities: Walking the Color Line (Routledge, 2012).

Michael Turk has lived at the intersection of politics, public policy and technology—crossing from the political to the commercial and into government. Turk is a public affairs and media consultant who focuses on using converged media to tell client stories. Previously, Turk served as vice president of Industry Grassroots for the National Cable & Telecommunications Association, the trade association that represents America's largest broadband providers. He has managed Internet operations for three Presidential campaigns—Fred Thompson 2008, Bush-Cheney '04, and Quayle 2000. He served as the Republican National Committee's first eCampaign Director following the 2004 campaign.

Clyde Wilcox is professor of government at Georgetown University. He writes on interest groups, campaign finance, religion and politics, gender politics, and science fiction and politics.

Part I

The New Political Campaign

CHAPTER 1

Introduction—Campaigns on the Cutting Edge

Richard J. Semiatin

TEN YEARS AGO, who would have imagined that a 4.5-inch smartphone would give you information about the most arcane subject in a flash? Today, campaigns are similar to the rest of the real world—acquiring knowledge is an instantaneous proposition. That means thrusts and counterthrusts by campaign organizations, which were the product of deliberate thinking over hours or days or even months in the past, now have to be decided in minutes. The eighteen-month hurricane of perpetual motion we call the modern campaign is driven, in large part, by technology. All campaigns have become more mobile, which has meant that more campaign functions have been integrated together to enable greater efficiencies. Those efficiencies save the precious commodity of time at a pace so swift that it would have been unimagined in the mid-1800s. Back in that era, campaigning was much more laid back as it was conducted on the front porches of candidates, through speeches and through the press. But speed has a danger as well, because too rapid a response can fatally injure a candidacy because there isn't time for a candidate and staff to think things through before they react. For better or worse, this is the world of campaigns today. Just ask Mitt Romney, Rick Santorum, Newt Gingrich, and Ron Paul about pivoting and responding as each one tried to secure the Republican presidential nomination in 2012.

Mobility has enabled campaign managers to have desktop-powered computers in their hands. They are able to get information on demographics, polls, videos, e-mails, speeches, and memos, among other information, at their fingertips. However, that availability can come at a cost—for as quickly as information comes in, decisions can be made under pressure—sometimes without reflection. But on other occasions a lightning-fast response can preempt a damaging blow from an opponent.

Technology has enabled the functions of campaigns to become more *integrated.* The distinct lines between polling, advertising, and mobilizing have become blurred. Pollsters no longer act only as pollsters, and media consultants (both traditional and new media) no longer are simply message and ad makers. All work on research aspects of campaigns—inform staff what is important to glean from surveys to operationalize an effective message. And those running the voter mobilization efforts advise both the pollsters and the media consultants which messages and ads work best to get their candidate's voters out to the polls. These have all been aided by smartphones, tablets, and laptops—where polling information, ads, and demographic maps are at the fingertips of all the consultants working together on a campaign. Consultants work together to determine the best venue for disseminating that information. Problems can arise when the Internet consultant seeks to edit, for space and production, the ad maker's work. As a result, the division of labor in campaigns is less neat than in the past, and that could spell trouble for the campaign. For if the campaign manager allows those lines to become too blurred, turf fighting within a campaign can be all-consuming. We are seeing a greater *convergence* in how technology is used in fundraising, in paid advertising, in new/social media, in voter mobilization, and by the various groups who participate in the political process.

Campaigns are becoming more individualized and tailored to *you*, the voter. For the first 150 years, campaigns were largely the domain of party organizations. The birth of television and the advent of advertising spawned personality-driven campaigns. Today, we see the next revolution—that campaigns are attempting to reach each voter individually. The campaign of the future (and to some extent the future is now) can target each household. Campaigns used to be about parties and candidates. Increasingly, campaigns will become about *you*, the voter, or what Madison Avenue would call *you*, the customer. This book is neither a review of the political science literature nor a major discourse on the democratic implications of elections and campaigns, although that latter discussion remains valuable and important and is addressed in the book's conclusion. Instead, this new edition focuses on evaluating current trends and assesses how national campaigns are making cutting-edge changes for today and tomorrow. We look at those changes on the presidential, congressional, and gubernatorial level. Moreover, this edition brings in new cutting-edge discussions about redistricting, the role of women in politics, and the role of minorities in politics.

What is most interesting is that technological changes have greatly benefited campaigns in their new traditional efforts to get-out-the-vote. The door-to-door ground game of the Obama operation was referred to as an army. In Virginia alone, the campaign had seventy offices![1] Tens of thousands of Obama workers used shoe leather to contact millions of voters in what became the largest get-out-the-vote operation in history. Personal contact made a difference—something that the Tea Party understood and picked up on in the 2010 midterm elections.

As a result, the book explores the most important facets of campaigns (fundraising, paid advertising, new media, polling, and voter mobilization): the institutions that work in campaigns (parties and interest groups), report on campaigns (the press), and govern the process of campaigns (campaign finance and redistricting) and emerging groups that are part of the change (women and minorities). Given the pace of new technology entering the political arena, it is often difficult to ascertain every possible trend on the horizon—the tablet of today could be wafer or paper thin in the not-too-distant future. The chapters on redistricting, women, and minorities are new to this edition.

With power increasingly in the hands of us, the users, campaigns we passively watched on our living room televisions just twenty years ago are now in our hands through new technologies, especially the new wave of handheld devices that work as phones, computers, and personal assistants. We have greater control of how we receive information. However, that information coming to us can be manipulated for better or worse as explained in the conclusion. We do know that campaigns that fail to adapt to the new world of politics will not survive.

The New Political Campaign

The new political campaign demonstrates the importance of contact, communications, and feedback with voters. Part I, "The New Political Campaign," discusses the various facets of campaigns from raising money, to communicating through paid and new media, to surveying voters, to targeting messages to mobilize citizens to vote. Campaigns not only are incorporating new technological changes but also must make them work seamlessly with the techniques of the past. Chapters examine what has worked in the past and present and, most important, speculate what the future may hold for national- and state-level campaigns.

"Money is the mother's milk of politics"; when California state legislator Jesse Unruh (D) uttered those words two generations ago, it was important.[2] Given the high cost of national campaigns today, whether it is presidential or even congressional, Unruh's words are more than important; they are prophetic. Money helps facilitate speech and amplify a candidate's message to a mass audience. Money helps to identify voters and to target them for mobilization.

Robert Boatright's chapter on fundraising (Chapter 2) demonstrates that the various techniques of traditional fundraising (direct mail, events, telemarketing) are increasingly integrated with appeals in the virtual world of new technology. In this edition, the author discusses the pioneering fundraising techniques used by the Obama campaign in 2008. He then goes on to discuss whether those techniques are replicable for future campaigns. Boatright shows that the distinction between presidential and congressional campaigns online is less so than in the past, especially in high-profile statewide races as discussed above. However, the author wisely points out that the Internet by itself is not enough. Technology adds more dimensions to fundraising than it does to traditional techniques.

Most of the money expended in major campaigns goes to advertising. The percentage can range from 50 percent up to more than 80 percent of the total budget in a presidential race. Tad Devine, one of the nation's leading campaign media consultants, discusses the role of paid advertising in political campaigns in Chapter 3. His career includes working as an ad maker and strategist for Al Gore (2000), John Kerry (2004), and Ted Kennedy. This time Devine not only provides insight into the work of ad maker and strategist but also draws on recent campaigns he worked on, including Lincoln Chafee for Rhode Island governor, Eliot Cutler for Maine governor, and Farouk Shami for Texas governor, all in 2010. Interestingly, both Chafee and Cutler were Independent candidates—Chafee won, and Cutler lost in a close race. Moreover, Devine points out that the smartphone may be the precursor of how television ads are viewed in the future.

The growth of online communications has exploded in the last decade. New media, as consultant Michael Turk points out in Chapter 4, change the way voters interact with campaigns. No longer is that communication one-way, as it was through traditional advertising. Campaigns now actively engage voters online. Turk draws on his experiences as a consultant working as the eCampaign director for Bush-Cheney 2004. He also served in that capacity for Fred Thompson's presidential campaign in 2008. As well, he served as the first eCampaign director for the Republican National Committee (RNC). He also shows how the Obama campaign's use of technology enabled it to maximize its efforts to contact, communicate with, and mobilize voters. Turk not only discusses the growing roles of new and social media but also brings up a discussion of whether there will be fewer centralized online platforms (such as campaign websites) and more use of social media websites, for example, in their place. Finally, he discusses how the growing mobility of online communications makes the impact of new and social media all the more important.

The campaign survey research world is changing where a mix of landline, cell, and automated phone samples is increasingly used. Campaign surveys provide the research that campaigns use not only to survey the electorate's preferences but also to gauge what messages and themes work in a campaign. This provides the campaign with an ability to develop a strategy and message based on research. The cutting edge of change in technology sometimes results in problems for pollsters as explained by Candice Nelson in Chapter 5. Nelson shows that cell phone users who do not have landlines are a growing proportion of the population. By the mid-2010 decade, she states, one-fourth of all phone samples will come from cell phones. That means that fewer voters are reached given that mobile telephone numbers are not widely available and that increasingly it becomes difficult for researchers to reach individuals under the age of thirty, although the cost is cheaper. Reaching voters online is fraught with problems too, as explained in Nelson's chapter. No matter how much technology has progressed since the last edition of this book, traditional phone surveys are likely to remain the staple of pollsters.

The new voter mobilization merges past with present. The 2008 Obama campaign demonstrated that the use of technology to precision target voters favorable to Obama was coupled with an in-field organization of thousands upon thousands in key states across the country who were able to read that information on their smartphones or BlackBerrys. As a result, technology actually enhanced personal contact of voters with campaign organization staff. The new (mobility) and old (door-to-door contact) techniques of identifying voters and getting them to the polls were seamlessly integrated by the Obama campaign. The Obama campaign built its strategy based on that used by the 2004 Bush-Cheney reelection campaign. The Bush-Cheney campaign and not the RNC supervised the party's major get-out-the-vote effort. Campaigns are now using "lifestyle" targeting, which melds consumer information with traditional political voting and polling data. These techniques known as "Customer Relationship Management" (CRM) have filtered down from the business world to permeate campaigns. This author argues that reinvigorating voter contact in the future might also involve social networking (Chapter 6).

The Evolving Campaign: Adaptation by Political Institutions and Groups

Part II, "The Evolving Campaign," features political parties, interest groups, and press coverage in the campaign process. Moreover, the administrative institutions that govern campaign finance and redistricting are also coping with new technologies, with cutting-edge changes coming at a rapid pace. Finally, the growing electoral power of women and minority groups is a result of utilizing cutting-edge change techniques to increase participation.

Both Chapter 7 and Chapter 8 address the Tea Party, which can be seen as a political party coalition (within the Republican Party) and as a third force in politics (hence, an interest group). Since the Tea Party has no central nucleus, Tari Renner in his chapter on political parties and Nina Kasniunas and Mark Rozell in their chapter on interest groups examine how the Tea Party's potency in the 2010 elections may have implications for the future. In a sense, parties and interest groups—whether it is the Democratic National Committee, the National Rifle Association, or a new super PAC, such as American Crossroads—are similar in that they are the organizational muscle in campaigns today. The difference today compared to the past is that there is greater and more involvement from more party and interest group organizations than ever before.

Political parties have moved beyond revitalization, argues Renner. While parties were still being revitalized as service organizations when we last examined them, today they are potent forces that provide a full spectrum of assistance to candidates. Campaigns are actively involved in recruiting, fundraising, and providing organizational services. Parties also use "earned" or free media to help gain exposure for themselves—today, that has become much more sophisticated with the array of technology available.

No entity has benefited more in recent years from the changing political landscape than the interest group. Kasniunas and Rozell point out that the U.S. Supreme Court's decision in *Citizens United v. Federal Election Commission,* 558 U.S. 08-205 (2010), resulted in associations or interest groups having an unlimited ability to spend money in campaigns. This has increased their ability to affect the on-air dialogue in campaigns competing with candidates and parties. Interest groups now have more tools at their disposal to maximize their influence within campaigns by serving as a third force interceding between two campaigns. The authors also take a somewhat different perspective in viewing changes in the campaign process from the premise stated by the book's editor—they argue that the change emerging from elections is toward group-centered politics.

Press coverage has become instantaneous. The filter of several minutes is gone today. The rush is to promote more headline news as Joseph Graf points out in Chapter 9 (updating the work of Jeremy Mayer). Graf argues that press coverage has become even more personality-driven than before, particularly in the electronic media where the sensationalism of stories, such as former presidential candidate John Edwards fathering a child out of wedlock, has become fodder for regular discussion on cable news networks. And technology enables campaigns to put extravagant rumors into the public eye, such as those regarding 2008 presidential candidate Fred Thompson—very similar to the role that partisan newspapers had in the early 1800s, when John Adams was criticized because of his weight and Thomas Jefferson was disparaged as an infidel.

Campaign finance has once again emerged as an issue affecting campaigns and elections. The *Citizens United* decision changes the ground rules for campaigns. The decision stated that limits of spending by associations of individuals violated the First Amendment because money helps amplify speech; and by limiting speech, you are limiting the voice of citizens individually or as a group. Peter Francia, Wesley Joe, and Clyde Wilcox argue in Chapter 10 that empirical evidence shows that associations, particularly businesses, have benefited most from the decision, and that the result may be a cause for concern by candidates and parties because their voices have more competition from outside organizations. The authors also draw on new plans such as the DISCLOSE Act to reform campaign finance. However, the chances of major campaign finance reform in the near future are slim. Instead, campaign reform may occur by thinking "outside the box." The difficulty in an era of divided party government is to put together a plan that has the possibility of attracting Republicans who support campaign finance deregulation and Democrats who support contribution limits—yes, the two philosophies seem to be at loggerheads.

Every ten years, according to Article I of the Constitution, a biennial census of the country is taken; in part, that census helps to apportion where the lines of congressional districts are in each state. This complex maneuvering is explained by Jeffrey Crouch in Chapter 11 on the biennial census and its implications for candidates and parties in the next decade. Crouch shows not only how the population shift to the South and West continues, but also how increasingly sophisticated states have become in mapping out districts. The author demonstrates what implications that has for Democrats and Republicans running for congressional seats and for the White House.

When we think of cutting-edge changes, we often think of techniques and tactics. But societal change over the last four decades has provided a new infusion—that of women, African Americans, Latino Americans, and Asian Americans into the mainstream of politics. In campaigns, each of these groups has increased its participation, not only as electoral and representational forces, but also as campaign managers, campaign staff, and consultants. It was Maggie Williams's entrance as campaign manager that infused the Hillary Clinton campaign with late energy in the 2008 nomination process, almost overcoming the advantage of Barack Obama.

In Chapter 12, Susan MacManus shows us that women candidates are still evaluated on their appearances; and in a sense, that is not a cutting-edge change but still a gender double standard. MacManus's enlightening chapter enables us to understand why that is true. It provides an additional hurdle for female candidates compared to male candidates. When a male candidate appears disheveled, he might be considered folksy or down-to-earth. For women, the standard is still different. Yet, MacManus points out that many successful female candidates have figured out creative ways to maximize their support without selling out, and some of those lessons do have cutting-edge implications. MacManus shows that there are now sophisticated efforts to get women out to vote—and that these efforts are very sophisticated and technologically savvy. Given that women represent over 50 percent of the turnout in most national campaigns for the House, the Senate, and the Presidency, understanding that women are interested in more today than just family issues is key to communicating and conveying messages, and ultimately persuading voters. Women are no different from men in their desire to be treated the same in the political arena.

Research shows that a majority of the U.S. population will be non-White and Latino by the 2040s.[3] In Chapter 13, Atiya Kai Stokes-Brown examines the role of minorities in campaigns. She shows us that the methods of communicating with minority groups converge with those of nonminorities—new and social media are increasingly used to communicate with minorities. Moreover, such techniques in campaigns have become mainstreamed for all groups no matter their ethnicity or race, as technology spreads and democratizes participation. The author provides a fascinating look at the changing demographic in some urban areas as Latinos are emerging as political force than African Americans. It is an example of a second stage of diversity, one that we may be seeing more of in the future.

The conscience of the book is still in its conclusion. Technology increases participation, but does it not also increase the ability to manipulate voters? Author Dick Simpson, who has politicked in the wards of Chicago, gives us reason in Chapter 14 to pause, stating that the wonderful cutting-edge changes discussed in the book, no matter how inviting and exciting, have the potential for great harm as well as hope—that democracy is fragile. Technology should be monitored so that it does not risk rights that we hold dear. Simpson points out that the importance of money has increased since the *Citizens United* decision, and that it gives pause for reflection whether candidates or groups are controlling the dialogue in campaigns. Consultants, citizens, and officeholders should understand that longtime rituals in politics are still virtuous. If they do, there is hope, and if they don't, the seeds of destructive politics will be sown for the future.

But the present does have great possibilities for the future. And the future is now. Several years hence, the "now" of today may already be passé.

Notes

1. "Obama's Get-Out-the-Vote Army" (*The Economist*, October 24, 2008). Accessed on August 9, 2011, from seattlepi.com.
2. "The New Jess Unruh" (*Time*, September 14, 1970). Accessed on September 6, 2007, from time.com.
3. Sam Roberts, "Minorities in U.S. Set to Become a Majority by 2042" (*The New York Times*, August 14, 2008). Accessed on September 2, 2011, from nytimes.com.

CHAPTER 2

Fundraising—Continuity and Change

Robert G. Boatright

DURING THE 2008 PRESIDENTIAL CAMPAIGN, Barack Obama raised a total of $765 million—more than twice what his opponent, Republican senator John McCain, raised, more than twice what either George W. Bush or John Kerry raised in 2004, and more than six times what Democratic nominee Al Gore raised in 2000. As the election was taking shape, few would have predicted that Obama, a first-term senator who had never actually run in a close election, would be able to eclipse veteran politicians such as his primary opponent Hillary Clinton. Yet there were signs long before 2008 that the Internet had already begun to revolutionize campaign fundraising, at least at the presidential level, and that once candidates figured out how to adapt to the new world of fundraising, the cost of running for office would skyrocket. The Obama campaign has set a goal of raising $1 billion in 2012, and it is certainly possible that the Republican nominee will raise nearly as much as well.[1]

Raising money for a run for office at any level is a time-consuming process. Candidates generally begin to think about fundraising long before their run, compiling lists of friends and acquaintances who might give, conferring with political leaders about potential supporters, and borrowing or purchasing lists of the contributors to past candidates. The idea behind this sort of fundraising is that there is a fixed universe of campaign donors, and that there are barriers to gaining access to these donors. This is still the case in some elections and for some candidates. But the political world was shaken in 2004 when Vermont governor Howard Dean raised $20 million on the Internet (and $53 million overall) in the process of going from long shot to front-runner in the 2004 Democratic presidential primary race.[2] What Dean demonstrated was that it is no longer as important as it once was to have accurate lists of past donors; a campaign that catches fire among party activists can raise a large amount of money in small amounts from nontraditional donors, and it can do this far more quickly than was once the case.

The Barack Obama campaign successfully integrated old and new methods of fundraising, seeking to harness the power of small contributors and online communities while exerting more control over the campaign's online presence. Future candidates of both parties will certainly try to emulate the Obama strategy, yet it is unclear how easy that will be. Since 2008 much has changed in the financing of campaigns and in the strategies candidates use to raise money. The standard practices of fundraising—personal solicitations to family and friends, phone calls to lists of consistent contributors, and invitations to fundraising dinners and the like—are still with us, and likely always will be. Yet innovations in the use of social media, the rise of a new cohort of Republican activists, and changes in the legal treatment of campaign spending have made it necessary to rethink some of the lessons of the 2008 election.

This chapter begins with a summary of traditional fundraising practices, and it then turns to a discussion of the ways in which fundraising has changed over the past decade. In this section, I pay particular attention to the differences between fundraising at the presidential and congressional levels. I then turn to changes since 2008 and to the question of what the successes of Republican candidates in 2010 can tell us about the diffusion of new fundraising practices. In particular, the chapter focuses on four different changes in campaign fundraising in 2010, and the consequences of these changes (for the 2012 election and beyond): the increasing use of social media sites such as Facebook to create fundraising "communities"; the increased speed at which candidates can raise money; the mobilization of the Tea Party and of conservative activists in general in 2010; and the Supreme Court's *Citizens United v. FEC* and its consequences for fundraising. These changes show that campaign fundraising has not changed as radically over the past few years as it did earlier in the decade, but fundraising has continued to become faster and more decentralized than it once was.

What Hasn't Changed: Traditional Fundraising Practices

Friends and Acquaintances

Before the campaign even begins, all potential candidates begin with an exhausting accounting of all of the personal and professional contacts who might be willing to contribute to the campaign. Those who have already held elective office, of course, have lists of people who have contributed to them before. For those who have not held office before, contacts made through professional associations, community organizations, and so forth can serve as the basis for developing networks—once a candidate has made appeals to his or her friends, these friends can turn around and enlist their friends, and so forth. The backgrounds of the crop of 2010 candidates show this—of the twenty most successful fundraisers among nonincumbent Senate candidates, sixteen had previously held elective office, two were prominent business executives, one was a political commentator, and one was the son of a member of Congress.[3] Among House candidates, only two of the twenty best fundraisers had held political office in the past, but five were business executives, one was a former talk show host, three had extensive military service, six were lawyers, two were physicians, and one was the son of a former member of Congress. In short, all of these candidates were well positioned to use their personal and professional connections to jump-start their campaigns.

While this sort of networking is easy to spot at the local level, it is important to emphasize that this sort of networking is relevant at the national level as well. In the case of President Obama, it is instructive to consider that many of his early donors were people who resided in the state senate district Obama represented in Illinois or had connections to the University of Chicago, where Obama taught before becoming a senator. All candidates have what Richard Fenno describes as a "personal constituency," and they begin their fundraising efforts here.[4] The people in this constituency are not just donors; they are ambassadors for the candidate to other groups, and this sort of a community also includes people who can provide advice for all aspects of the campaign. This circle of friends and acquaintances will likely include many who have made the maximum permissible donation—$2,500 per election cycle as of 2012—but these people are valuable above and beyond the dollars they personally give to the campaign.

Bundling

While candidates will likely be personally involved in the solicitation of contributions from their friends and acquaintances, the scale of campaigning for most offices precludes having the candidate play a direct role in soliciting all, or even most, of the money that will be needed to be competitive. Once a candidate has identified his or her most connected supporters (that is, people who know a lot of other people who might give), these people may either formally or informally gather contributions for the candidate. The practice of formally doing this (that is, personally collecting checks and forwarding them to the campaign) is known as *bundling*. The Federal Election Commission (FEC) requires that candidates report to the government the names of individuals or groups who have bundled contributions for the campaign. Some candidates encourage bundlers to provide other, less formal, means of letting the campaign know when they have recruited donors. For instance, the Bush and Kerry campaigns set fundraising goals for individuals and reported on their websites the names of people who had hit particular benchmarks. The Bush campaign created categories for those who bundled $50,000 ("Rangers"), $100,000 ("Pioneers"), and $200,000 ("Mavericks"). Supporters who wanted to try to bundle for Bush received a tracking number from the campaign, solicited contributions from friends, and asked these friends to put the tracking number on their checks. The John Kerry campaign had a similar bundling program, and many of the 2008 presidential candidates followed suit as well. Contributors who meet these goals are usually pleased to be recognized for their accomplishments, but campaigns have also provided various perks to these people in appreciation for their fundraising, including dinners with the candidate and other forms of recognition.[5]

Interest groups can also bundle money for candidates. In some instances, they do this without ever actually discussing their efforts with the candidate. Groups, as well, are required by law to disclose the amount of money they have bundled, but they are generally pleased to give some indication of what they have done since the ability to bundle a large amount of money sends a signal about the group's goals and its financial clout. Like individuals, groups can also bundle contributions in a less formal sense, by sending letters or e-mails to members encouraging them to give directly to the campaign or use an online portal such as ActBlue to contribute. Organizations as varied as the Human Rights Campaign and the National Association of Realtors run informal programs of this sort, and then track their members' giving using FEC data.

Campaign Events

Campaign events have always been a common way for candidates to raise money. These events range from relatively casual "meet and greet" events that may cost only $50 or $100 per person to fancier $2,500-per-person dinners. Contributors at these events get the benefit of meeting the candidate and mingling among others who share their financial means and interest in the campaign. The Democratic and Republican parties hold regular fundraising dinners in many parts of the country— the Jefferson-Jackson Day dinners for Democrats and the Lincoln Day dinners for Republicans—that are regular gatherings of regular party contributors.

Among the most lucrative fundraising events for candidates are events featuring political "superstars." In the fall of 2006, in the run-up to her own presidential bid, New York senator Hillary Clinton reportedly headlined campaign events at which over $5 million was raised for Democratic candidates.[6] Clinton's husband, former president Bill Clinton, has also been a reliable draw for Democratic candidates' fundraisers. On the Republican side, former vice presidential nominee Sarah Palin has headlined many fundraising events since 2008.[7] Nonpolitical celebrities such as actors and athletes are also excellent draws for fundraisers; for instance, Massachusetts Senate candidate Scott Brown (R) held several fundraisers that featured former Boston Red Sox pitcher Curt Schilling. The headliners at these events can then use the capital they have generated for their own purposes—were

Sarah Palin to run for president, candidates whose fundraisers she headlined would certainly remember the help she provided.

Phone Banks and Direct Mail

Telemarketing was one of the most dependable means of fundraising during the 1980s and 1990s, and it remains important today. Telemarketers rarely raise large individual contributions for their efforts, but a well-targeted telemarketing operation can be profitable. The quality of the lists used for telemarketing matters greatly, however. Telephone calls to a candidate's prior supporters, or to people who supported a similar candidate, may simply jog the memory of someone who contributes regularly. Incumbent members of Congress engage in "dialing for dollars" regularly, using dedicated telephones at their party's headquarters to keep in contact with people who are not necessarily close acquaintances but who have some connection to the candidate. Telemarketing firms that have access to lists of people with strong partisan views or views on controversial issues (such as abortion or guns) have had success in using more incendiary scripts to solicit contributions from people who may have no prior connection to the candidate. Telemarketing can also be done as an event; just as colleges conduct "phone-a-thons" to raise money over a few days, so candidates can hold one-day telemarketing events to reconnect with donors. Republican Mitt Romney, for instance, raised over \$10 million during a one-day phone-a-thon to start his 2012 campaign.[8]

Direct mail serves a similar purpose; a well-executed direct mail campaign can use partisan rhetoric and appealing graphic design to lure potential contributors into opening the letter and perusing the contents. Direct mail remains a staple of congressional campaigns and local campaigns, where it serves the triple purpose of soliciting contributions, mobilizing voters, and informing voters about campaign issues.

Both telemarketing and direct mail are expensive, low-yield activities, however. A substantial amount of money must be spent ensuring that lists are accurate and are targeted to people who are at least somewhat receptive to the campaign's message. Estimates of the cost of direct mail fundraising, for instance, suggest that even a well-run effort can cost between 35 cents and 65 cents per dollar raised.[9] More refined microtargeting can further ensure that the phone calls or direct mail pieces are tailored to the recipient. Even then, however, caller ID reduces the number of people who will even answer the phone when they see an unfamiliar number, and the volume of junk mail people receive makes it likely that even a well-designed direct mail piece will never be opened. Many campaigns have reportedly spent more money on fundraising by mail or phone than they bring in. This is no surprise—the benefits to contributors of responding to direct mail or telephone solicitations are small. They do not get to interact with the candidate or become involved in the campaign beyond sending a check.

PACs

Some candidates can also raise a large amount of money with minimal effort. Most individual contributors do not give without first being asked. Organized interests, on the other hand, have reasons to seek out candidates. This is particularly true at the congressional level. For incumbent officeholders, there are established political action committees (PACs) that will give money without any sort of direct solicitation from candidates. For nonincumbents, the parties may help to line up meetings with PAC directors; a showing that the candidate is viable and sympathetic to the group's objectives may yield PAC contributions. PAC contributions do not comprise a large percentage of the receipts of nonincumbent candidates simply because most PACs prefer to play it safe, to prioritize gaining access to legislators who are already there. PAC support can send a message to other contributors, however; if one influential PAC is convinced to give to a candidate, other PACs or individual supporters may see this contribution as a stamp of approval and give as well.

Innovations in the 2000s

The activities described above are arranged in order to show the degree of "community" involved in soliciting or making campaign contributions. Some of them, like campaign events or personal conversations with friends, bring the candidate into contact with his supporters, while others, like direct mail, phone banks, or PAC fundraising, do not. Traditional theories of political participation emphasize that people become involved in politics because they are seeking individual benefits. In the case of campaign contributions, some donors give because they hope to receive some sort of specific favor in return, but these types of contributors are rare. Most people give because they are seeking the social benefits of feeling like they are a part of the campaign and connecting with other people involved in the campaign, or they are seeking the expressive benefits of feeling like they are standing up for something they strongly believe in. These two types of benefits are not mutually exclusive, but as the above discussion seeks to make clear, people who give more tend to give in part because the candidate has invited them into his or her community of supporters.

The great innovation of the 2000s was the use of new technologies to create a sense of community among supporters. At the start of the decade, the conventional wisdom was that candidates with a large number of wealthy supporters could generally raise large enough war chests early in the campaign, thus scaring away competitors. At the presidential level, this is what George W. Bush did in 2000, and it has been standard practice for many congressional incumbents as well. To frame this in terms of the fundraising strategies discussed above, a candidate with a large enough stable of personal acquaintances who are willing to contribute can begin with enough of an advantage to run television advertisements and to bankroll extensive direct mail fundraising and telemarketing. To many, this practice was a sign that political "insiders" started with a strong advantage over outsiders, unless those outsiders had a lot of their own money to spend.

There were exceptions to this pattern, but these exceptions prove the rule. Among the most successful candidates at raising small contributions during the 1990s were Representative Robert Dornan (R-Calif.), Senator Paul Wellstone (D-Minn.), and unsuccessful Senate candidate Oliver North (R-Va.). What these three had in common was that they had strong grassroots followings, drew attention from beyond their states or districts, and had a strong personal appeal. All three stood at the extremes of their parties, as well. While candidates such as these tended to do well at raising contributions of $50 or less through direct mail or telephone appeals, two studies at the time estimated that it costs a campaign 50 cents per dollar for contributions of under $50, but only 20 cents for contributions over $50.[10] These candidates, then, were exceptions—most candidates solicited small contributions only after they had generated momentum for their campaigns.

The Internet and Presidential Campaign Fundraising

This conventional wisdom was upended by the Howard Dean campaign. The best fundraising efforts prior to 2004 were centralized, top-down efforts run by fundraising professionals. The Dean campaign sought to present itself as a decentralized "movement" and accordingly gave supporters much of the responsibility for fundraising. The campaign sought to use e-mail to remove the barrier between fundraising and other types of campaigning. That is, people on the Dean e-mail list would receive several messages from the campaign each month; some of these would be solicitations, but other e-mails would encourage supporters to attend local campaign events, to view videos the campaign had posted to its website, or to discuss aspects of the campaign online with other supporters. The Dean campaign was able to constantly monitor the success of different fundraising pitches, modifying them in an ad hoc way to see what worked and what didn't.[11] It could tie fundraising goals to campaign events or deadlines, in the same manner as televised "phone-a-thons" do. These frequent contacts made even small donors feel like part of the campaign team.

Barack Obama's campaign resembled Howard Dean's campaign in several ways. Like Dean, Obama presented himself as an outsider, and like Dean, Obama sought to present his campaign as a movement, as something larger than the candidate. Obama encouraged supporters to set up their own fundraising pages and to combine fundraising with both online and off-line activism. The personal pages Obama supporters set up served as a sort of internal version of Facebook, complete with blogs supporters could maintain and with ways to link to other supporters who lived nearby or who had similar interests.[12] The fundraising success of the campaign made it easy to raise and spend money in places where Democrats had previously been unorganized. Throughout the primary and the general election campaigns, the Obama campaign experimented with a variety of different e-mail approaches, carefully monitoring what worked. And it regularly sent videos to supporters of campaign manager David Plouffe discussing the plans for the upcoming week. These videos reassured contributors that the campaign was using their money wisely, and it gave them the sort of access that was once given to only the biggest donors.[13]

The "rock star" nature of the Obama campaign also made fundraising easy. The campaign did a brisk business selling campaign-related merchandise; this was a way of raising money while also advertising the campaign.[14] And Internet fundraising could be effectively organized around the large campaign events Obama held as the campaign went on. While the long Democratic primary certainly wound up being very costly for both Obama and Hillary Clinton, it provided an opportunity to continually raise money because of the media focus upon the race and the excitement generated by the primary.

How Replicable Is the Obama Fundraising Machine?

It remains to be seen what sort of lessons can be drawn from the Obama campaign. Obama's Democratic opponents, as well as the contestants for the Republican nomination, also adapted their campaigns to the new world of Internet fundraising, but less successfully than did Obama. Mike Huckabee used his website to set fundraising goals and create the sort of "phone-a-thon" atmosphere that Dean had, and Ron Paul's supporters organized a series of "money bombs," efforts to organize large numbers of contributions to the campaign on given days. For instance, Paul raised $4.3 million on November 5, 2007 (the first day of the year leading up to the 2008 election).[15] Paul's money bombs served a dual purpose—they raised money for the campaign, and they drew media attention to the campaign.

For the most part, though, attention in 2008 was paid to the difficulties other candidates would have doing what Obama did. Obama and Dean were distinctive enough personalities that they could expect that people they had not ever asked for money would be driven to their websites merely out of curiosity. Presidential elections draw more attention than do congressional elections, so congressional candidates would have difficulty garnering enough attention to steer people to their websites. In 2006 and 2008, many congressional candidates began placing advertisements on political blogs that might draw potential supporters. By 2010, many candidates had moved beyond political blogs to other websites where potential supporters might browse. These sorts of advertisements, because in many instances they were aimed at people who didn't even reside in the home state or district of the candidate, were aimed more at fundraising than at gaining votes. But some have argued that in any election there are simply too many congressional candidates competing for the same pool of dollars, so the sorts of communities created by Dean and Obama are less likely to occur.

Obama and Dean were also Democrats, and they were insurgent Democrats. This is significant for two reasons. First, some have argued that Republican candidates have been averse to running the sort of decentralized, "movement" campaigns run by Dean and Obama. Second, some have also argued that the enterprise of blogging and forming Internet communities is simply more attractive to people on the left than to people on the right. Four of the six most trafficked political blogs as of early 2008 were left leaning, and one of these, Daily Kos, had more than three times as many unique visitors than any other blog.[16] The most successful Republican candidate on the Internet in 2008, Ron Paul, was a libertarian, a niche that one might also expect to be well populated by online activists. Thus, after 2008 it was unclear how much fundraising would change in 2012.

What the 2010 Elections Tell Us About Changes in Fundraising

Few people would argue that changes in candidates' fundraising practices were the cause of the large Republican gains in the 2010 election. As was the case for Democrats in 2006 and 2008, there were several races in which challengers who raised only a fraction of what their opponents raised won simply because of the prevailing partisan winds. Nonetheless, in 2010 there were several noteworthy signs of the fundraising trends we should watch in upcoming years.

The Speed of Internet Fundraising

Ron Paul's campaign in 2008 demonstrated that a short-term burst in fundraising can have ripple effects—it can generate media coverage, it can build the enthusiasm of a candidate's supporters, and it can pull other potential contributors off of the sidelines. Furthermore, a quick burst of fundraising can catch one's opponent off guard. This was demonstrated early in 2010 in the special election in Massachusetts to fill Senator Ted Kennedy's (D) seat. The Democratic primary for the special election had featured three strong candidates, and these three candidates had received a substantial amount of media attention. The victor, Attorney General Martha Coakley, was considered a shoo-in in the general election. Coakley did little fundraising or campaigning between the December 8 primary and the January 19 general election. Republican nominee Scott Brown, however, campaigned aggressively. Brown solicited support from a variety of conservative organizations outside of Massachusetts, telling them that although he was an underdog, the potential of a Republican winning Kennedy's seat was worth investing money. Brown raised $16 million during the election; $13 million of this came from out-of-state donors, and $14 million arrived between January 1 and January 19. In fact, Brown raised so much money so quickly that Coakley (who raised $9 million for the primary and general elections) was unable to respond. Brown succeeded in large part because his personality and pitch were tailor made for Internet fundraising. Brown arguably would have been far less successful in a general election, where he would have needed to campaign over several months, would have competed with other Republican candidates for money, and would have lost the element of surprise.

The sort of stealth fundraising practiced by the Brown campaign was, however, replicated in a number of Republican primaries that pitted "insider" candidates against insurgents. The rise of the Tea Party certainly helped these insurgents, but the ability of these candidates to raise money quickly and quietly also mattered in primaries. Primaries are often low-turnout affairs, and the fact that they are spread out over several months enabled candidates who had access to national networks of ideological donors to advertise and solicit contributions at times when other candidates were not aggressively doing so. In 2010, two races where a network of national donors mattered were the Nevada Republican senate primary, in which Sharron Angle upset establishment favorite Sue Lowden; and the Delaware Republican senate primary, in which Christine O'Donnell beat Rep. Mike Castle. Notably, both of these primary victories happened in low-population states, in which a rapid fundraising haul can upend the race in a very short time. It is also important to note that these were hardly the sorts of candidates one associates with the Internet; by 2010, the Internet was not exclusively the province of techno-logical sophisticates.

Citizens United v. FEC (2010)

A second surprising development in 2010 was the Supreme Court's *Citizens United v. FEC* decision. In January, the Court overturned a prohibition of the Bipartisan Campaign Reform Act that limited so-called "electioneering" advertisements, interest group advertisements shortly before the election that discussed candidates in positive or negative terms. Moreover, the Court struck down a 1990 Court decision that prohibited corporations from running advertisements that expressly endorsed candidates. Following the decision, many feared that corporations would now fill the airwaves with election ads. While there has been much debate over whether this happened, the Court's decision has arguably made interest groups and interest group fundraising far more important than they once were.

While corporate and interest group advertising is beyond the scope of this chapter, it is important to note that the rise of organizations such as American Crossroads GPS in 2010 has important implications for the ways in which candidates raise money. There were several congressional races in 2010 where outside groups spent more money than did the candidates themselves. Candidates cannot directly coordinate with outside groups; that is, a candidate could not encourage contributors who had maxed out to turn around and give to groups that were spending on his behalf, and a candidate cannot give a group the names of his supporters. Yet in an age when information of this sort is available online, and when the activities of groups and candidates are easily observable, it is not difficult for groups to figure out how to reach a candidate's supporters and vice versa. Two races from 2010 show this. In Pennsylvania, former Club for Growth chairman Patrick Toomey secured the Republican nomination for the Senate. Toomey stepped down from his position at the Club for Growth before beginning his campaign, but the Club spent $5.3 million on his campaign. Did Toomey solicit contributions from people who had been financial supporters of the Club for Growth? Undoubtedly, although many of these donors may well have given to him even without being asked by Toomey. Did the Club raise money from people who had first given to Toomey? Probably.

Alaska's 2010 Republican Senate primary was won by a candidate who spent only $198,000. That candidate, Anchorage lawyer Joe Miller, defeated incumbent senator Lisa Murkowski in large part because of a $300,000 independent expenditure by the Club for Growth and a $600,000 independent expenditure by the Tea Party Express. Miller would go on to raise a total of $3.5 million in the race, so much that he was unable to spend it all, ending the race (which he lost narrowly after Murkowski opted to run in the general election as an Independent) with over $800,000 left in his campaign treasury. Miller was able to capitalize on the excitement generated by these outside groups to increase his own fundraising. He ultimately raised 65 percent of his money from out-of-state donors.[17]

Social and Mobile Media

By 2010, candidate websites had begun to have a sort of cookie-cutter look to them. While in 2004 the Howard Dean website stood out because of its user-friendly nature and the variety of ways in which it sought to engage the public, by 2010 most websites included a variety of interactive features. Candidates had begun to experiment with a variety of other media, however, to reach voters. It is unclear how much of this experimentation has to do with fundraising or how successful fundraising by these means will be. Some of these efforts stand out simply because of their experimental nature—Republican Tim Pawlenty's 2012 presidential campaign, for instance, developed an online game that awarded points to players according to what they do for the campaign.[18]

Many candidates who used social media platforms such as Facebook and Twitter in 2010 used them as a means of providing information about their campaigns or of gathering information about potential supporters. As one Democratic consultant notes, lists of Twitter followers for people who are similar to a candidate provide an excellent list of people for microtargeting efforts.[19] Few campaigns have the ability to use these lists systematically, but they can selectively start to assemble lists or think about targeted advertising. Likewise, a candidate's Facebook page is an excellent way to connect with supporters and to provide information about campaign events. Some candidates in 2010 even developed iPhone apps to distribute campaign information. California Republican gubernatorial candidate Carly Fiorina, for instance, developed an app that allowed users to track where Fiorina was or what sorts of information had just been released by her campaign.[20] And the Obama campaign, needless to say, has developed several different apps that distribute information about activities at the White House.

All of these strategies illustrate the ways in which fundraising has become integrated into campaign communications. If all supporters receive are requests for money, they will become annoyed and stop responding. If, on the other hand, supporters are effectively targeted by the campaign, are given information that is tailored to their interests, and are encouraged to participate in ways other than giving money, they will probably be more likely to give money at least some of the times they are asked. Given the ways in which online activity by campaigns has expanded since 2004, candidates do not necessarily know how effectively their online presence has satisfied their contributor base, but political consultants are now encouraging candidates to maintain as many different online activities as possible, while still directing supporters to their webpage as frequently as possible. After the 2010 election, many consultants were telling newly elected politicians how important it would be to maintain contact with their supporters throughout the upcoming year; this way, supporters would not feel they had been forgotten when candidates came back to them in 2012 to ask for money again.[21]

Emerging Trends and Implications for Future Elections

What does all of this mean for upcoming elections? It is tempting in each election cycle to write off some of the changes as results of personality or of short-term political effects. The 2010 election does seem to have shown that while the innovations of the Dean campaign and the Obama campaign were a preview of future Internet fundraising efforts, claims that the Democrats would dominate online fundraising likely were not accurate. The year 2010 may have shown that successful fundraising does not necessarily win races; but it did show that there are lessons to be learned about campaign fundraising that go beyond the successful strategies of candidates from 2008 and years previous.

Speed Matters

As the 2012 presidential race developed, many observers noted that the major Republican contenders sat on the sidelines well into 2011; in contrast, in the last election the Democratic and Republican primary fields were well established by early 2007. While certainly some of the events of early 2011 played a role in this—aspiring Republican nominees did not want to be upstaged by the 112th Congress or the capture of Osama bin Laden—the slow start to the election was also a reflection of the lessons from the Obama campaign, and perhaps the Scott Brown campaign as well. It simply does not take as long for the right sort of candidate to raise money as it once did, and candidates who can slowly build support among $2,500 donors, as Hillary Clinton did and as Republican "insider" candidates like Haley Barbour or Mitch Daniels might have done, no longer hold a prohibitive advantage. Candidates who can generate grassroots enthusiasm for their campaigns on the Internet can afford to raise money late.

Stealth and Timing Matter

Correspondingly, the fundraising battle involves at least two players. Candidates who can outraise their opponents while their opponents are not paying attention can engage in late campaign spending that can sink an opponent. Conventional wisdom has always held that incumbents can safely build a campaign war chest through contributions from PACs and regular donors, and thus scare off strong opponents. The 2010 elections, in which Democratic incumbents comfortably outraised their Republican opponents yet found themselves at a disadvantage late in the election, show the limits of this strategy. For an incumbent, it is still better to begin the campaign using such safe and predictable means of raising money, but this may not be the insurance policy it once was. In addition, candidates of all types can exploit campaign events and FEC reporting deadlines to rally supporters for brief surges in fundraising. During the presidential primaries for both parties in 2008, candidates effectively communicated to their followers the implications of showing robust fundraising numbers by each of the FEC deadlines—impressive numbers would generate media coverage, would enhance the perception that the candidate was viable, and would inspire others to donate. Congressional candidates successfully used this strategy in 2010 as well.

Finding a Niche

As the Internet has come to dominate campaign fundraising, the line between fundraising and campaigning has blurred. This has several implications. First, candidates cannot separate their fundraising pitches from their efforts to provide issue information to supporters and the public or from their efforts to encourage people to vote for the candidate or volunteer for campaign activity. All are one and the same. Candidates who raise money successfully must convince supporters and potential supporters that money is essential to the campaign but that they are valuable to the campaign for reasons other than their money.

Second, candidates must work to create a group identity (or several group identities) among their supporters. Candidates who brand themselves—for instance, as Tea Party candidates or as "grizzly moms"—can tap into political networks well beyond the districts or states in which they are running. Candidates can also seek to create different identities among groups of supporters; the Obama campaign's encouragement of different user groups on the website can also be effective. Creating multiple groups can foster a healthy competition among groups in terms of who can get the most people to events, who can give the most money, and so on. In the context of a presidential campaign, this can give a candidate useful information about strategy and get supporters involved in discussions about the campaign's priorities. This sort of competition used to happen in an informal sense in earlier campaigns, but the Internet has brought it out into the open.

Third, candidates who have successfully defined their niche or niches can engage in microtargeting, via the careful use of Internet advertising. Google ads or ads placed on selected blogs or other websites are not nearly as expensive as other types of advertisements, can be effectively targeted and differentiated, and provide feedback on the ad's success in the number of click-throughs.

Authenticity

A final implication of the changing fundraising landscape is one that has held true for some time. Candidates who succeed at raising money must also be candidates who truly seek to engage their supporters, not those who create a façade of community. Voters quick to notice when candidates are actively engaging with their supporters through the web and various forms of social media. They are aso adept at discounting the efforts of candidates who have set up Facebook pages because their consultants told them to but have not actually sought to use them for dialogue with supporters or the public. It is not hard to distinguish candidates' own blog posts from the campaign's press releases. Scott Brown's 2010 Senate campaign proved that voters will often overlook ideology if they are convinced that a candidate is to some degree like them. Candidates for office, incumbents and nonincumbents alike, have contended for years with low citizen support for Congress and the low esteem in which citizens hold politicians. There are multiple ways for candidates to think about this—certainly not all candidates can define a unique niche for themselves—but it is not difficult for candidates to present themselves in an authentic manner.

Conclusions

There are many uncertainties about campaign fundraising as we enter the 2012 elections. Most notably, it is not at all clear how candidates will use mobile media to raise money or how they will measure their success in doing so. Many of the questions raised in the past decade about fundraising, however, have now been answered. Is there anything about Internet fundraising that favors the left? There is little evidence that this is the case. Are insurgent or nontraditional candidates advantaged in Internet fundraising? This may be true, although such candidates have generally had an advantage in raising small contributions. And is there anything unique about Barack Obama's fundraising machine? Every major candidate likely provides something unique in terms of his or her fundraising skills and coalition of supporters, but going into 2012 it appears merely that the Obama campaign is particularly good at raising money, not that there is anything to the campaign's strategy that cannot be replicated by the right candidate at some point in the future.

Despite all of the changes in fundraising practices, it must be kept in mind that many aspects of campaign fundraising have not changed. A successful campaign must start with the traditional strategies of buttonholing friends, neighbors, or influential party members. This sort of fundraising is a prerequisite to the more exotic sorts of fundraising discussed above. It is also worth remembering that fundraising through the Internet is not always a means of reaching new people. Many Americans today do their banking and pay their bills on the Internet, so it is only natural that more are giving money online.[22] This suggests that the same people who once put a check in the mail to support a candidate are now going online to do so. This is not necessarily a revolutionary change in campaigning, then. What is revolutionary is that now candidates can easily and inexpensively communicate with these people—they can say "thank you" for the contribution by giving contributors access to more information about the campaign than was once possible. To the extent that candidates do this honestly and with the aim of making the campaign a more inclusive sort of community, this is a positive development. And at a minimum, this sort of approach can help candidates raise more money.

Notes

1. Jeff Zeleny, "An Obama Insider, Running the Race from Afar" (*The New York Times*, April 2, 2011).

2. Pew Internet and American Life Project, *Election 2004 Online* (Washington, DC: Pew Internet and American Life Project, 2005).

3. Author's calculations using FEC data.

4. Richard Fenno, *Home Style: House Members in Their Districts* (Boston: Little, Brown, 1978), 24–27.

5. John C. Green and Nathan S. Bigelow, "The 2000 Presidential Nominations: The Costs of Innovation," in *Financing the 2000 Election*, edited by David B. Magleby (Washington, DC: Brookings Institution Press, 2001).

6. Catrin Jones, "Hillary Clinton's Home Stretch Appeal" (ABC News Political Radar Blog, September 28, 2006). Accessed on November 4, 2011, from http://abcnews.go.com/blogs/politics/2006/09/hillary_clinton-4/.

7. See, e.g., "Palin to Appear at Rand Paul Fundraiser in Louisville This Week" (Associated Press, September 13, 2010). Accessed on October 19, 2011, from http://www.courier press.com/news/2010/sep/13/palin-appear-paul-fundraiser-louisville-week/.

8. Jonathan Martin, "Mitt Romney's Money Machine Cranks Up" (*Politico*, May 17, 2011).

9. Larry Biddle, "Fund-Raising: Hitting Home Runs on and off the Internet," in *Mousepads, Shoe Leather, and Hope: Lessons from the Howard Dean Campaign for the Future of Internet Politics*, edited by Zephyr Teachout and Thomas Streeter (Boulder, CO: Paradigm Press, 2008), 166–78.

10. Michael John Burton and Daniel M. Shea, *Campaign Mode: Strategic Vision in Congressional Elections* (Washington, DC: CQ Press, 2003), 105; Dennis J. McGrath and Dane Smith, *Professor Wellstone Goes to Washington* (Minneapolis: University of Minnesota Press, 1995), 183.

11. See Biddle.

12. Jose Antonio Vargas, "Obama's Wide Web" (*The Washington Post*, August 20, 2008).

13. Ryan Lizza, "Battle Plans: Finding the Right Way to Run" (*The New Yorker*, November 17, 2008), 46–55.

14. David Plouffe, *The Audacity to Win* (New York: Penguin, 2009), 51.

15. Jose Antonio Vargas, "Ron Paul Beats Own Fundraising Record" (*The Washington Post*, December 17, 2007).

16. Matthew R. Kerbel, *Netroots: Online Progressives and the Transformation of American Politics* (Boulder, CO: Paradigm Publishers, 2009), 45.

17. Data from Open Secrets, http://www.opensecrets.org/races/geog.php?cycle=2010&id=AKS2. It should be noted that because Alaska is a small state, politicians tend to raise a higher proportion of their money from out-of-state donors than is the case for other races. Nonetheless, Miller raised a larger percentage from out-of-state donors than Murkowski or their Democratic opponent.

18. Jennifer Preston, "Republicans Sharpening Online Tools for 2012" (*The New York Times*, April 20, 2011).

19. Natch Greyes, "The Untapped Potential of Social Media: A Primer for Savvy Candidates" (*Campaigns and Elections*, March 2011). Accessed on November 4, 2011 from http://www.campaignsandelections.com/magazine/us-edition/175967/the-untapped-potential-of-social-media-a-primer-for-savvy-campaigners.thtml.

20. Eric Kuhn, "Carly Fiorina Campaign Launches Location Based App," *CNN*. Accessed on December 28, 2011 from http://politicalticker.blogs.CNN.com/2010/10/13/carly-fiorina-campaign-launches-location-based-app/

21. Steve Pearson and Ford O'Connell, "Down Home Digital: Staying Online" (*Campaigns and Elections*, December 2, 2010). Accessed on November 4, 2011, from http://www.campaignsandelections.com/magazine/us-edition/255073/down-home-digital-staying-online.thtml.

22. Susannah Fox and Jen Beier, "Online Banking 2006" (Philadelphia: Pew Foundation, 2006). Accessed on October 19, 2011, from http://pewinternet.org/Reports/2006/Online-Banking-2006/Online-Banking.aspx.

CHAPTER 3

Paid Media—In an Era of Rapid and Revolutionary Change

Tad Devine

Paid political advertising, which has been the centerpiece of campaign communication in the United States for decades, has entered a period of rapid and potentially revolutionary change. From the Obama campaign's innovative use of the Internet and social media, to mobile election tools, such as Gov. Sam Brownback's (R-Kans.) campaign app "SamForGov," and YouTube sensations like Alabama agriculture commissioner candidate Dale Peterson, campaigns are communicating with voters in ways that were not available or even conceivable only a generation ago. Practitioners of politics at all levels must recognize that the rapid changes in campaign communication are a wildfire on the political landscape—a fire that will not be contained.

For more than four decades, political advertising has been the most powerful vehicle for a candidate to deliver an unfettered message directly to voters. From the landmark "Daisy" ad in 1964 to the high-definition and interactive ads of today, political advertising has fundamentally changed and is fundamentally changing. Advances in research, technology, and the sophistication of targeting are leading ad makers to develop increasingly individualized advertising tailored to niche audiences. With these innovations, campaigns are using paid media to communicate their message to a more diverse cross-section of the voting electorate than ever before.

The purpose of this chapter is to review paid media in political campaigns, to show how they became powerful and how they are changing. It begins with an examination of the role of media consultants, and then looks at the way research-based message development informs ad making. The chapter then reviews message development by looking at specific campaigns and ads. Finally, the chapter looks ahead at the cutting edge of campaign advertising, focusing on the way digital technology, the Internet, conversion technology, and media targeting are affecting the way political ad makers work and deliver messages to voters on behalf of campaigns and candidates.

Most of the examples, and all of the case studies, are ads that I have made or worked on with my past and present partners. My perspective is that of a practitioner spending the last two decades writing, directing, and producing television ads here in the United States and around the world. That perspective is undoubtedly biased toward the power of television advertising. But until campaigns—from presidential races to statewide and even local elections—begin to concentrate their resources on paid communication other than television advertising, TV's primacy as a means of communicating with voters will remain obvious. And while rapidly evolving technologies may soon fundamentally change this calculation (as the first screen of television is rivaled, and perhaps someday eclipsed, by the second and third screens of the computer and the smartphone), for today at least, television advertising is still king.

Paid Television Advertising

Campaign television ads are the most powerful tool in modern American politics.[1] That is why major statewide and national campaigns spend more on paid media than on anything else.[2] Some may dispute that statement, and with the emergence of the Internet and other means of communication it is a legitimate debate. But until statewide and national campaigns start spending up to half or more of their resources in areas other than television advertising, it is difficult to dispute that paid ads are more powerful than any other tool in a campaign's arsenal.[3]

Paid advertising can have an impact that ripples throughout a race. In 2010, businessman and corporate lawyer Eliot Cutler ran for governor of Maine as an Independent. Without the support of a political party behind him, and having never run for elected office before, Cutler faced an uphill battle. Before the campaign started paid advertisements, Cutler's name recognition was in the single digits among likely voters.[4] On Election Day, after five months on TV, Cutler won 208,270 votes, coming in a close second and surpassing the Democratic nominee. For Eliot Cutler, television advertising was key to connecting with voters.

Given the power of television advertising and the need of a campaign to reach many people in a short time, paid television ads will likely remain the dominant communications medium in campaigns through this next decade. In many ways, alternative media will enhance the power of TV advertising, but they have not yet replaced it.

Increased Internet fundraising is already providing campaigns the capital needed to buy more television time, and there is now the possibility of interactivity between television advertising and campaigns. Ads now drive viewers to campaign websites to do everything from contributing to friending the candidate on Facebook. Finally, as more and more people have access to lightning-speed Internet connections, and as those connections extend to handheld devices beyond computers, the likelihood increases that voters will one day watch ads, or even longer-format communications, as they commute to work on a train or sit in a doctor's waiting room. Perhaps one day truly undecided voters will make up their minds while standing in line at a crowded polling place and watching an ad on a handheld device.

The Role of Media Consultants

Media consultants have two main roles in campaigns: First, as creators of television ads, we write, direct, produce, and deliver campaign advertising. We team up with other skilled professionals, such as film crews, producers, editors, and media time buyers. These production specialists typically work not only on political campaigns but on other kinds of advertising as well. They bring their skills in editing and filmmaking, as well as media placement and time buying, to political campaigns under the direction of media consultants, who are typically the people who work most closely with the candidates and campaigns. In order for everything to run smoothly, successful media consultants need the political know-how to read and interpret polls, understand demographics, and assimilate voting patterns, as well as the artistic and people skills to create ads and communicate personally to voters with substance, passion, and/or humor.

The second principal role of media consultants is as campaign strategists. In that capacity consultants are among the architects of a campaign's message. Media consultants collaborate with pollsters, campaign managers, candidates, and others to develop a message. For example, the slogan of the 2010 gubernatorial campaign of Independent candidate Linc Chafee in Rhode Island was "Trust Chafee." Research showed that voters were sick of the cronyism and corruption that had become synonymous with state politics, and were desperate for an honest leader they could trust. By sticking to our message—that Chafee was the only candidate with the independence and integrity to break from party politics and be honest with voters—the campaign was able to use Chafee's status as a third-party candidate to its fullest advantage. Strategic discipline led to the defeat of both the Republican and Democratic nominees, and the election of Rhode Island's first Independent Governor in modern times.

In addition to research, media consultants use their experience in campaigns to anticipate likely lines of attack and to react quickly to changing circumstances. After many years and many campaigns, situations that have occurred previously

---

BOX 3.1:   Becoming a Political Media Consultant

Political consulting is a niche field. I did not move into my current career full-time until I was almost forty. That is not to say I wasn't involved in politics or campaigns. I got my start in politics as a delegate counter for President Jimmy Carter's 1980 reelection campaign while I was a law student on summer break. I then stayed involved with the Democratic Party, working on other presidential elections, before joining a political advertising firm in the early 1990s. Many media consultants enter the field from political backgrounds like mine, but another successful route comes from working in television production. The first political advertising consultants were real-life Mad Men from agencies in New York. In 1952, the Republican National Committee hired the Madison Avenue firm of Batten, Barton, Durstine & Osborn to help polish the image of presidential candidate Dwight Eisenhower.[5] Pursuing a degree in filmmaking and working as a television producer are now popular and viable paths to becoming a political media consultant.

---

inevitably reemerge. Experience can be useful in making the quick decisions necessary in the short time frame of a typical campaign. For example, in 2010 my firm worked for clients across the United States, among them Eliot Cutler in Maine and the House Democratic Committee in Illinois. Having worked previously in both states, my partner and I could advise our clients about the tone and tenor of the advertising, not just the issues in the ads. That experience led us to produce entirely positive ads in Maine and many tough, negative ads in Illinois. This kind of battle-tested experience is particularly useful because campaigns frequently involve changing circumstances. Decisions have to be made quickly and decisively for candidates to win or to deal with fast-unfolding events.[6]

Writing Campaign Ads

Writing is the essential starting point of almost all television and radio advertising. Political consultants write scripts that are typically made into thirty- or sixty-second ads read by a narrator, a third party (such as a person who knows the candidate), or the candidate.[7]

Scripts provide a focal point at which strategy and research converge to create a deliverable message. Scripts also embody the reality that television ads are typically limited to a very short format—in the United States, almost always thirty seconds.

Sometimes ads are not scripted and are the result of a cinema verité technique of filming the candidate. These ads are typically made by filming a live event, such as a speech; by simply following the candidate around as he or she campaigns; or by interviewing the candidate and using his or her unscripted responses to questions asked by an interviewer. Cinema verité provides a way of communicating with voters that tends to depict the candidate in a more real and less formal light. The message discipline required for making these ads usually is applied not at the front end (as when the candidate would read a script), but at the back end, when the consultant must cut and assemble the candidate's (or third party's) words and phrases in the studio. The ad maker then uses the tools of editing to ensure that the spot makes the intended point in the short time allotted.

As of 2002, ad makers actually have less than thirty or sixty seconds due to regulations in Congress's Bipartisan Campaign Reform Act (BCRA), which requires federal candidates to "stand by their ads." That requirement means that a candidate saying something like "I am Jane Jones, and I approve this message" takes up four seconds of each ad. The consequence for media consultants is that ads have less time to present persuasive information and content to voters, truncating not only the visual aspects of the ads but the written aspects as well. Interestingly, media consultants have gotten creative with this constraint, adding personalized statements that fit within BCRA's rules. For example, in Kentucky's hotly contested 2010 Senate race, Rand Paul (R) ended the ad "Rand's Plan" with "I'm Rand Raul, and I approve this message because government is the servant, not the master."[8]

The Importance of Audio and Video

Other powerful tools used by media consultants are the images and sounds at the heart of television advertising. Television is primarily a visual medium, and television ad makers look for strong visuals and credible sources of authority to make their case visually. Television and radio are also auditory media, in which everything from the sound of the candidate's voice to the soundtrack behind an ad can have a powerful impact with voters. In many ways, music is the secret weapon of television political advertising, since it can evoke a mood or underline the message being delivered through words and images.

Research for Message Development

One of the keys to media production in political campaigns is the use of research to develop a message. Campaigns and consultants review the research and based on that research develop concepts for television, radio, and other forms of advertising.[9] Typically this takes the form of converting short narrative statements about a candidate or set of issues into an ad. The statements are road tested in polls before they are written as a script for broadcast ads.[10] Successful political campaigns almost always emanate from a disciplined regime of research, where tools such as polls, focus groups, people-metered ad testing, opposition research, and issue or candidate record research provide the basis for a message.

At the presidential level, where the resources and the stakes are highest, almost all advertisements are subjected to both pre- and post-production research. Research includes polling that occurs prior to the development of scripts, and detailed focus group testing of ads after preliminary versions of the ad have been produced. Campaigns also use online media testing of ads: preselected online groups see the advertising and are asked to comment on its impact. In almost every major U.S. campaign today at the statewide level, campaign advertising is tested in one way or another prior to broadcast. Although there are exceptions to the rule, pre- and post-production testing is the industry standard. By gauging the impact of messages on voters in preproduction polls, or by showing preliminary versions of a commercial to focus groups, ad makers can get a good sense of the impact on potential voters before making the costly commitment to broadcasting the spot.

Projective Research

Perhaps the most important development in the last three decades in U.S. political campaigns is the use of *projective research* in the production of television advertising and in message development. This technique, pioneered in the United States and used extensively in political campaigns, allows researchers to push and probe respondents with a variety of questions to gauge how voters will respond to issues and arguments. By determining whether voters are impacted, either positively or negatively, by a particular argument, projective research can inform media consultants about what ads are likely to be most powerful in moving the voters who emerge as the primary targets of campaign communication strategies. If the research is well conceived and executed, campaigns can avoid the costly mistake of putting enormous resources behind messages that do not have a good chance of succeeding with voters. Developing winning messages in a poll and successfully testing the depictions of those messages in a qualitative focus group setting are the best way to ensure success in the real world of elections.

Quantitative and Qualitative Research

Polling is the form of quantitative research that campaigns use the most (see Chapter 5 for more analysis on survey research). Polls—either a random survey of respondents or a discrete panel back survey of a previously identified group whose members are contacted more than once—are at the heart of modern research.[11]

Campaigns essentially play out the election in polls, testing to see not just where the electorate is today but how voters will be affected by issues and information.

Focus groups and other forms of qualitative research are the other tools that media consultants use to determine which ads will work and why. Focus group research typically occurs after TV production, when at least a preliminary version of an ad has been made. By letting a selected group of target voters evaluate an ad prior to broadcast, campaigns can avoid running an ad that may not produce the desired effect.

Communicating the Message Through Different Ads

The skills and tools of experience, writing, and research enable the media adviser to craft a message for a campaign. Political ads communicate that message to voters in a number of forms: biographical, issue, accomplishment/vision, and negative ads. The appendix at the end of this chapter provides case studies for all four types of advertisements.

Typically in a campaign, candidates introduce themselves to the voting public in terms of their biography. One of the most important qualities that they can communicate is shared values. Biographical advertising opens a window into the lives of candidates so that voters can better understand and relate to them on the basis of shared values. Biographical ads help to frame the narrative of a campaign. Sometimes the biographical ads are deeply personal, and sometimes the narrative is directed toward accomplishment, agenda, or vision. Farouk Shami, a Democratic candidate in Texas's 2010 gubernatorial primary, used his biographical ad to show that while he may look or speak differently, his personal realization of the American dream actually embodies the story of Texas itself (illustrated in the first case study).

Issue ads tend to be more about policies than people. The issues may be important to a particular place or demographic group. These ads are typically informational, supplying voters with facts and a candidate's position on issues that he or she is putting at the center of the campaign. For example, Americans United for Safe Streets made an independent expenditure ad (I talk more about this type of ad later in the chapter) in support of Gerry Connolly (D-Va.) during his close 2010 reelection campaign. The ad focused on closing a legislative loophole that makes it easier for criminals to obtain weapons at gun shows where they can avoid background checks (illustrated in the second case study).

Another category of advertising focuses on the accomplishments of candidates and looks ahead to future achievements. I believe that almost every campaign is really about the future. It is critical for candidates, particularly incumbents seeking reelection, to remind voters of what they have done and of the bonds that exist between the candidate and the electorate, but also to focus on the fights that lie ahead. This formula of accomplishment and vision is a winning one that ad makers try to utilize in campaigns. Accomplishment and vision ads are critical to inoculating incumbents against attacks from challengers, and are useful in introducing political outsiders with experience from the private sector who are running for office. Eliot Cutler (I-Maine) had never run for public office before his 2010 gubernatorial bid. His final ad, titled "Future," made the case that he was the only candidate with the vision and skills to make Maine work again (illustrated in the third case study).

The final category of political ads is the most famous (or infamous): negative ads. If TV ads are the most powerful force in politics, then negative ads may be a campaign's A-bomb. The most notorious negative ad was, and still is, the "Daisy" spot, televised on September 7, 1964.[12] In that ad, President Johnson's campaign showed a young girl plucking petals from a daisy juxtaposed with a countdown to a nuclear explosion. The spot left the impression that if Johnson's opponent, Sen. Barry Goldwater (R-Ariz.), was elected president, he might actually lead America into a nuclear confrontation with the Soviet Union. Even though the ad was only aired once during the 1964 presidential race, it had a tremendous impact, felt even to this day. Indeed, some advocacy groups are still using remakes of that ad to make points on issues such as the 2010 START treaty.[13] The fourth case study recounts Linc Chafee's (I-R.I.) 2010 campaign for governor, which employed negative ads to connect his opponents to the political machine Chafee was running against.

Cutting-Edge Changes in Advertising

Technological changes that will affect paid advertising in the 2012 presidential election will transform the way candidates communicate with voters in the next decade. Not only is the digital process changing the quality of the product, but also the means of communicating information are becoming more and more diverse. Media consultants no longer make ads just for television and radio; they also make them for a new screen—the Internet. And they make them for distinct audiences of potential supporters and persuadable voters.

Digital Technology

Advances in digital technology have fundamentally changed the political consulting business in recent years. In the last decade, political ad makers have moved from producing television ads in either videotape or film to using high-definition video (HD) for most production. HD allows media consultants to have high-quality, clear images. It is also much more convenient for producing and editing ads. Instead of shooting in film, where there is a time-consuming physical demand of changing the film cartridge after only several minutes of filming, an

HD camera will usually run for an hour of continuous filming. And the image quality of HD is superior to lower grades of video. That is important when you consider that political ads must compete not only against other political ads for audience attention, but also against the more expensive production value of ads for financial institutions, auto companies, and other high-end consumer marketers. Those ads run before and after political ads in front of the same audience, and a drop in production quality can adversely affect the way viewers perceive the lower-quality ad.

The change in editing in recent years has been as dramatic as the change in filming. Political ad makers moved from large-scale online editing, which typically occurred in big studios, to PC/Avid digital editing, which can be done on hardware as small as a laptop computer. Similarly, ads can now be delivered to television and radio stations anywhere almost instantly using digital transfers. An ad can go from concept to execution, to delivery, to broadcast, all in the same day. And in many senatorial or gubernatorial campaigns today, particularly at the end of a closely fought race, that is precisely what happens.

Technology is also making big changes in the content of advertising. Ads can direct viewers to campaign websites and create the potential for interactive communication driven by the power of paid media. Once this interactivity occurs— when a viewer responds to a call to action by going to a website as directed in an ad—campaigns can capture the e-mail addresses of people who are interested in candidates or particular issues, allowing them to continue to speak directly to those voters at will and for almost no cost.[14] In one of his ads, Eliot Cutler asked viewers to "read my plan at cutler2010.com."[15] Once on the website, voters could sign up for electronic and mobile updates, donate to the campaign, and connect with the candidate through social media venues like Facebook, YouTube, and Twitter.[16]

As digital technology changes the way ads are filmed, edited, and delivered to voters, media consultants and campaigns must adjust to a faster and more efficient process. As more and more people have access to editing technology, the process of making political ads may even become more homegrown. We've already seen competitions in which ad makers working at home have sent in ads for various causes.[17] This is happening in web venues like obamain30seconds.org and elsewhere. It is not surprising that Madison Avenue is following suit, with ads made by amateurs featured in the Super Bowl and entire agencies, such as Idea Bounty and Victors & Spoils, built on the principles of *crowdsourcing,* which utilizes the inexhaustible supply of eager Internet users, on a per-contract basis, instead of hiring full-time employees.[18]

In the future, the media consultant in some campaigns may become the volunteer with a laptop, a creative young person who has the ability to edit images either captured by personal digital video cameras or selected from the vast expanse of imagery available now to almost anyone, anywhere, at the click of a mouse.

The Internet and Advertising

The powerful connection between the Internet and campaign advertising has been established in modern campaigns, and that connection is only likely to be enhanced in the future. Announcement videos released online have now become the norm for campaign kickoffs as opposed to press conferences and set-piece events. Additionally, campaigns looking to make a splash are now harnessing the power of the Internet to spread video at lightning speed by creating advertisements that they hope will "go viral." With social networking sites like Facebook and Twitter encouraging users to share video through easy uploading systems, political ads can now reach an unprecedented number of viewers in record time. In order for an ad to be forwarded it must strike a special chord with viewers, oftentimes being quirky, funny, or just plain ridiculous. It is the job of the media consultant to incorporate the candidate's message into the ad, while still maintaining a viral appeal. This type of ad was used heavily in the 2010 election cycle. We saw it from candidates who did not have large war chests (Dale Peterson's video for Alabama Agriculture Commissioner), to candidates with millions to spend on advertising (California Senate candidate Carly Fiorina's "Demon Sheep" web video).

While the two ads mentioned above were among the most talked about political videos released during the 2010 election, gaining an enormous amount of free media from the press, neither candidate realized victory at the polls. Millions of people around the globe saw these ads online, but in the end, the only viewers that matter to a campaign are the voters where the candidate is running. That is in part why television, which can be purchased by geographic area, still trumps the Internet in terms of reaching targeted voters.

Reaching Niche Markets

As the delivery of television advertising and the research behind campaigns become more and more sophisticated, the demand to reach niche voters will grow. As campaigns identify voters and categorize them, it has become easier to reach them with television advertising, just as direct mail has been delivered to voters on a highly segmented basis for many years. In the future more campaigns will use niche marketing for advertising on television and the Internet.

Cable channels, with their multitude of format and geographical options, are already giving political advertisers ways to reach different groups of people. For example, an ad can be delivered on a cable system that only broadcasts in a specific geographic area. This type of geographic niche advertising is important in campaigns where media markets spill over from large states to smaller states. For campaigns in New Hampshire, where so much advertising occurs every four years in presidential races, the Boston media market (of which southern New Hampshire is a part) is much more expensive than the Manchester market. As cable systems become pervasive, political ad makers use them to deliver messages to voters who live in places like New Hampshire or southern Vermont at a fraction of that larger broadcast market's cost. The ability to penetrate only New Hampshire counties, instead of paying for Massachusetts voters to see an ad intended for the New Hampshire primary, saves enormous amounts of money for campaigns. Likewise, groups of voters may congregate around certain television shows or television channels. If the research for a campaign shows that a certain demographic of voters lines up with particular TV venues, then the campaign not only can deliver messages to them through the broader advertising on network television, but also can tailor discrete messages to be delivered to a target audience via cable.

The Next Wave: The Future of Media Advertising

Television advertising in the future will have to adjust to a more rapid pace of delivery. It's simply a faster world, in which ads on TV compete with other forms of communication, such as the Internet, direct mail, and paid telephone banks, to deliver and amplify the message of a campaign. Perhaps the biggest adjustment that television advertising will have to make will be the move to "convergence technology." Advertising in future political campaigns is not likely to be limited to the single screen of television, but may appear on the second screen (the computer) and the third screen (the smartphone).

The Smartphone as a Precursor?

Smartphones and tablets are precursors to what may become an everyday means of firsthand communication with voters. Now that voters can easily view videos through their telephones, and the images are so clear that they can have the kind of powerful impact that television advertising first had thirty-five years ago, political ad makers may decide they need to move to these screens even more. If so, it will create an interesting new way of communicating with voters. Campaigns may begin to use text services to disseminate videos to subscribers. We've already seen campaigns use texting to reach voters, such as in 2008 when the Obama campaign chose to text Obama's vice presidential pick, rather than use a traditional media outlet to release the breaking news. Campaigns used to go door-to-door with candidates and ground troops. Now they may go hand-to-hand with video images and sound bites.

Tablets are also contributing to the changing landscape. The iPad has revolutionized the way media consultants do business. We are now able to carry around high-tech presentations, embedded with quality video, which can transform a business meeting into an advertising pitch at the drop of a hat.

Independent Expenditures

One of the most important developments in political advertising in recent years has been the growth of *independent expenditure* advertising in political campaigns. While this phenomenon has existed for many years (examples include the "Willie Horton" spot from 1988 and the "Swift Boat" ads from 2004), the 2010 Supreme Court ruling in *Citizens United v. Federal Election Commission* changed the game. For the first time, corporations and unions are able to spend unlimited sums to support or denounce political candidates in elections. They cannot give money directly to campaigns, but they can exert influence in other ways—the primary way being independent expenditure ads.

By the November 2010 election, just a few months after the *Citizens United* decision, outside interest groups had already broken spending records. They quadrupled their spending since 2006 and in 2010 funneled about $105 million more into political advertising than party committees.[19] Interestingly, 72 percent of the advertising money from outside interest groups came from places that were prohibited from spending money in 2006.[20] I saw the boom of special interest advertising in campaigns firsthand through my work on a 2010 judicial retention election in Illinois. In that race, the group JUSTPAC spent over $600,000 on vicious negative advertising in an unsuccessful bid to defeat Illinois Supreme Court chief justice Tom Kilbride.[21] Throughout the course of the campaign, over $3 million was spent by both sides making it the most expensive retention election in Illinois history.[22] Given the floodgates opened by the U.S. Supreme Court, massive spending of this kind by special interest groups is only likely to increase in the years to come.

Independent expenditure advertising is something engaged in not only by groups distinct from campaigns, but by political parties and by the political party committees established at a national level to support candidates for the House and Senate. At the heart of independent expenditure advertising are firm rules and laws that forbid the independent groups and committees from coordinating, or even communicating in most cases, with political campaigns. This division between campaigns and the independent actions of groups choosing to exercise their right to political free speech in American constitutional democracy is making it more difficult for political campaigns to control the message being delivered to voters.

Voters naturally attribute or impute any political advertising they see (whether or not it contains a particular disclaimer) to a campaign and not to an independent expenditure group to which the candidate has no connection. Thus, a campaign that may have decided strategically to pursue positive advertising to introduce a candidate may have to engage in a battle over tone, and groups mounting their own highly negative campaigns may undermine the content of the campaign's message. Unfortunately, the campaign, and not the independent expenditure group, may pay the price because many voters believe that candidates control everything that is being said by their side.

Conclusion

Political advertising remains the most powerful tool in a campaign's arsenal of communication, but as technology changes the way we communicate, political advertising will also change. Soon political ads' main venue may be by popping up on your smartphone or through newscasts to your iPod. Whatever the future holds, one thing is certain—as long as we have political campaigns, we are likely to have political ads. Others will debate the impact of that reality on American democracy. For now, those who want to win campaigns will try to understand and exploit the power of political ads.

For now, the future of political campaigns is not just on the web. Even the Internet giant Google continues to advertise itself not just in cyberspace but on television as well.[23] This is because the Internet requires motivation by the user to seek out information in a way that television does not. In politics, people who consume news on the Internet tend to have much higher political interest, awareness, and participation. Political advertisers, however, must still reach that enormous segment of voters who are less involved than activists but still believe that the act of voting and the choices made for political offices are critical. For the foreseeable future, the most powerful way to reach those voters is through television advertising. To those who posit that old-fashioned political ads don't matter, that the future of political persuasion lies solely on the Internet and other technological highways, perhaps the best rejoinder is the ancient chant: "The king is dead. Long live the king."

Appendix to Chapter 3 begins on the next page.

Appendix to Chapter 3: Contemporary Case Studies of Paid Advertising

You can view all the ads at <*www.devinemulvey.com*>.

Biographical Ad

Case Study: Farouk Shami for Governor, Texas, 2010

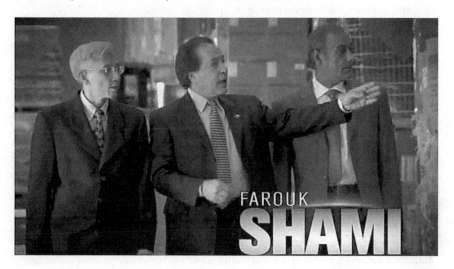

Farouk Shami is a Houston businessman who ran for governor of Texas in the 2010 Democratic primary. A self-made billionaire who made his fortune developing and marketing hair-care products, Shami was able to finance his own campaign. From the start, he faced enormous challenges. First, Shami is an immigrant from Palestine who speaks with an accent. In a place where immigration ranks among the top "problems" facing the state, Shami's status as a Palestinian American did not work in his favor.[24] Second, Shami had zero political experience, had never run for elected office, and was virtually unknown. Despite these setbacks, Shami entered the race, and we used our first ad, "Big as Texas," to introduce him to voters.

To tell Shami's story, the campaign employed a biographical ad. The spot ran heavily at the beginning of the campaign, and featured images of different cities depending on the broadcast market. It was scripted, and narrated by a booming voice with a Texas drawl. Many of the biographical ads I make are narrated by the candidate him- or herself, which I feel creates greater authenticity, but because the state of Texas was a main character in this ad, we decided a narrator with a local accent was a better way to connect Shami with voters.

The ad begins with a sweeping shot of an open highway. The narrator begins, "It's a story as big as Texas. A story of hope, opportunity, and the American dream." Iconic images of Texas throughout its history flash before the screen. A bus passes by the Texas state line, and the narrator begins to tell Shami's life story. Our campaign sought to link Shami's amazing personal narrative of coming to America with $71 in his pocket to build a multibillion-dollar company with the story of Texas itself. In this way we argued that even though Shami may look or speak differently, he shares values with Texan voters.

After explaining Shami's background, the ad reveals him as a successful businessman, walking through his factories and speaking with workers. Research showed that job creation was the most important issue in the race, so even in our biographical ad we incorporated a jobs theme: "Farouk Shami. He just brought 1,200 jobs to Texas by moving his factories here from Korea," the narrator explains.

The ad culminates with a scene that had a powerful visual and symbolic impact for Texans: Shami surrounded by his large family at his ranch. It ends with Shami resting against a fence as the narrator delivers the tagline of the campaign: "Farouk Shami. The day he becomes governor is the day business as usual ends in Texas." Farouk Shami's biographical ad told his story, laid out his plan for the future, and linked his personal narrative to the state he sought to lead. While Shami's long shot campaign would not end in victory, "Big as Texas" went on to win Best Statewide Advertisement in America at the annual Reed Awards for excellence in political communication, and the Spanish language version of the ad "Grande Como Texas" won a Gold Pollie Award from the American Association of Political Consultants for the best foreign language ad in America that year.

Issue Ad

Case Study: Americans United for Safe Streets, Virginia, 2010

In Virginia's 11th district, incumbent congressman Gerry Connolly (D) was facing a serious challenge by businessman Keith Fimian. Connolly had beaten Fimian in 2008, but Fimian had gained a great deal of momentum in two years, and in 2010 he was lifted by a strong Republican tide. Fimian was picked as one of the GOP's "young guns" and received funding and support from the party as a result.

Toward the end of the campaign, Fimian participated in a televised interview where he advocated allowing guns on college campuses and declared that college students should "pack heat" to prevent gun violence. He said he believed that the 2007 Virginia Tech massacre, in which thirty-two people were shot dead, would not have happened if "one of those kids in one of those classrooms was packing

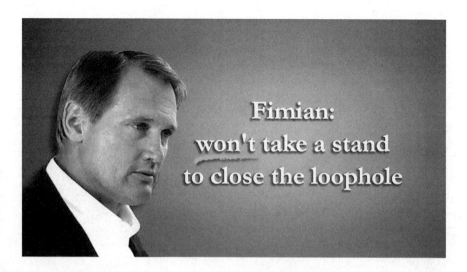

heat."[25] This was an incendiary comment concerning a tragedy that was close to the hearts of all Virginians.

The group Americans United for Safe Streets got involved in the race with an independent expenditure ad, which our firm produced to raise awareness of Fimian's extreme views. In the spot "Next," Omar Samaha tells the tragic story of his sister Reema who was a victim of the Virginia Tech shootings. The ad, narrated by Omar, focuses on the "gun show loophole," which allows convicted criminals to purchase guns without a background check. Keith Fimian did not support closing this loophole, so the ad asks viewers to call the Fimian campaign to confront him on this issue.

While the advertisement does not specifically reference the on-air comments Fimian made, "Next" kept the issue of gun control fresh in the minds of voters. After the first Election Day count, Gerry Connolly led with only 487 votes. After provisional ballots were counted, Connolly increased his lead to 981 votes (just .43%) and eked out a razor-thin win. "Next" is an example of how an independent expenditure ad can go on-air at the end of a campaign and help sway an undecided electorate.

Accomplishment and Vision Ad

Case Study: Eliot Cutler for Governor, Maine, 2010

In 2010, Eliot Cutler ran as an Independent in Maine's gubernatorial election. He was a unique candidate, having never sought or held elected office and having spent

most of his adult life outside of Maine. It was our job to show voters that despite his nonpolitical background, Cutler had the vision and skills to pull Maine out of the recession that had devastated the state's economy and drained people's spirit. A successful lawyer and businessman, Cutler had worked at the highest levels of government. In Washington, he was part of Jimmy Carter's White House budget team, and he worked for Senator Ed Muskie (an iconic figure in the state's political history). Cutler's closing ad, "Future," which was produced by our firm, communicated his unique qualifications, while asking the people of Maine to believe in their state again.

The ad starts with Cutler speaking directly to the camera. He begins by saying, "This year's election for governor is about changing direction." As Cutler continues, images of real Mainers are interspersed with images from social networking sites utilized throughout the campaign. For example, one scene shows a computer mouse clicking the "Like" button on Cutler's Facebook page. The campaign's expert use of social media helped it to stand out as new and innovative, and we wanted to highlight that in our ad by showcasing new media and the connections it had forged between Cutler and his followers.

Halfway through the sixty-second spot, a narrator takes over to talk about Cutler's experience and credentials. Every major newspaper in the state endorsed Eliot Cutler, so instead of praising him in our words, we used the language from the newspaper endorsements to make our case. Images of Cutler with Mainers are integrated with text from Cutler's endorsements. Quotes like "deep experience"[26] and "a skillful negotiator"[27] flash across the screen. The clear message is that Cutler is both qualified and innovative enough to solve Maine's problems. The most compelling part of this ad is its sense of optimism. The goal of "Future" was to inspire the people of Maine to believe in their state and to choose a leader who had the credentials to make Maine work again, even though that leader did not come from one of the two major political parties.

While the campaign did not achieve victory on Election Day, "Future" helped continue the momentum that brought Cutler from single-digit name recognition five months before the election to within two percentage points of winning. The campaign did this all without airing one negative ad.

Negative Ad

Case Study: Linc Chafee for Governor, Rhode Island, 2010

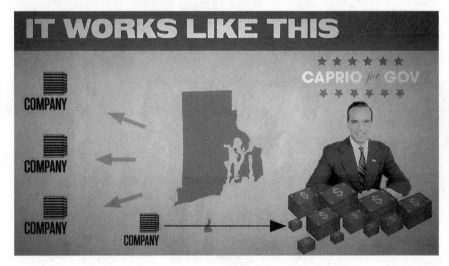

A recent example of negative advertising comes in the form of an exchange from the 2010 gubernatorial race in Rhode Island. Taxes were a huge issue throughout the campaign. Independent candidate Linc Chafee had proposed a 1 percent sales tax on currently exempt items to help the state out of its gaping budget hole. His opponents seized on the mention of increased taxes and attacked Chafee relentlessly with ads featuring working mothers to the camera expressing their hardships in the struggling economy. The most notorious of these ads came from Democratic nominee Frank Caprio's campaign and featured Rhode Islanders saying, "Lincoln Chafee just doesn't get it." The attacks were relentless, and internal polling showed they were having a negative impact on Chafee's standing.

The Chafee campaign decided to respond with a negative ad of its own. It chose to target Caprio, portraying him as a typical politician with a record of political cronyism and a scandal involving a "pay to play" scheme. The ad "Pay to

Play" explains what a pay to play scheme is through simple narration and graphics. "In the world of old politics it's called pay to play," the narrator begins. We then attack our opponent, adding a graphic of his face as the narrator says, "And Frank Caprio is a master of the game." The ad continues, "It works like this: Caprio puts out a request for a proposal to do state business. Companies contribute cash to Caprio's campaign. Companies then get millions in state business." To bolster our attack, we cited the *Wall Street Journal* article that accused Caprio of engaging in pay to play while serving as Rhode Island's general treasurer. The ad ends with Chafee working at a desk. "Linc Chafee: A new way forward," the narrator concludes. The "Trust Chafee" logo then appears on the screen.

The purpose of "Pay to Play" was to portray Caprio as an old-time politician who was part of the political machine, while presenting Chafee as an honest, trustworthy leader who represented "a new way forward" for Rhode Island. "Pay to Play" ran for two weeks on broadcast and cable and had a substantial impact on the horse race, as well as Caprio's favorable/unfavorable rating. In the end, the one-time front-runner, Frank Caprio, finished a distant third, and Linc Chafee was elected the only Independent governor in America.

Notes

1. See Edwin Diamond and Stephen Bates, *The Spot: The Rise of Political Advertising on Television* (Cambridge, MA.: MIT Press, 1992).
2. Federal Election Commission, Campaign Disclosure Reports, cir. 2010, 2008, and 2006, www.fec.gov/finance/disclosure/disclosure_data_search.shtml.
3. In 2008, the Obama presidential campaign spent $244.4 million on broadcast advertising and only $26.6 million on Internet media and $20.5 million on print media according to the Center for Responsive Politics' OpenSecrets.org. For more information, see Patricia Zengerle's article "How to Spend a Billion: Obama Will Lavish on Ads," *Reuters,* April 6, 2011.
4. Supported by internal polling. Discussed publically by Cutler's campaign manager in Susan M. Cover's article "Lead Grows for LePage in Latest Poll" (*Morning Sentinel,* September 9, 2010).
5. See Herbert S. Parmet, *Eisenhower and the American Crusades* (New Brunswick, NJ: Transaction, 1999).
6. See Robert J. Huckshorn and Robert C. Spencer, *The Politics of Defeat: Campaigning for Congress* (Amherst: University of Massachusetts Press, 1971).
7. W. I. Romanow, *Television Advertising in Canadian Elections* (Waterloo, Ont.: Wilfred Laurier University Press, 2003).
8. The Strategy Group for Media produced Rand Paul's advertisements. "Rand's Plan" was uploaded to YouTube by randpaul on September 21, 2010. Accessed on June 13, 2011, from http://www.youtube.com/user/RandPaul#p/u/8/uVorVi8gCJM.
9. For more information about the use of research in campaigns see Douglas E. Schoen, *The Power of the Vote* (New York: William Morrow, 2007); and Frank Luntz, *Words That Work* (New York: Hyperion, 2007).

10. Ivor Crewe, Brian Gosschalk, and John Bartle, *Political Communications: Why Labour Won the General Election of 1997* (London: Routledge, 1998), 56–57.

11. A panel "back survey" refers to a survey of a discrete group of voters who are established initially as a random group and who are subsequently recontacted by the same pollster and asked to give their opinions on new issues, as well as on previously asked questions such as candidate support. Panel back surveys allow pollsters and campaigns to follow the dynamic within a discrete group of respondents, which may be different from what is happening at the same time with the electorate at large.

12. See Kathiann M. Kowalski, *Campaign Politics: What's Fair? What's Foul?* (New York: Twenty-First Century Books, 2000).

13. Michael D. Shear, "New 'Daisy' Ad Warns Against Delay in Arms Treaty" (*The New York Times*, "The Caucus Blog," November 19, 2010).

14. Steve Davis, Larry Elm, and Grant Reeher, *Click on Democracy: The Internet's Power to Change Political Apathy Into Civic Action* (Boulder: Westview Press, 2004), 30.

15. "Opportunity" was uploaded to YouTube by EliotCulter on August 23, 2010. Accessed on June 14, 2011, from http://www.youtube.com/watch?v=9S9oYcGgAts&feature=player_embedded#at=45.

16. See www.cutler2010.com. Accessed June 14, 2011.

17. See MoveOn.org's "Obama in 30 Seconds Contest" at obamain30seconds.org.

18. See Jeff Howe, "The Rise of Crowdsourcing" (*Wired*, June 2006).

19. See Spencer MacColl's report, "A Center for Responsive Politics Analysis of the Effects of: *Citizens United v. Federal Election Commission*," available at OpenSecrets.org.

20. Ibid.

21. Abdon M. Pallasch, "State Bar Condemns Ads Attacking Sup. Court Justice" (*Chicago Sun Times,* November 4, 2010).

22. See the *Chicago Sun Times'* editorial "Rewrite the Rules on Judge's Recusal," May 26, 2011.

23. See the Google Chrome "offline" campaign, "The Web Is What You Make of It," which is profiled in Claire Dain Miller's article "Google Takes to TV to Promote Browser" (*The New York Times,* May 4, 2011).

24. See the University of Texas/*Texas Tribune* statewide survey of registered voters taken February 11–17, 2011, in which immigration ranked highest when respondents were asked to rank the "most important problem facing the state of Texas today."

25. Keith Fimian in an interview with reporter Mark Segraves on Channel 50's NewsPlus, October 25, 2010.

26. "Cutler for Governor" (*Portland Phoenix*, October 20, 2010).

27. "Maine Needs Cutler in Blaine House" (*York Weekly,* October 20, 2010).

CHAPTER 4

Social and New Media—An Evolving Future

Michael Turk

AS CAMPAIGNS HAVE EVOLVED OVER THE YEARS, changing media platforms have challenged the unprepared and presented opportunities to the bold and innovative. The story of the first televised presidential debate in 1960—the clean-shaven John Kennedy sparring with the scruffy Richard Nixon—has become the stuff of legend. Those listening via radio gave the win to Nixon; those watching television scored it for Kennedy.[1] In the end, the Nixon campaign was caught flat-footed by the new technology and paid the price by a defeat of 100,000 votes out of 68 million cast.

As a medium for disseminating information, the Internet is unrivaled in the modern communications era. Breaking stories today routinely pop first on the Internet, and get the attention of television and radio shortly thereafter. When the U.S. assault began on Osama bin Laden's compound, a Pakistani citizen named Sohaib Athar tweeted the events live before the rest of the world learned of their significance.[2] When Sen. John Kerry (D-Mass.) toured a space shuttle during the 2004 campaign, and NASA put photos of the visit on the agency's website, bloggers and political partisans found the images in short order and began mocking the Democrat's campaign.[3]

In the earliest days of the Internet, the media asked if the next campaign cycle would be the one in which the Internet came into its own and made the difference between winning and losing for a presidential candidate. As the media looked on with anticipation, voters looked for more information about elections and candidates—with exponentially more going online in pursuit of politics each cycle. Between 2000 and 2010, the percentage of adult Americans using the Internet to research the election grew from 18 percent to 73 percent.[4]

As the electorate looked to the Internet for information, the technologies available to both watch and participate in the election increased and improved. No longer content to sit on the sidelines, voters became active participants. Some of the best, most talked about videos from the 2006, 2008, and 2010 campaigns were not produced by campaign consultants, but came from amateur videographers with names like S. R. Sidarth and Internet handles like ParkRidge47 or BarelyPolitical (aka ObamaGirl).[5] These activists were both producers and consumers of political messaging, contributing their own voice to the broader message and changing the way voters participate in the electoral process. Voters now take to the Internet to make political ads, framing candidates in ways not always appreciated by the official campaign committees.

Campaigns are also changing their tactics based on the new capabilities afforded by the Internet. Candidates and committees have made voter empowerment a cornerstone of their technology initiatives. In 2003, the Dean campaign made effective use of Meetup (one of the earliest social media) to mobilize activists. In 2004, the Bush campaign's Personal Precinct program allowed volunteers to print maps of their neighborhood to walk, generate call sheets for phoning from home, or organize house parties to spread the campaign's message to friends and family. In 2008, the Obama campaign used its activist platform at mybarackobama. com to build on those earlier efforts and coordinate a national field organization using online tolls. The campaign granted activists a greater level of access and involvement than ever before, and used its Internet presence as both a hub of activity and a recruitment tool to grow its offline organization.

This chapter seeks to explore the benefits campaigns can recognize with innovative application of new and social media. The chapter will cover the rise of the Internet and new media in campaigns, how the Internet evolved into a potent communications and mobilization tool for campaigns, how new media and social media have transformed campaigns, how mobility is changing and may further change the role of communications, and what campaigns of the future may look like. The one constant in technology is change. The one constant in campaigns is the unending quest for the technology, idea, or message that will give campaigns an electoral advantage. As we look toward the 2012 campaign, we can make some educated predictions of what technology changes we will see, and how campaigns may use them.

The Rise of the Internet and New Media in Campaigns

In the mid-1990s, the Internet was a new frontier, largely unheard of by most Americans. Political use of the Internet, however, had been a staple of the nascent network since its earliest days. Usenet groups—discussion forums visited by the Internet's pioneers and academics who were frequently given access through university networks—had been a hive of political activity for nearly fifteen years before the first presidential campaign went online. Users had discussions about topics ranging from Reagan's arms control policy to a campaign to cryogenically freeze the Reagan-Bush ticket.[6]

Despite the proliferation of political discourse online, such discussions on the Internet would remain the realm of computer science students until the invention of the browser and commercialization made the network accessible to the mainstream. As companies like AOL and Prodigy opened the door to consumers, and the ease of navigation born of HTML gave way to "browsing" the web, the growth of politics online exploded.

Campaigns began taking simple steps to extend the reach of their communications efforts with the Republican National Committee (RNC) going online in 1994, followed by a handful of state political parties and grassroots organizations like Free Republic.

In the 1996 campaign, presidential websites were little more than brochureware with limited navigation options for things like press releases, issue papers, and campaign updates. The "advanced" features of the site included things like quizzes and a brief audio clip.[7]

As the millennium dawned, campaigns began to recognize the Internet's ability to organize and rolled out websites with rudimentary volunteer tools like Steve Forbes's e-Precinct, George Bush's Team Leader, and the Gore-Lieberman iTeam and GoreNet offerings. These tools laid the framework for more sophisticated tools that would come in later cycles. Party committees began to invest in similar tools to encourage political participation. During the early years of the twentieth century, affinity programs created by political parties and campaigns rewarded activists in much the same way frequent-flier programs reward repeat business.

The RNC's Team Leader program combined political action with affinity rewards like Velcro wallets and PDA covers. For completing certain tasks, activists would receive points they could trade in for merchandise emblazoned with the Team Leader logo. The program was initially mocked[8] but eventually was recognized for the significant role it played in the party's political operation. During the 2004 campaign, Team Leader, together with the Bush volunteer initiative, was tied to walk and phone programs. Campaign volunteers were no longer beholden to campaign infrastructure if they wanted to get involved.

While the Bush campaign and the RNC were focused on driving action and rewarding activists, the Dean campaign was making use of early social media platforms like blogs and Meetup.com. Dean supporters put Meetup's fledgling service on the map by using the site to coordinate political events. The campaign used its blog to speak directly with the activists and draw inspiration from supporters. After the campaign had developed an interactive graphic of a baseball player to track online fundraising, supporters on the blog suggested the candidate go on stage carrying a big red bat, if donors could raise $1 million online. Joe Trippi, Dean's campaign manager, directed a staffer to find a red bat. When the donations rolled past the million-dollar total, Dean strolled on stage with bat in hand.[9]

The 2004 and 2008 campaigns proved beyond any reasonable doubt the old adage that knowledge is power. Especially compared to the relative simplicity of early campaign websites, modern presidential campaigns combine cutting-edge digital marketing tactics, best-of-breed software, and specialized, and frequently custom, call and walk programs, affinity efforts, and community engagement tools. Presidential campaigns can be as sophisticated as any Fortune 500 company or Silicon Valley startup in terms of the platforms they develop and innovative tactics they employ.

While campaigns previously focused on GRPs, or television's gross ratings points, and could calculate media budgets with relative ease, today's campaign has to contend with CPA (cost per acquisition), CPM (cost per thousand ad impressions delivered), ROI (return on amount invested in campaign advertising), e-mail list size, open rates, click-throughs, bounce and unsubscription rates, traffic metrics, friend counts, and countless other metrics. Campaigns look closely at traffic to their website for patterns they can exploit. For instance, in 2004, the Bush campaign received an average of one donation for every hundred visitors. The average donation was $100. This understanding can aid the campaign in increasing the number of site visitors or raising the average donation amount.

For the campaign manager, the wide array of metrics available with web tools provides a clearer view of success and cost than traditional media. Campaign metrics can identify ways to maximize benefits and accountability. New media investments provide a level of feedback and reporting campaigns can count on. The ability to track outcomes does not change the fundamental goal of political campaigns—organizing a winning coalition. It does, however, make that job somewhat easier. While television advertising can tell you the number of viewers tuned to a program or channel at any point in time, it cannot tell you if the voter you are trying to reach actually saw the ad.

New media, in this way, are more sophisticated than television in that they can be targeted to specific users. Online destinations can match voter files against their registered subscribers to ensure that the voter you are attempting to reach is the one who views your ad.

As users of social networks like Facebook and Google+ share more information about themselves and their interests, political advertisers can target their messages very narrowly based on those characteristics. Social networks, and the rich information they provide, have become valuable tools for reaching voters.

New Media and Social Media

While the terms *new media* and *social media* are often used interchangeably, for the purpose of this chapter, *new media* will be used to describe communications and mobilization efforts that are delivered via the Internet. This is as opposed to traditional media like television, radio, and direct mail. Social media would technically be a subset of new media and include platforms that rely on interconnections between people to share and distribute information or coordinate activity.

In the most recent presidential campaign cycle, the rise of social media has played a significant role in campaigns. Platforms like Facebook, Twitter, YouTube, and Myspace were used by campaigns to coordinate supporters, and were used by supporters to self-direct their own efforts independently of the campaign. The impact of social media became so great that the number of friends and followers of a campaign became a metric by which campaign success and failure were judged. Nonpartisan blog techPresident, created to assess how campaigns were using the Internet, featured a permanent count, updated daily, of how many fans the respective 2008 candidates had.[10] The use of fans as a gauge of electability continued during early coverage of the 2012 campaign, with Barack Obama's 22 million Facebook fans being frequently contrasted to the 3 million fans of his closest Republican rival—Sarah Palin.[11]

While *new media* has become a generic term for Internet-based communications in recent years, campaigns have used the web to deliver information and engage activists for some time. Indeed, political discussion and organization can be traced back to before the rise of the web we know today. In fact, discussions of campaigns were taking place on bulletin board systems years before the development of the browser.

The Role of New Media in Campaigns

The technological convergence society has witnessed in recent years has made many distinctions between new and traditional media relatively meaningless. Cell phones have become mobile Internet access platforms. Tablets have made the personal computer a portable experience. Voters are using these tools to engage in politics like never before. As noted earlier, in campaign 2010, 73 percent of American voters went online for political information or activism.

Technology has changed the way voters get information as well as the way campaigns provide it. Online campaign operatives are the first to tout the benefits the Internet brings to campaigns, but are also the first to note that the organizing aspects of campaigns haven't changed; only the tools have. Campaigns are still tasked with identifying the coalition they will need to assemble in order to win. They must still develop a coherent message that appeals to the audience that makes up that coalition. They must work to identify supporters and volunteers and mobilize those individuals to give money, contact other voters, and otherwise do the heavy lifting of the campaign. The shift toward online fundraising is illustrated by Sen. John McCain (R-Ariz.): "In his 2008 presidential campaign, 33 percent of his online fundraising came through e-mail marketing, while 58 percent came through his campaign website. By contrast, in McCain's 2010 Senate campaign,

83 percent of his online fundraising came through e-mail, and only 15 percent through his website."[12]

Attracting someone who will carry your water, without tire, day in and day out, is no small task. Fortunately, it is made easier with technology. Online tools allow you to see who is doing the work and reward them. They allow you to automate the process of tracking volunteer performance and, if used correctly, to see any shortfall in your model before it becomes an issue.

In a campaign e-mail sent during the 2008 election, Barack Obama's campaign made the following statement: "We need to fill 845,252 volunteer shifts in battleground states."[13] That the campaign could tell precisely how many volunteer shifts it had to fill, communicate that rapidly to supporters, and see in real time the progress toward its goal is a testament to the power of these tools.

Harnessing New Media for the Campaign Organization

Technology facilitates almost every aspect of campaign organization, from attracting new activists to turning out dedicated supporters on Election Day. Campaigns still rely on offline events, rallies, and campaign offices to attract supporters, but new media tactics like online advertising and list matching can augment organic list growth through site traffic to grow substantial rolls of supporters.

Online advertising puts the campaign message directly in front of potential supporters with banner, search, television, radio, and print ads. The ads typically direct viewers to a campaign site, a Facebook page, a YouTube video, or another campaign message. Once there, the visitor is encouraged to sign up for campaign updates or to volunteer. This type of campaign is usually more effective as the visitor has already (a) seen the campaign message, (b) found it compelling enough to take action, and (c) actively chosen to join the cause. The action rate for these supporters will almost always far exceed the rate of e-mail addresses purchased through list exchanges. In 2008, the Obama campaign spent roughly $8 million on online ads on its way to amassing an e-mail list of 13 million supporters.[14]

The disadvantage of online advertising, versus purchased lists of supporters, is typically the cost. Campaigns may spend between $2 and $10 (or more) per qualified supporter attracted through online ad buys. Previously, such campaigns had high upfront fees for the advertising, and there was little recourse if a given campaign failed to attract supporters. Recently, however, firms have begun adopting "cost per acquisition" (CPA) or "cost per donor" (CPD) models where the campaign pays only for converted addresses—that is, supporters who complete the whole process. This allows campaigns to budget more accurately, but often CPA or CPD campaigns have higher minimum spend levels.

Campaigns have generally tended to limit television advertising to persuasion messages, rather than recruitment. If ads contained the campaign's URL at all, it was a cursory mention, rather than prominent placement or tied to the message. In 2004, Sen. John Kerry (D-Mass.) used specific landing pages with friendly URL to drive television advertising to a specific page on the campaign site. One such ad even featured an appeal specifically for donations. The ad drove to a donation page at JoinJohnKerry.com.[15] These ads, and the landing pages to which they drove voters, allowed the campaign to provide additional context, supporting materials, and registration components tied to the content of the commercial. Such tactics, while still not widely employed, could lead to significant recruitment gains and give campaigns a way to gauge television ad effectiveness by tracking donors, supporters, and traffic originating at that URL.

List matching provides campaigns with another method of recruiting supporters. Vendors match voter information to e-mail lists and provide the campaign data including the voter's e-mail address and possibly consumer behavior. These list matches can give the campaign a very large list with very little effort. The disadvantage of list matching is that the resulting list the campaign receives will likely have very poor open and response rates. Because the list is composed of people who didn't take steps to remove themselves, or "opt out," they are quite likely people who either didn't open the vendor's message to begin with or who actively chose not to take action. Some vendors will provide an "opt-in" basis for building your list—in which activists must affirm their desire to receive your e-mails. Such services are typically more expensive and result in smaller list matches.

Having built an e-mail list, campaigns will typically interact with those supporters, while highly effective campaigns will use that list to grow their field staff. While much of the coverage surrounding Barack Obama's campaign focused on the campaign's technology, to some extent the story of how well the campaign blended the technology with tried-and-true tactics went untold. Zack Exley managed the Kerry campaign's Internet operation in 2004 after coming to some prominence in 2000 because of a lawsuit filed against him by the Bush campaign over a mock website. Exley spent time with the Obama campaign's field team in 2008 and saw firsthand the campaign's marriage of technology and traditional organizing. He suggests that the campaign took two big risks—"risking everything on the effectiveness of masses of volunteers, then . . . risking everything again by relying on volunteer teams to lead those masses."[16]

Not only did the Obama team find that volunteers could be trusted to manage activities, but the top-to-bottom integration of their field organizers allowed the type of management that a bottom-up organization like Howard Dean's lacked. Further, it allowed a "promote from within" strategy that groomed eager volunteers for larger management roles and put power closer to the teams on the ground.

One complaint frequently heard in campaign circles is the dearth of talent that can manage campaign activities. Obama's team demonstrated that volunteers could be trained to excel in management tasks.

Maximizing the Effectiveness of Communications

Sending supporters timely messages with relevant content will help you keep them connected to the campaign and energized to take action. For campaigns, maximizing the effectiveness of those campaign messages can mean the difference in election outcomes. Determining the best placement of donation buttons or images, and variables like text color and word choice, can increase the amount of money raised or the number of activists willing to do something on behalf of the candidate.

The tools available for mass communication allow a level of message testing and delivery that is unmatched. A/B or multivariate testing allows campaigns to try different messages, different imagery, different color schemes, and countless other variables to get the message that will generate the highest action rate.

Rumors of the complexity of the Obama team's message testing have created an almost mythical air around the campaign's e-mail program. Reporting on the effort apparently ranges from 7,000 different messages tested to 7,000 different instances of a single e-mail. What is clear, however, is that the campaign spent a great deal of time and energy honing the messages to make them more interesting to supporters and more effective for the campaign.

Many commercial e-mail platforms now allow campaigns to very easily accommodate multivariate testing. Campaigns are given template e-mails that are customized with different colors, copy, pictures, and subject lines. Merge fields that allow the insertion of specific text based on supporter characteristics provide the campaign the flexibility to target the message to the specific voter, should it choose.

Campaigns can develop a few variations of messages. Those messages are then sent to small subsets (typically no more than a few hundred or a thousand) of the e-mail universe. The responses to those messages—including open rate, click-through on specific links, clicks on individual images, and so on—are tracked, and the components that perform best are then compiled into a single message that is sent to the rest of the audience. An example of that was Pat Toomey's (R-Pa.) successful campaign for the Senate in 2010. Toomey's message was very simple: "More Jobs, Less Government."[17] Strategically, this enabled Toomey to maximize his background as a small businessman and opponent of big government.

The benefits of multivariate testing are significant. The messages received by your broadest audience have already been adjusted to ensure the best action rate. This maximizes click-through and conversion, resulting in more money raised, more actions taken, and so on. The only real disadvantage is the amount of time it takes to test and send messages. The time constraints may place multivariate testing out of reach for smaller campaigns with less staff capacity. Ironically, it's these campaigns, due to their hunger for funds and support, that would most benefit from the approach.

The Modern Campaign Website

E-mails typically drive supporters to the campaign's website for further information or activism opportunities. Presidential campaign platforms have become incredibly sophisticated—providing supporters with custom tools to generate maps for walking their neighborhood, and online phone banks that allow volunteers to work from home. These platforms can also serve as sophisticated nerve centers for the entire campaign. Michael Palmer, eCampaign director for John McCain's 2008 campaign, described the campaign's web platform as the nerve center through which all of the committee's field organization was run.[18] The platform allowed volunteers and field staff to feed all voter data into a centralized database, rather than multiple different systems.

Fred Thompson's (R-Tenn.) campaign used the phone tools developed for volunteers to manage its phone banks in primary states. In addition, the campaign website was built with a social network that allowed supporters to connect and a news feed that would recommend content to visitors based on what their friends were reading.

MyBarackObama.com, on the Democratic side, was recognized for its ability to organize, but more importantly for its ability to allow supporters to organize themselves. The campaign gave supporters the ability to create their own groups and freely coordinate amongst themselves.

How New Media Are Changing the Role of the Voter

The very nature of the voter is changing as campaign platforms and the Internet have become open platforms through which voters can direct their own activities. The line between producer and consumer of political messaging has become blurred, if it hasn't disappeared altogether. In early 2007, a young activist named Philip de Vellis created an Internet firestorm by creating a web video called "Vote Different."[20] The ad was a mash-up of Apple's 1984 ad mixed with campaign video of Hillary Clinton superimposed into the ad as the "big brother" figure. The video concluded with the Obama campaign logo and became an instant hit. That de Vellis had released the video under the pseudonym ParkRidge47 and hid his identity helped drive the rapid viral spread of the video. The blog techPresident organized the online political community in a digital manhunt to identify the video's anonymous creator.[21]

In the earliest days of the 2008 campaign, it was not a paid campaign spot that had the largest impact, but a video whose creator says it took only a few short hours in his apartment on a Sunday afternoon. More important, though, de Vellis predicted the video would be just one of a coming wave of user-generated contributions to political messaging, saying, "There are thousands of other people who could have made this ad, and I guarantee that more ads like it—by people of all political persuasions—will follow."[22]

As if to punctuate de Vellis's prediction, in the spring of 2008, pop singer will.i.am gathered a group of Hollywood celebrities and singers to record a song and video called "Yes We Can." The video became a rallying cry of sorts for the campaign's supporters. Howard Dean's former campaign manager saw it differently. The Obama campaign was, at the time, trying to push the narrative that Hillary Clinton should withdraw from the campaign. Because of the popularity of the video, that message was lost, and the primary dragged on much longer. Trippi suggests, "The one thing we haven't figured out is the tool that lets all those people know now, we need to turn this way."[23]

It is exactly this challenge that new media campaigns are concerned with addressing. The one-way campaign was easier than a two-way campaign. Campaigns controlled the message voters heard. Voters had little or no ability to dramatically shift the campaign dynamic by creating content that forced campaigns to respond. The process favored candidates with money who could afford to spread their message via the best media.

Video, especially, is both a powerful tool and one that is now in the hands of campaigns and a large number of content creators looking to make a political point. The rise of YouTube has given way to the downfall of more than a few candidates.

Campaigns have begun sending young staffers with video cameras to film their opponents in the hopes of catching an unguarded moment. These "trackers," as they are known, rarely make news themselves, but their work often does. In 2006, Senate candidate George Allen (R- Va.) made a possibly derogatory comment about his opponent's tracker at a stop in southern Virginia.[24] That comment was caught on film and became a major issue that eventually derailed not only Allen's hopes for the U.S. Senate but also his chances at a White House bid.

In 2009, Virginia gubernatorial candidate Creigh Deeds was caught on tape trying to equivocate on tax increases.[25] The caricature of Deeds the video created was too much to overcome, and his Republican opponent won in a rout. The power of video is hard to overstate, and it is power that is in almost everyone's hands—not just the hands of campaigns.

BOX 4.1:   An Accidental Career

Like many people involved in politics, I became a campaign operative almost completely by accident. I had always been interested in politics and technology, but it wasn't until the 1994 campaign that I decided to get off the sidelines and into the game. Because of my background building, repairing, and using computers, in 1995 a former boss at the New Mexico GOP told me, "That thing called 'The Internet'—go figure that out." A copy of a *Teach Yourself HTML* book and time spent coding my first GOP website set the stage for a life spent trying to use the power of the web to elect Republicans. It's a career choice I'll never regret, and one I would highly recommend. The power of the Internet and technology will continue to change the way we connect to our elected officials. If you are technically inclined, harnessing that power to help shape our government is an amazing feeling.

The Rise of Social Media Platforms

Nowhere is the power of the empowered voter more apparent than in the rise of social networks. Social networks and social sharing sites allow influential voters to curate their own content—creating, aggregating, and disseminating news and information to their circle of friends and contacts.

Sites like Facebook, Twitter, and YouTube bring friends together and make the sharing of political news easier. Users of Facebook, for instance, can create events, allowing supporters to organize themselves to conduct offline events or even just to repeat important news. Twitter, originally dubbed a "microblogging" service, provides a platform for rapid distribution of short-form news. The 140-character messages can be received via a variety of desktop and smartphone applications or as text messages. As of August 4, 2011, Twitaholic, which tracks online usage of Twitter, found that mybarackobama had 9.4 million followers, ranking it third behind Lady Gaga and Justin Bieber. No other political candidate ranked in the top 100.[26]

Twitter messages are grouped by conversational threads using a marking standard known as hashtags. The hashtag for discussion of conservative information is #tcot, while progressives mark their messages with #p2. Searching Twitter for these tags yields a nearly endless flow of information, discussion, and debate. So powerful are these threads in delineating the discussion that Facebook status messages and other social network updates are frequently tagged with them as well.

These powerful networks provide new opportunities for voters to engage with one another and to find new networks of supporters. Other networks such as Digg, Delicious, or Reddit can also be used effectively to distribute a campaign's message.

As supporters read information they find valuable, they can "tag" or "bookmark" the page. Their collection of bookmarks is viewable to friends and available for others to subscribe to.

Even fundraising has gone social with fundraising companies like Kimbia developing a method to allow individual supporters to embed fundraising widgets on their own websites in much the same way YouTube allows sharing of video. These widgets make anyone with a webpage a potential fundraiser. Other companies, like Rally.org, are tying fundraising and social networks together to allow organizations and campaigns to feed both news and finance requests through the same platform—using their social content as the hook to attract donors.

These social networks have had two surprising outcomes. First they have given rise to a new type of influential—call them the social media mavens. These are people who attract large groups of followers, who are seen as sources of news and information, and who develop reputations for the quality of the information they curate. Second, these networks draw significant audiences composed of younger voters. More and more, these younger voters are eschewing traditional media (television, direct mail, and radio) and get much of their entertainment online.

As younger audiences move away from television viewing and focus on Internet consumption of media through YouTube, Netflix, and Hulu, they are also more difficult to reach with traditional ad buys. Direct mail has consistently lost audience as more and more junk mail fills our mailboxes. Efforts to cut through the clutter are marginally effective. A study for Rock the Vote found that technologically savvy voters were significantly less likely to respond to direct mail solicitations.[27]

As more voters raised on technology come of age, and replace voters comfortable with direct mail and television, the continuing shift to mixed media appeals will become more critical. Social media sources will become increasingly important as voters look to the online influential for political news. As a result, effective marriage of cross-platform and targeted messaging could replace direct mail and television as the norm.

The Mobile Voter

Further complicating the modern campaign's effort to reach voters is the increasingly mobile nature of the populace. In 2012, campaigns are likely to spend more effort testing different messages to different audience segments on an ever-wider array of technologies. Campaign messages aimed at voters on platforms like Facebook and YouTube will be dramatically different from messages delivered via telephone and the mailbox, which will differ still from appeals delivered to mobile devices.

In addition to the challenges of delivering a message to a mobile audience, voter turnout becomes increasingly challenging. Fortunately, mobile technologies also provide a wealth of opportunities for mobilization. For instance, pairing voter data with geolocation-aware applications can enable supporters to go door-to-door on their lunch hour by using a walk app to find the closest undecided voters. Supporters can also be empowered to find and connect with each other based on location data. Applications like Foursquare allow campaign supporters to check in from campaign events—sharing their location, involvement with the campaign, and current activities with friends. These updates can be distributed via Twitter, Facebook, and other social platforms to promote the event, and help build an audience for future occasions.

Mobile technologies like QR codes will allow yard signs and bumper stickers to become mobile messengers that connect interested individuals with campaign-specific messaging. QR codes are read by the camera on smartphones and can instantly bring the interested voter to the campaign's website or another landing page once scanned. These applications could connect mobile supporters with opportunities for activism based on their current coordinates. According to online writer Ben Donahower, "A third of smartphone users scan QR codes and by Christmas 2011, 1 in 2 Americans will have a smartphone." He goes on to say that "a majority of the population could be scanning QR codes by the presidential election (2012)."[28]

Another significant recent development is the rise of mobile payment solutions like those provided by Square. A small reader can be attached to the candidate's phone (or phones owned by staff) and provide payment processing on the go. The campaign's cell phones become a platform for taking donations at any time or place. As the candidate walks a rope line, if someone asks how to give, the answer no longer has to be "visit my website" but can instead be "John will be happy to take your credit card right now."

The combination of technologies available to campaigns makes it easier than ever to reach voters, and just as easy for voters to engage with the campaign. These new applications are changing the way campaigns operate today, but also hold great promise for the future of campaigns.

The Online Future

The early online campaigns of the 1990s, discussed at the beginning of this chapter, were rudimentary by today's standards, but seemed revolutionary at the time. Today's online campaigns, similarly, will look relatively uninteresting by the benchmark of future campaigns.

As campaigns innovate, the continuing convergence of technologies will make mobile the focal point of campaigns. It's no longer enough to simply try to reach voters. It will be critical to reach voters no matter where they are. Campaign offices will be supplemented with powerful mobile apps that make supporters an office unto themselves. Voter data, and the applications they power, will significantly change the way we communicate with, mobilize, and raise funds from supporters. These changes will impact not only the Internet, but the traditional media we take for granted today—things like direct mail, television, and even the web.

Personalized Direct Mail

Direct mail today is typically anything but glamorous. If voters even bother to read their mail, the messages are often irrelevant. To appeal to the lowest common denominator, direct mail is generic and may have little personal impact for the recipient.

Personalized direct mail tied to Internet landing pages will likely change the way campaigns use the postal service to reach voters. These messages contain tailored messages specific to individual voters. While the mail piece still qualifies for the bulk rate preferred by campaigns, each individual piece can contain different messages, different images, and a URL for a personalized landing page customized to the voter's issue preferences. On that landing page a web video tailored to match the voter's key issues will accompany an appeal to give, get active, or spread the word.

For instance, voters living next door to one another could get a mail piece that shared the same structure, image placement, and areas for copy. The two pieces of mail, however, could not be more different. The first voter would receive a message about military spending and support for our troops while the second contained a message on tax cuts and economic issues. Each of the voters would see a message tailored to his or her interests, complete with custom landing pages tailored to what that user would want to see.

The direct mail piece may even contain a QR code the recipient could scan to reach the web component. The union of offline formats with online technologies will create more engaging and highly relevant messaging for voters and invite them into the campaign, rather than pushing them away.

Toward Integration—Advertising Across Platforms

In much the same way, political advertisers in the future will be able to target specific voters across platforms—delivering a consistent message regardless of the platform. Cable television, for example, has been working on a new model for delivering advertising based on each voter in the household. Viewing patterns indicate the person watching the TV in the bedroom is a female over 45, while the TV in the bedroom belongs to her 19-year-old son. If both are registered to vote, they may see completely different appeals—even if watching the same program on different TVs. By delivering specific messages to different members of the household, even as they consume the same content, campaigns will be able to target specific voters, while ignoring all others.

Like direct mail, television currently delivers a message that broadcasts the same generic appeal to all viewers at once. An ad delivery system tied to the individual set-top box or addressable TV could deliver completely different ads to different televisions during the same program.

Further, new developments in Internet-connected televisions could allow viewers to "click through" from their television programming to web-based content on the TV. The content would load alongside the program allowing audience members to browse information about the campaign without having to step away from their favorite show.

Campaign communication strategies will be driven no longer by the media, but by the audience. Voters will be matched to the media they consume. Young men, who are increasingly turning away from linear television, will be reached on platforms like Hulu or Facebook, while older voters will get highly targeted mail. All voters, however, will see consistent messaging across all channels, tied to a personal profile of interests.

Will Candidate Websites Become Obsolete?

As social networks like Facebook continue to connect audiences on platforms that allow for fundraising, voter mobilization applications, and content sharing, candidates will have to decide whether they should even bother investing money in a website of their own. After all, the old adage in marketing is "go where the people are." Facebook's audience has eclipsed 750 million people. More than 141 million Americans now use Facebook.[29] With that many potential voters in one place, there is little need to drive them to a competing site.

Campaigns can spend less time and money trying to attract supporters and more time working with supporters on centralized platforms to build networks of people to carry their message. For instance, the campaign may provide a Facebook app that asks supporters to message their friends based on which are in target states. The campaign may develop an app that allows people to do virtual phone banking or generate walk lists all without ever leaving Facebook. With an open platform connected to millions of voters, the possibilities are almost endless.

Conclusion

Today's campaigns are more complex than ever before due largely to the sheer volume of information to which voters have access, and to the increasingly mobile nature of our society. When voters were content to stay home and watch the "big three" networks, they were much easier to reach, and broadcast media ruled the political landscape. Now that voters consume news and information on a 24/7 basis, and use mobile devices that are permanently connected to broadband Internet, the challenge is often not just persuading them, but reaching them and being relevant. Breaking through the clutter of our always-on media requires an integrated communications strategy that leverages traditional and new media to make campaign messages personally meaningful.

The future of campaigns is as much about the voter as it is about the candidate. The messages that will move the voter of the future will be relevant, compelling, and delivered in a way that reaches the audiences no matter where they may be. Voters will interact with the campaign, create and distribute their own content, and become both messengers and recipients in a two-way dialogue between the elected and the governed.

At the end of the day, the distinctions between new media and old will disappear, and we will be left with just media, and the desire to use them effectively to reach an audience.

Notes

1. Theodore H. White, *The Making of the President 1960* (New York: Atheneum House, 1961), 348.
2. Melissa Bell, "Sohaib Athar's Tweets From the Attack on Osama bin Laden" (*The Washington Post,* May 2, 2011). Accessed on May 22, 2011, from washingtonpost.com.
3. Amit Asaravala, "NASA Waffles on Kerry Photos" (*Wired,* July 31, 2004). Accessed on May 24, 2011, from wired.com.
4. "Youth Vote Influenced by Online Information" (Pew Internet and American Life Project, December 3, 2000); and "The Internet and Campaign 2010" (Pew Internet and American Life Project, March 17, 2011). Both accessed on May 24, 2011, from pewinternet.org.
5. S. R. Sidharth, "George Allen's Listening Tour" (August 15, 2006); Philip deVellis, "Vote Different" (March 5, 2007); and Amber Lee Ettinger, "Crush on Obama" (unknown publication date). All accessed on May 30, 2011, from youtube.com.
6. Search of Usenet's net.politics thread courtesy of Google archive at groups.google.com. Accessed on May 30, 2011.
7. "1996 Presidential Campaign Websites." Accessed on June 1, 2011, from 4president.us/1996websites.htm.
8. Paul Boutin, "Grand Old Protest: A Republican Web Site Even Bush-Bashers Can Love" (January 24, 2003). Accessed on June 1, 2011, from slate.com.
9. Garrett Graf, "The Dean Campaign Finds Treasure on the Internet: Lessons for the Social Sector Change" (November 2004). Accessed from proxied.changemakers.net/journal on June 2, 2011.
10. Friend and Follower Data Archive. Accessed on May 27, 2011, from techpresident.com.
11. Barack Obama's Facebook page at facebook.com/barackobama, and Sarah Palin's Facebook page at facebook.com/sarahpalin. Both accessed on August 9, 2011.

12. Jen Stolp and Eric Frenchman, "Want to Raise Money Online in 2012? First Learn the Lessons of 2010 . . ." (*Campaigns and Elections*, May 17, 2011). Accessed on August 3, 2011, from campaignsandelections.com.

13. Obama campaign e-mail (October 22, 2008). Accessed on June 2, 2011, from barack obama.com.

14. "Obama's Online Spend: Actually Tiny" (*Business Insider*, November 6, 2008). Accessed on June 2, 2011, from businessinsider.com.

15. Kerry-Edwards 2004, from JoinJohnKerry.com. Accessed on June 3, 2011, from you-tube.com.

16. Zack Exley, "The New Orgnizers: What's Really Behind Obama's Ground Game" (*The Huffington Post,* October 8, 2008). Accessed on June 1, 2011, from the huffingtonpost .com.

17. See homepage, toomeyforsenate.com. Accessed on August 3, 2011.

18. Michael Palmer, director, Intell360. Interview conducted April 11, 2011, Washington, DC.

19. Based on author's experience as Internet Advisor for the Thompson for President Campaign in 2008.

20. Philip deVellis. "Vote Different" (March 5, 2007). Accessed on May 27, 2011, from youtube.com.

21. Micah L. Sifry, "Who Is ParkRidge47?" (March 7, 2007). Accessed on June 2, 2011, from techpresident.com.

22. Philip de Vellis, "I Made the 'Vote Different' Ad" (March 21, 2007). Accessed on August 3, 2011, from the huffingtonpost.com.

23. Micah L. Sifry, "Getting the Download From Joe Trippi" (Personal Democracy Forum, March 30, 2008). Accessed on June 3, 2011, from personaldemocracy.com.

24. S.R. Sidharth, "George Allen Introduces Macaca" (August 15, 2006). Accessed on June 4, 2011, from youtube.com.

25. Vagoptv.com, "Deeds on the Ropes on Taxes" (September 17, 2009). Accessed on June 4, 2011, from youtube.com.

26. Twitaholic.com. Accessed on August 4, 2011.

27. "Keeping Young Voters Engaged: 2007–2008 Re-Registration Test Program" (Rock the Vote). Accessed on June 3, 2011, from rockthevote.org.

28. Ben Donahower, "Four Ways Political Campaigns Can Use QR Codes." Accessed on August 3, 2011, from e.politics.com.

29. See "Timeline" on Facebook.com for the number of active users. Quantcast, which monitors usage and demographics of the Internet, says that there are 141 million users of Facebook, as of August 2011. See Quantcast.com/facebook. Both sites accessed on August 4, 2011.

CHAPTER 5

Polling in the Twenty-First Century— Part Past, Part Future

Candice J. Nelson

POLLING WAS THE FIRST INDICATOR that the Democratic nomination for president in 2008 would not be decided on February 5—Super Tuesday. Though national polls showed Hillary Clinton as the presumed front-runner for the nomination throughout most of 2007, polls by the Clinton campaign, the Obama campaign, and the *Des Moines Register* in the fall and prior to the Iowa caucuses all pointed to an Obama victory in the caucuses. In October, Joel Benenson, Obama's pollster, assured Obama that, despite the national polls, Obama could win in Iowa.[1] An internal Clinton tracking poll in early December showed Clinton and Obama tied with 29 percent of the vote.[2] On January 2, the day before the caucuses, the *Des Moines Register* published a poll showing 32 percent of likely Democratic caucus-goers supporting Obama, compared to 25 percent supporting Clinton.[3]

Seven months before the 2012 caucuses and primaries began, polling again signaled a possible intraparty fight for the Republican nomination between Tea Party supporters and more traditional Republicans. Twenty-six percent of Republicans and Republican-leaning Independents favored Mitt Romney for the nomination, more than any other candidate, but almost one quarter (23 percent) of strong Tea Party supporters supported Michele Bachmann.[4]

Between the 2008 and 2012 presidential elections, campaign surveys have become more difficult to conduct. Since the mid-1970s, when the telephone spread to over 90 percent of households, landline telephones have been the mechanism of choice for the vast majority of surveys, including campaign surveys.[5] However, the increased use of answering machines, caller ID, and cell phones has made calling landline phones a less reliable method of reaching potential respondents. Technological advancements have called the future of random digit dialing (RDD), the standard method for telephone surveys, into question, presenting campaign pollsters with their biggest challenge for the future—how best to reach prospective voters. That is the question for the survey research community today, and likely in the years to come. Are phones still the best way to conduct surveys, and, if so, how does the survey community deal with the increasing number of households without landline phones? This chapter will examine the current state of phone surveys, the challenges for the future, and the alternatives to the traditional landline phone surveys.

Phone Surveys: Practices and Problems

Phone surveys' major advantage is their ability to randomize the survey respondents, which enables pollsters to generalize from the survey sample to an entire population. Pollsters can survey as few as 400 respondents and generalize to an entire congressional district or state. National surveys typically have approximately 1,000 respondents, largely to allow some comparisons among demographic groups (men compared to women, Democrats compared to Republicans, and age, income, and educational level comparisons, for example). Since telephone surveys became the methodology of choice for campaign pollsters, telephone surveys have relied on RDD to select respondents in a particular population. RDD uses the area codes for the geographic population being surveyed. Computers generate random numbers that allow survey administrators to call random respondents within the survey population. Among the many advantages of RDD is that it enables pollsters to reach potential respondents with unlisted phone numbers. The advent of computer-assisted telephone interviews (CATI) allowed computers, rather than individuals, to place the calls, reducing the time needed to make phone calls and thus complete interviews.

But pollsters have begun to find it difficult to get people to answer phone surveys. With answering machines and caller ID, potential survey respondents are able to screen their calls and simply not answer when the caller seems to be a polling organization. In order to get 500 completed interviews, pollsters may need to call twenty to twenty-five times that number of phone numbers.[6] For people ages 18–30, that number can double.[7] That obviously increases both costs of surveys and the time they take.

A second, and growing, problem for phone surveys is the increased use of cell phones, particularly the growing number of individuals who only have cell phones. A National Health Interview Survey between January and June 2010 found that slightly more than one in four Americans (26.6 percent) had given up their landline phone and lived in households with only a cell phone.[8] The cell phone–only phenomenon is most problematic for surveys of young people. The National Health Interview Survey found that over half (51.3 percent) of young people between the ages of 25 and 29 years lived in wireless-only households, and almost 40 percent

(39.9 percent) of 18- to 24-year-olds only had cell phones.[9] The Institute of Politics at Harvard University has conducted its Biannual Youth Survey on Politics and Public Service online since the fall of 2006, because of the unreliability of using landline phones to reach 18- to 24-year-olds.

Complications With Cell Phones

Currently, almost all, if not all, survey firms use some form of automated dialing device to make their calls. However, federal law prohibits making CATI calls to cell phones, so all phone calls to cell phone users must be dialed manually. As a result, sampling cell phone users is twice as expensive as sampling landline phone users.

There is also the problem of acquiring cell phone numbers. For any survey in which the geographic location of the respondent is important—and that would include all campaign surveys—using cell phone numbers creates problems. Because cell phones are portable, they go with their owners when they move from one jurisdiction to another. A cell phone owner may move from one state to another, but not change his or her cell phone number. Landline phone area codes represent real physical jurisdictions. This problem is greater, once again, with respect to young people, who often have cell phone numbers tied to their parents' home address, even when away at school or working in a different area or state. In order to compensate for this problem, screening questions have to be built into cell phone calls to ensure that the respondent actually lives in the area code of his or her cell phone number. This is less of a problem in statewide and national races, but a considerable problem in congressional and legislative races.[10]

Cell phones pose additional problems for campaign pollsters. While landline surveys can be as long as 18 to 20 minutes, cell phone surveys must be shorter. It is almost impossible to do message testing, an important part of initial campaign surveys, on cell phones.[11] Also, when calling a cell phone, there is no way to know where the respondent is. With landline surveys, the survey researcher knows that the respondent is at his or her residence. When a respondent answers a cell phone, he or she could be anywhere—driving in a car, in the school carpool line, at a restaurant.[12]

Landline- Versus Cell Phone–Only Users

Surveys by the Pew Research Center for the People and the Press and the Pew Internet and American Life Project conducted in 2009 and 2010 found substantial demographic differences between landline- and cell phone–only individuals. Not surprisingly, cell phone–only users were younger than landline users; 41 percent of cell phone–only users are 18 to 29, while only 7 percent of landline users fall in this age group.[13] Landline users are better educated (38 percent are college graduates, compared to 27 percent of cell phone users) and have higher incomes. Twenty-seven percent of landline users have incomes of $75,000 or more; just 16 percent of cell phone users have incomes in this bracket. Conversely, 43 percent of cell phone users have incomes under $30,000, compared to just 26 percent of landline users.[14] There are also significant gender, racial, and ethnic differences between landline and cell phone users. Men make up 60 percent of the cell phone–only population, while 59 percent of women use landline phones. African Americans and Latinos make up 14 and 17 percent, respectively, of cell phone users, compared to just 5 percent of Latinos and 9 percent of African Americans in the Pew survey who reported using landline phones.[15]

The main advantage of surveys using RDD is the ability of the survey to generalize from the sample to the entire population. Because the cell phone– and landline-only populations are different, generalizing from landline phone users to the entire population mischaracterizes the cell phone–only population. With the cell phone–only population exceeding 25 percent, surveys that use only landline phones risk bias in their results. By 2010, most campaign pollsters included cell phone numbers in their RDD surveys;[16] by the 2012 election cycle all surveys will have a cell phone component.[17]

Random Digit Dialing or Voter Files

As response rates to traditional RDD phone calls decline, pollsters have sought alternative means to reach sample respondents. Campaign pollsters today have the option of reaching survey respondents either by random digit dialing or by using voter files. State election agencies compile lists of registered voters, called a voter list. A voter file is an enhanced voter list that provides additional information about registered voters beyond that on the voter list. For most campaign pollsters, the decision to use RDD or a voter file depends on two factors: the type of race and the quality of the state voter file. Bob Carpenter, senior vice president at American Viewpoint, a Republican polling firm, said in an interview for this project that for statewide surveys, he still uses random digit dialing, but for congressional or legislative races, he would use a voter file.[18] Sarah Simmons, senior research analyst at Harris Interactive, concurs that voter files make the most sense in smaller races, while RDD is still preferable for statewide races and most congressional races.[19] Yet Fred Yang, a principal at Garin Hart Yang, a Democratic polling firm, said he used only voter files for political campaigns in 2010.[20] David Winston, president of the Winston Group, said that his decision to use a voter file depends on the quality of the voter file in the state. For states with high population turnover, such as Arizona and Nevada, the voter files are less reliable, but in a state like Iowa, with low population change, the file is much more reliable.[21] While the quality and accuracy of voter files still vary across states, the Help America Vote Act (HAVA), passed in the aftermath of the 2000 presidential election in Florida, has at least created state voter files in all 50 states, which has made using voter files in campaign surveys much more viable for pollsters.[22]

In June 2007, for an earlier version of this chapter, I discussed the advantages of doing surveys from voter files with Bob Blaemire, then the president of Blaemire Communications, and Bill Russell, then the firm's marketing director. Blaemire Communications was one of the most respected Democratic voter file companies in the United States, and counted as its clients some of the major Democratic polling firms.[23] Blaemire and Russell pointed out that voter files contain party identification (in states where there is party registration) and voting history, including frequency of voting. Pollsters therefore have on the voter file information that they would have to obtain by using screening questions in an RDD sample. Blaemire and Russell argue that although drawing a sample from a voter file is more expensive than drawing an RDD sample, the advantages of having information on the voter file that would otherwise have to be asked for in a survey make sampling from a voter file more cost-effective.[24] Given that the costs of phone surveys are determined largely by the number of phone calls made and the length of the survey, Blaemire and Russell argue that voter file surveys are less expensive for two main reasons. First, fewer questions need to be asked. Second, because the phone numbers on the voter file are the residential numbers of registered voters, fewer phone calls have to be made to get the sample.[25] Blaemire and Russell confirm, however, what survey researchers have found: Young people are harder to reach by phone. They find that it is harder to get phone matches for young people than other age groups.[26]

The Future of Campaign Polling—Phone Surveys

Most campaign pollsters still think that phone surveys are the most reliable for predicting voter behavior and campaign outcomes. Yet these same pollsters also recognize that the use of phones is going to be more problematic in the years to come, particularly because of the proliferation of cell phones. So, what form is survey research likely to take in the coming years?

Polling in a Changing Electoral Base—Case Study of the Reid Senate Campaign

As it gets harder and harder to reach potential voters by phone, campaign pollsters need to be more and more creative in their polling. One example of such creativity occurred in the Nevada Senate race in 2010. Going into the 2010 elections, Senate majority leader Harry Reid was viewed as one of the most vulnerable, if not the most vulnerable, incumbent senator. While the economic picture nationwide was not favorable for the Democratic Party, the situation in Nevada was particularly grim. Unemployment, at 14.5 percent, was the highest in the country.[27] Sixty percent of Nevada homeowners had mortgages that exceeded the value of their homes. Forty-eight percent of Nevadans thought their families were worse off economically than they had been in the past. Fifty-five percent disapproved of President Obama's job performance; 61 percent disapproved of Senator Reid's job performance. Reid had not had a competitive race since 1998; two-thirds of the 2010 electorate had not lived in the state in 1998.

Despite these grim numbers, The Mellman Group, the polling firm for the Reid campaign, consistently had Reid ahead in its polls. In October, The Mellman Group had Reid ahead by 5 percent (which was Reid's margin of victory); every other public poll had Sharron Angle, Reid's Republican opponent, ahead by 3 or 4 percent. Mark Mellman, president of The Mellman Group, credits his correct prediction of the race to three methodological factors in his firm's polling: the definition of likely voters, the inclusion of cell phones in its surveys, and its inclusion of hard-to-reach voters in the polls.

While pollsters are reluctant to publicly describe exactly how they define "likely voters," it is often some combination of past voting history and interest in the current race. Mellman found that if he defined likely voters as those survey respondents who said they had voted in 2006 *and* 2008, Reid trailed Angle by 1 percentage point. However, among respondents who had voted in 2006 *or* 2008, Reid was ahead in the polls by 17 percentage points. A discrepancy also occurred between easy-to-reach and hard-to-reach respondents. Those who could be reached after one or two calls supported Reid by 1 percent over Angle; those respondents who could only be reached after three or more calls supported Reid by 9 percentage points. Finally, there were substantial differences in Reid's support between those survey respondents reached by landline phones and those reached by cell phones. Respondents reached on their landline phones supported Reid by 4 percent; those reached on cell phones supported Reid by 25 percent.[28]

Not only did the growing population in Nevada require creative approaches to polling, but so did the large Latino population. Latinos comprised just over 25 percent of the population in Nevada in 2010, an almost 82 percent increase since 2000.[29] Mellman conducted surveys in both Spanish and English. These bilingual surveys produced two important pieces of information. One, support was higher for Reid among those surveyed in Spanish than among those surveyed in English, so the English-only surveys conducted by other polling operations underestimated Reid's support among Latinos. Second, the economy, jobs, and education were more important to Latinos than immigration reform, information that was important to the campaign's messaging to this demographic group.

Recognizing that the electorate had changed between 1998 and 2010, Mellman created a methodological approach to reach prospective voters who might be missed with more traditional survey approaches and, in doing so, correctly predicted the outcome of the election.

Another example of the importance of recognizing changes in the electorate for accurate surveys occurred in 2008, prior to the Iowa caucuses. Ann Selzer, the pollster for the *Des Moines Register*, correctly predicted that Obama, not Clinton, would win the Iowa caucuses, and that there would be a large turnout.[30] Selzer interviewed 800 Democratic caucus-goers, but assumed 60 percent of the caucus-goers would be first-time caucus-goers, and only 54 percent would be Democrats (the remainder would be Independents—40 percent—and Republicans—5 percent),[31] a very different caucus population than in past elections.

Reaching Cell Phone Users

In the realm of phone surveys, random digit dialing continues to be the gold standard for campaign surveys.[32] Political campaigns are risk averse and reluctant to move away from something that has worked so well for forty years. In the near future, it seems that phone surveys, either using RDD or voter files, will continue to be the mechanism of choice in political campaigns. However, pollsters may need to call more phone numbers to reach their sample size, which means surveys will become increasingly more expensive.

Given the increasing prevalence of cell phone users, cell phones will have to be a part of surveys in the 2012 election cycle and beyond. Bob Carpenter predicts that in 2012 cell phones will be 10 to 15 percent of most surveys; by 2014 and 2016 cell phones could be 25 to 35 percent of surveys.[33] Other pollsters estimate the percentage of cell phones in any given sample in 2012 between 20 and 30 percent.[34] Yet the portability of cell phone numbers, the fee structure for calls to cell phones, and the prohibition on using computer-assisted dialing to call cell phone numbers mean cell phones will increase the costs of survey research in campaigns.

The Future of Campaign Online Surveys

The question of where survey research will be in the future inevitably raises the question of online surveys. However, for any survey that wants to generalize from the sample to the entire population, the lack of randomness in most online surveys is a serious problem. That we can generalize from phone surveys is still their greatest strength. The lack of the ability to generalize from Internet surveys remains their biggest weakness.

Harris Interactive was one of the pioneers in online survey research and is still one of the largest online polling firms. The Harris Poll Online currently has about

5 million participants.[35] All online polling firms use a variation of a technique called "opt-in"; the firms solicit respondents through a variety of means—websites, advertisements, and sweepstakes, for example. Respondents who agree to be part of these large surveys are periodically sent surveys online, and the respondents choose whether or not to participate in any particular survey. Many of these large online surveys are done for market research, but many also have some political content.

The opt-in component is what critics of online polling see as these polls' greatest weakness. Because respondents opt to participate, the sample is not random, and thus generalizations cannot be made. Moreover, individuals who are online are not representative of the entire population; the online community is younger, whiter, more affluent, and better educated than the population at large. According to a survey by the National Telecommunications and Information Administration in the Department of Commerce in October 2010, 81 percent of 18- to 24-year-olds used broadband Internet in their homes, compared with just 50 percent of those 55 and older.[36] Sixty-eight percent of whites had broadband Internet in their homes, compared to 45 percent of Hispanics and 50 percent of African Americans.[37] Fifty percent of Americans with incomes between $25,000 and $34,999 have broadband Internet in their homes, compared to almost nine in ten Americans with incomes of $150,000 or more.[38] Eighty-four percent of those with college degrees have broadband Internet access in their homes, compared to just 30 percent of those with less than a high school degree.[39]

Accuracy of Online Surveys

Online surveys claim that they are able to correct for the lack of a probability sample in a variety of ways. One way is to use a mathematical procedure called weighting to correct for the underrepresentation of certain demographic groups.

Other online polling organizations have tried other innovative ways to make online surveys representative of the general population. Knowledge Networks uses random digit dialing to recruit a panel of respondents to survey online. For those in the survey who do not have Internet access, Knowledge Networks provides the respondents with technology that allows them to respond to surveys online.[40] In return for the equipment, panel members agree to participate in an agreed-upon number of surveys.[41]

The Advantages of Online Surveys

The previous discussion has illustrated how a number of online polling firms try to correct for the main disadvantages of online polling—the lack of randomness in the sample and the disproportionate reach of the Internet to some demographic populations. However, online polling was initially thought to bring some very important advantages. One of the initial advantages of online surveys was thought to be cost savings, because once the survey is posted on a website or e-mailed to respondents, there is virtually no cost to the administration of the poll, unlike phone surveys, which require phones and interviewers. However, increasingly online surveys are conducted through vendors, which increases the cost of the survey. Fred Yang finds that online surveys are not much less expensive than land-line surveys; if a phone-only survey costs $30,000, an online survey could be $25,000.[42] A second initial advantage of online surveys was speed. However, in the heat of a campaign, when results are needed in only a few days, many pollsters think that online surveys are not fast enough.[43]

The Next Five Years—Online Surveys

Although online surveys may not be part of the campaign polling equation in the next five years, it seems inevitable that online polling will play more and more of a role in survey research in the future. One key to online polling is the availability of e-mail lists. For example, if e-mail addresses could be appended to voter files, it would be possible to pull random samples of e-mail addresses off a voter file and conduct random sampling online.[44] However, Bob Blaemire thinks that voter files cannot now be matched with e-mail addresses in a way that is useful to campaign pollsters. Catalist, the largest voter file firm used by Democratic candidates and progressive organizations, has an 82 percent phone match on its voter file, but only a 42 percent e-mail match.[45]

Another problem with using e-mail addresses for survey research is that many people have several of them—in Bill Russell's words, "One they give out, and others that they use when they actually want someone to contact them."[46] People are also more likely to change e-mail addresses than they are to change phone numbers, particularly landline phone numbers. People do not have to give an address to obtain some e-mail accounts, such as Gmail, Hotmail, and Yahoo, so there is no way to know where they live, making those e-mail accounts useless for survey research in political campaigns. As Blaemire points out, campaigns are unlikely to spend money to get e-mail addresses if they cannot be sure the person is registered to vote, and without an address, there is no way to verify registration.[47]

The Future of Interactive Voice Response Surveys

Interactive voice response (IVR) surveys, more commonly referred to as robocalls, have become increasingly common in recent years. Of the approximately 1,500 statewide polls conducted in 2010, over half, 54 percent, were IVR surveys.[48] While at first dismissed by pollsters as unreliable, by 2010 some surveys using robocalls proved to be surprisingly correct in predicting election outcomes.[49] A study of IVR surveys in 2010 found they were no less accurate in predicting the outcome of elections than were live interviews.[50]

Yet automated calls still have real problems that make pollsters wary of using them in campaigns. For example, with an automated call there is no way to know who the respondent is. Also, because cell phones have to be hand dialed, they are not included in IVR surveys. Because of the differences in landline and cell phone users, discussed above, that can create bias in IVR surveys. Finally, because it is easier to hang up on a computer than a real person, it is difficult to do surveys of any length, which means IVR surveys are not useful for message testing.[51] Automated calls are most useful for short surveys, such as those asking the "horse race" question near the end of a campaign.[52] Yet Fred Yang predicts that automated calls are "here to stay," and will be a part of survey research going forward, if for no other reason than their costs—they are less expensive than a live call.[53]

Between Now and the Future: Survey Research Possibilities

For at least the next few election cycles, blended surveys are likely to be the norm. The basic component of the survey will be RDD or a voter file to a landline phone, with a cell phone or Internet component. The initial problems with cell phones continue to exist, as do the problems with Internet surveys. The purpose of the survey may also dictate the method used for the survey. For longer surveys, such as benchmark and trend surveys, landline phones are most desirable. For shorter surveys, such as tracking surveys near the end of the campaign, cell phone and IVR surveys may be used.

Understanding Voters and Candidates

In thinking about the future of survey research, it is important to keep in mind the purpose of a survey in a campaign. The primary reason campaigns use survey research is to understand voter attitudes about candidates and issues and then use those attitudes to predict candidate choices at the polls. For these purposes, landline phone surveys with a live interviewer are still the best way to survey potential voters. Landline surveys can last 18 to 20 minutes, which is the time necessary to do message testing in a poll. With a live interviewer, the interviewer can encourage the respondent to stay on the line, using phrases like "We're almost done" or "Just three more minutes." Cell phone surveys need to be shorter; people won't stay on the line for 20 minutes in a cell phone survey.

Dan Balz and Haynes Johnson, in their study of the 2008 presidential election, describe how polling helped the Obama campaign craft its message going into the 2008 primaries and caucuses:

Out of that autumn research [October 2007] came three pillars of an Obama message: First, bring the country together to usher in a new politics . . . Second, strongly emphasize the need to fight the special interests . . . Third, level with the people . . . Obama's advisers believed it was time to start drawing contrasts with Clinton, to heighten voters' doubts about her and to cement her image as the insider in a year of change.[54]

Two years later, polling helped Republican candidate Rand Paul craft his successful message in the Kentucky Senate race. Polling showed that the citizens of Kentucky wanted Congress to control spending, which led Paul to develop a message overwhelmingly focused on domestic and fiscal issues.[55] Paul won the Republican primary against Kentucky secretary of state Trey Grayson, who had been endorsed by Senate Republican leader Mitch McConnell and retiring senator Jim Bunning, and went on to win the general election.

Phones Are Still King

Because online polling, with its lack of randomness, cannot accurately predict attitudes, opinions, and behaviors, it is not likely to supersede phone surveys for political campaigns. However, there are many other uses for Internet surveys in campaigns.

Because of time and cost constraints, questions on phone surveys generally force the respondents to select one of a set of responses predetermined by the pollsters. There are few open-ended questions that ask, for example, why a respondent holds a particular attitude or opinion. A common survey question is "Generally speaking, would you say things in this country are heading in the right direction, or are they off on the wrong track?" Rarely is there an open-ended follow-up question that asks the respondent why he or she believes the country is heading in the right direction or on the wrong track. Yet online surveys could allow for such follow-up questions, because time would be less of a constraint for the respondent. The respondent could answer the survey at a time that fit into his or her schedule, rather than having to respond when the interviewer phoned.

Today, research into the "why" behind attitudes and opinions is done in focus groups. Focus groups bring together ten to twelve people to enable survey researchers to probe why different demographic groups hold the opinions they do. Focus group participants typically share a demographic characteristic—gender, age, or race, for example. The small size of focus groups and the lack of randomness of the participants (focus group members are usually recruited by advertisements and paid a modest honorariam) prevent generalizing from their comments. However, they enable the moderator to probe the attitudes and opinions of a small group of people to try to understand why people hold the opinions expressed in larger surveys. For example, it was a focus group held in New Jersey in 1988 that led Republican operatives to discover the voter anger over a Massachusetts furlough program supported by then-governor Michael Dukakis that allowed convicted felons in Massachusetts prisons weekend furloughs. One prisoner, Willie Horton, furloughed as part of the program, did not return to prison at the end of the weekend. Ten months later he raped a Maryland woman and stabbed her fiancé.[56] The results of the focus group led to the infamous advertisement in the 1988 presidential election focusing on the Willie Horton case.

More recently, David Winston used focus groups to coin the phrase *security moms* in the 2004 election. Listening to mothers talk in focus groups following 9/11, he found their greatest concern on September 11, 2001, was having to decide which child to pick up first at school or day care after the attacks. These moms never wanted to feel like that again. Winston believes that detail of concern would not have come through in a survey.[57]

The Value of Online Focus Groups

The Internet presents opportunities for online focus groups. Without the time and expense of flying to a city or cities to do focus groups, pollsters can recruit and conduct focus groups online, saving the campaign valuable dollars. Recruiting participants may also be easier, as participants can participate from their homes rather than having to travel to a focus group session. The demographics of the online citizenry, however, discussed earlier in this chapter, make online focus groups more feasible among some demographic groups than others for the immediate future.

Another option for focus groups is phone conference calls. Fred Yang has experimented with using conference calls for focus groups and finds that conference calls have both advantages and disadvantages. Like online focus groups, conference call focus groups are less expensive than in-person focus groups, and Yang also finds that it is less likely for one person to dominate the discussion, which sometimes happens with in-person focus groups. One the other hand, conference calls make it impossible to see facial expressions and physical reactions, an advantage of in-person focus groups.[58]

While randomness is important for generalizing the attitudes and opinions of a survey population, it is less important in testing campaign messages. Through online focus groups, pollsters can test campaign messages and campaign advertising. Participants in an online focus group can be shown campaign ads. Mark Putnam, the founder of Putnam Partners, a Democratic media firm, has found web testing of political ads to be very useful.[59]

The Growing Integration of Polling and Microtargeting

A part of campaigning that has received substantial attention in recent elections is microtargeting, which is described in more detail in the voter mobilization chapter of this volume (Chapter 6). Microtargeting can complement survey research but not replace it. Indeed, the success of microtargeting is based in polling. During the 2004 election, the Bush campaign polled 5,000 people from a consumer database on their political attitudes and behavior.[60] An important attribute the Bush campaign was looking for was "anger points"—issues that would motivate survey respondents to turn out to vote.[61] The campaign then used those anger points to target messages to potential Bush voters to motivate them to turn out on Election Day. Sosnick, Dowd, and Fournier, the authors of *Applebee's America*, a study that describes how the Bush campaign used microtargeting in 2004, acknowledge the importance of polling to microtargeting in their critique of the Kerry campaign, commenting that "Kerry's team failed to do the polling and analysis required to segment the electorate into like-minded groups and determine what issues angered or excited them."[62]

Given the costs of phone surveys and the limited number of questions that can be asked, it is unlikely that lifestyle questions, like those used in microtargeting, will find their way into phone surveys. For every lifestyle question asked, one attitude or opinion question would have to be dropped. However, if and when Internet surveys become more commonplace, lifestyle questions could become part of the question bank. Because they lack the time and cost constraints of phone surveys, it may become more cost-effective for campaigns to ask lifestyle questions in online surveys rather than acquire costly consumer databases.

Conclusion

Online surveys are not likely to replace phone surveys in the next five years. Phones will still be the primary means to survey voters in political campaigns, with cell phones slowly becoming a larger and larger part of the sample. How much of a role IVR calls will play in the future is still uncertain, but they likely will be part of the mix.

Five years ago, landline phone surveys seemed to be headed to extinction, yet today they are still the most prominent way surveys are conducted in political campaigns. The problems of cell phone and Internet surveys that existed five years ago still exist today, so their use in campaigns has not increased as quickly as might have been predicted.

The biggest unknown in survey research may be the role of social networking. Rather than using online focus groups to test campaign ads, it may be that Facebook, or other social networking sites, could be used. Ad testing could become the purview of the new media department of a campaign, and not the responsibility of the pollster.[63] At this point, a great deal more is known about the problems and questions that survey research faces in the coming years than is known about the solutions.

Notes

1. Dan Balz and Haynes Johnson, *The Battle for America 2008* (New York: Viking, 2009), 116–117.
2. Balz and Johnson, *The Battle for America 2008*, 121.
3. Mark Blumenthal, "Poll: Des Moines Register/Selzer & Co" (January 1, 2008). Accessed on November 7, 2011, from http://www.pollster.com/blogs/poll_des_moines_register selzer_1.php?nr=1.
4. Jon Cohen and Dan Balz, "Poll: Romney Is Still GOP Front-runner" (*The Washington Post*, July 21, 2011), A3.
5. Robert P. Berrens, Alok K. Bohara, Hank Jenkins-Smith, Carol Silva, and David Weimer, "The Advent of Internet Surveys for Political Research: A Comparison of Telephone and Internet Samples" (Political Analysis, 2003).
6. Interview with Bob Carpenter, senior vice president, American Viewpoint, March 15, 2011.
7. Bob Carpenter interview, March 15, 2011.
8. Stephen J. Blumberg and Julian V. Luke, "Wireless Substitution: Early Release of Estimates From the National Health Interview Survey, January–June, 2010" (Centers for Disease Control and Prevention). Accessed on November 7, 2011, from http://www .cdc.gov/nchs/data/nhis/earlyrelease/wireless201012.htm.
9. Blumberg and Luke, "Wireless Substitution," 3.
10. Bob Carpenter interview, March 15, 2011.
11. Interview with Fred Yang, principal, Garin Hart Yang, May 18, 2011.
12. David Winston, president of The Winston Group, a Republican polling firm, describes what is common practice in cell phone polling. Respondents are asked if they are in a place where they can safely answer the survey on their cell phone. Phone interview with David Winston, June 20, 2011.
13. "Assessing the Cell Phone Challenge to Survey Research in 2010" (The Pew Center for People and the Press and the Pew Internet and American Life Project, May 20, 2010), 5.
14. "Assessing the Cell Phone Challenge," 5.
15. "Assessing the Cell Phone Challenge," 5
16. Blumberg and Luke, "Wireless Substitution," 3.
17. Bob Carpenter interview, March 15, 2011.
18. Bob Carpenter interview, March 15, 2011.
19. Interview with Sarah Simmons, March 31, 2011.
20. Interview with Fred Yang, May 18, 2011.
21. Interview with David Winston, June 20, 2011.
22. Interview with Bob Blaemire, May 10, 2011. The Help America Vote Act required all states to develop statewide computerized voter registration lists.

23. In 2007, Blaemire Communications merged with Catalist, and Blaemire became Catalist's director of business development.
24. Interview with Bob Blaemire, president, Blaemire Communications, and Bill Russell, marketing director, Blaemire Communications, June 14, 2007.
25. Blaemire and Russell interview, June 14, 2007.
26. Blaemire and Russell interview, June 14, 2007.
27. The information for this section comes from Mark Mellman and Jim Margolis, "Harry Reid: Withstanding the Wave" (November 18, 2010). Accessed on November 7, 2011, from http://www.pollingreport.com/a2010nv.htm; and Mark Mellman's presentation, "Why the Public Polls in Nevada Were Wrong: Mistakes to Learn From" (Workshop on Political Polling, American University, June 17, 2011).
28. The Mellman Group also polled for the Barbara Boxer for Senate campaign and found the same discrepancy. Boxer led Carly Fiorina, the Republican nominee for the Senate in California, by 6 percent among landline respondents, but 36 percent among cell phone respondents.
29. "2010 Census Data" (U.S. Census Bureau). Accessed on November 7, 2011, from http://2010.census.gov/2010census/data/.
30. Balz and Johnson, *The Battle for America 2008*, 123.
31. Blumenthal, "Poll: Des Moines Register/Selzer & Co."
32. Interview with Sarah Simmons, March 31, 2011.
33. Bob Carpenter interview, March 15, 2011.
34. Interview with David Winston, June 20, 2011.
35. Interview with Sarah Simmons, March 31, 2011.
36. "Digital Nation: Expanding Internet Usage" (An NTIA Research Preview, February 2011, U.S. Department of Commerce, National Telecommunications and Information Administration), 10.
37. "Digital Nation," 11.
38. "Digital Nation," 8.
39. "Digital Nation," 9.
40. Dotty Lynch, American University, interview, April 10, 2007.
41. Berrens et al., "The Advent of Internet Surveys for Political Research," 14.
42. Fred Yang interview, May 18, 2011.
43. Interviews with Bob Carpenter, March 15, 2011, and Sarah Simmons, March 31, 2011.
44. Dotty Lynch interview, April 10, 2007.
45. E-mail to the author from Bob Blaemire, May 11, 2011.
46. Blaemire and Russell interview, June 14, 2007.
47. E-mail to author, July 18, 2007.
48. Mark Blumenthal, presentation at Workshop on Political Polling, American University, June 17, 2011.
49. Dotty Lynch interview, April 10, 2011.
50. Mark Blumenthal presentation, Workshop on Political Polling, June 17, 2011.
51. Randall Guttermurth, vice president, American Viewpoint, presentation at Workshop on Political Polling, American University, June 17, 2011.
52. Fred Yang interview, May 18, 2011.

53. Fred Yang interview, May 18, 2011.

54. Balz and Johnson, *The Battle for America 2008*, 117.

55. Joel Turner and Scott Lasley, "Randslide: Tea Party Success in Establishment's Backyard," in Charles S. Bullock, III, ed., *Key States, High Stakes: Sarah Palin, The Tea Party, and the 2010 Elections* (Lanham, MD: Rowman and Littlefield, 2012), 83–85.

56. "Independent Ads: The National Security Political Action Committee 'Willie Horton.'" Accessed on August 6, 2007, from http://www.insidepolitics.org/ps111/ independentads.html; "Willie Horton" (Wikipedia, October 29, 2011). Accessed on August 6, 2007, from http://en.wikipedia.org/wiki/Willie_Horton.

57. David Winston, comments at Workshop on Political Polling, American University, June 17, 2011.

58. Fred Yang interview, May 18, 2011.

59. Mark Putnam, presentation to the Campaign Management Institute, American University, May 17, 2011.

60. Douglas B. Sosnick, Matthew J. Dowd, and Ron Fournier, *Applebee's America* (New York: Simon and Schuster, 2006), 36.

61. Sosnick et al., *Applebee's America*, 36.

62. Sosnick et al., *Applebee's America*, 43.

63. Interviews with Fred Yang, May 18, 2011, and Bob Carpenter, March 15, 2011.

CHAPTER 6

Voter Mobilization—Into the Future

Richard J. Semiatin

THE PAST IS PROLOGUE to the future.[1] And paradoxically, the future is prologue to the past when it comes to voter mobilization. With new technology, campaigns and parties are rediscovering their roots to maximize get-out-the-vote (GOTV) efforts. The technology that is emerging has put a reemphasis on voter mobilization as epitomized by the Obama campaign for president in 2008. "The Obama campaign built an unprecedented network of support, which included an e-mail list with 10 million names and cell phone numbers, (and) had . . . 1.5 million active volunteers."[2] While technology plays a tremendous role, old-fashioned planning and personal contact remain a critical element of success. Senate majority leader Harry Reid's (D-Nev.) reelection victory in 2010 was rooted in a long-term GOTV plan that rebuilt the Nevada State Democratic Party in the early 2000s.[3] Getting voters to the polls means that campaigns are using new technology and traditional GOTV tactics to get voters to the polls. How this is being accomplished differs dramatically from the pasts.

Up until recent decades, political parties served as the engine to deliver votes for candidates from the presidency all the way down to the local level. Today, campaigns are much more on their own—campaign staff members use iPhones, tablets, and BlackBerrys to call up voter information in households. While precincts were the level of analysis of campaigns for decades, that level of analysis is now down to neighborhoods and individual households. Campaign staff will know what people eat, where they shop, and what they watch on television. Given all the personal information out in public and cyberspace, presidential, senatorial, congressional, and gubernatorial elections will become more individualized. The process of voting will become less of a civic ritual, less communal, and more personalized. The future of campaigns is showing that candidate organizations, not national parties, are becoming the primary delivery vehicle of identifying citizens, targeting them, and getting them out to vote. For instance, in 2010, Republican successes in gubernatorial races could be tied to state GOTV efforts that promoted early voting in states such as Florida.[4]

Thus, the chapter begins with a look at the background of GOTV operations, then proceeds to the current state of affairs of traditional and new methods of voter mobilization, and finally discusses where such efforts are headed in the future.

The Tradition of Parties Delivering Votes

The political science literature and history books of presidential campaigns have focused on the long, historical, and central role of parties, which candidates could rely upon to bring out their voters on Election Day. Political scientists of the 1950s and 1960s discussed the symbiotic bond between candidates and parties—that candidates owed their allegiance to parties and supported the platform accordingly; parties would then provide the organizational muscle to bring enough of their voters to the polls to help win elections.[5] The long-standing model of party-driven politics was ended by the era of television, as candidates, beginning with John Kennedy, became their own electoral entrepreneurs. With television, candidates no longer needed ambassadors to introduce themselves to voters in presidential and later on other federal elections (Senate and House).

The model of candidate-driven politics emerged, but still parties played a role in delivering votes. A hybrid system emerged where parties would provide a basic organization and delivery system for each campaign. Campaigns would then supplement that effort with their own campaign workers who would target key precincts and neighborhoods—identifying likely voters and marginal voters for their candidate.

Parties under the Federal Election Campaign Act (FECA) Amendments of 1974 were given the power to provide coordinated expenditures to help candidates for Congress, the Senate, and president get out the vote. The expenditures were based on population and for general election purposes.[6] That expenditure could extend to advice, tactical planning, and organizational help to identify, contact, and get-out-to-vote key groups essential for victory.

Traditional Model of Targeting Voters

Campaigns have utilized voting data, voter registration lists, voter registration, turnout mail, radio, and ID calls as part of their voter contact operation for the last several decades. Such tactics are used as the basis for a voter identification and GOTV operation. Each party and its candidates (Democrats and Republicans) seek out their voters in precincts throughout the congressional district.

They then prioritize those precincts depending on their partisanship and voter turnout rates.

Voting Data

The voting data from the past several elections are distilled, and the campaign identifies precincts on a zero- to ten-point scale. Ten is a maximum-performing district for the candidate, and zero is a district where there is no hope. Thus, for a Republican, a ten-point district would be classified as the strongest Republican and a zero-point district as the weakest Republican; Democrats classify their districts in a similar way. The precincts that are rated in the middle—four, five, and six—are dominated by neither party and are called "swing" precincts.[7] If the election has a high number of undecided voters (such as the 1992 presidential election between Bush Sr., Clinton, and Perot), then swing precincts are the focus of both parties as they seek to persuade undecided or weakly identified voters of their own party. However, in base-driven elections (such as the 2008 presidential campaign between McCain and Obama), where there are few undecided voters, the emphasis for Democrats and Republicans is more firmly focused on squeezing every vote out of high-performing partisan precincts. The reasoning is simple: In swing precincts you have to inform, convert, motivate, and turn out voters. In partisan districts, there is one less step: You do not have to convert potential loyalists. That saves both cost and time. The calculation of registration efforts will change once again based on the 2010 U.S. Census, which will reapportion congressional districts for the 2012 election.

Federal party organizations play a coordinated effort with campaigns to identify voters, often assisting them (as an in-kind service) with voting lists and advice for how to develop a voter contact list. Parties have also served as the source to find individuals who can run the field operation for important campaigns. For example, the Bush campaign of 2004 drew on the services of Terry Nelson, who served as deputy chief of staff at the Republican National Committee in 2002 and 2003. Nelson then moved to the Bush-Cheney reelection campaign as political director in charge of the massive field operation for the campaign.

All targeting operations begin by looking at the average vote of the party. In statewide federal races, that would be the average performance of the party in senatorial and presidential races over a three-to-five election cycle. For example, if we were to average the performance from 2004 to 2010 in statewide federal races in Missouri, the data would show Republicans averaging approximately 52 percent and Democrats 45 percent.[8] Since congressional races often traverse county lines, it is slightly more technical to obtain and compute average performance data in congressional districts, but not a barrier.

Voter Registration Lists

Supplementing voting data are voter registration lists. The voter registration lists are matched up with voting data for precincts to see where candidates perform as well as expected, underperform, or overperform. For example, a precinct of 500 voters might show that Republican candidates in federal races are winning on average 60 percent of the vote, compared to 40 percent for Democrats. However, if the voter registration figures show that the precinct has 70 percent registered Republicans, then that district is underperforming for Republicans, meaning that Republican candidates are averaging 10 percent less than they should.

Underperforming precincts are of highest concern to a candidate because they are potentially the greatest source of votes. After identifying the problem, the party and candidate have to figure out why the district is underperforming. Is it because candidates are out of step with their own voters? Is it because of neglect from previous campaigns? Has the district started to change behaviorally (voting for the opposing party's candidate) even though party registration is still in the present party's and candidate's favor? The campaign then has to decide what tactics it will employ to target that district (statewide or national federal races) or precinct (congressional races).

Voter Registration

Increasing party registration is key for any voter mobilization effort. Parties, partisan interest groups, and "527" organizations (i.e., independent political organizations) work at increasing their voter bases. In particular, the Democratic Party has conducted extensive voter registration drives in the past focusing on the African American and Latino communities in urban areas, which tend to have lower voter registration rates, and thus lower voter turnout rates. Republicans will sometimes counter with voter registration efforts in rural areas to offset increased registration of Democrats in urban areas. The U.S. Census Bureau reported that in 2008, 146 million adults—or 71 percent of the adult population—were registered to vote. The percentage of registered voters who voted on Election Day was 89.7 percent, an increase of 1.2 percent from 2004. There is no mistaking that voter registration is highly predictive of who turns out.[9]

Turnout Mail

Turnout mail is critical to GOTV plans for candidates and parties because it plays two roles as Election Day approaches: It advertises candidates to citizens, and it reminds those citizens to vote on Election Day. Sometimes mail comes in the form of a literature drop at your doorstep by the candidate. Candidates and parties partake in these endeavors. Usually campaigns will send out five to ten mailers to get the desired effect of maximizing their vote on Election Day. The message conveyed by the direct mail piece is about the importance of voting. For example, Creative Direct, which did the direct mail for Republican gubernatorial candidate Bob McDonnell in Virginia, successfully portrayed him as a mainstream candidate in 2009. McDonnell had a problem with women voters as evidenced by a 93-page master's thesis he wrote while attending Regent University in 1989. The thesis called for covenant marriage and restricted abortions. The thesis also stated that a 1972 Supreme Court decision in favor of contraception between two unmarried adults was "illogical." Creative Direct designed a direct mail campaign that would show that his views toward women today were moderate. One direct mail ad featured his daughter, Lt. Jeanine McDonnell, who had served in Iraq. The cursive style one might see in a Hallmark card quoted Lt. McDonnell as saying, "My Dad always respected and supported me, encouraging me to be a leader." The point was that if McDonnell were so against women, why would he have ever encouraged his daughter to become an officer in the military? In the end, McDonnell won not only the election but 54 percent of the women's vote.[10]

Radio

Radio has served as a classic method for GOTV, especially for niche populations, which are hard to influence by turnout mail or phone banks. Lower-middle-class or poor voters, as well as African American and Latino communities, are often targeted for radio ads. Promos run on hip-hop, rap, R&B, soul, and gospel stations with messages urging people to vote. Other promotions have included hip-hop conventions urging people to vote. On November 2, 2010, President Barack Obama did interviews on hip-hop stations such as WGCI in Chicago, urging young voters and minorities to vote in the closely contested senatorial and gubernatorial elections in Illinois to help elect Democrats to those posts.[11] (A Democrat won the governorship but not the Senate seat.) Obama is the first president to speak extensively to rap and hip-hop stations, demonstrating that reaching voters goes beyond the news station interviews of the last century.

ID Calls

ID or identification calls help to locate supporters, ascertain their voting plans, and finally ensure that they get out to vote. ID calls are the surest and most direct method to reach voters personally, and voter registration lists plus available voter lists are used to help ensure that the population they reach can vote. The calls help to identify the candidate citizens might vote for and assess the likelihood of their voting. The purpose of ID calls is to build a relationship between the voter and the caller (whether the latter is from a candidate or party organization). Wally Clinton, a consultant who specializes in phones and communications for Democrats, has said that building a relationship with a potential voter is "about listening, not yelling."[12] Given caller ID on home and cell phones, a lower response rate and less patience by respondents demonstrate how much more difficult it is for candidates and parties to reach voters directly.

ID calls normally begin several weeks before the election to determine the level of support, where it is located, and where the candidate has to go to increase support. As the election approaches, the campaign ascertains the likelihood of whether individuals on the list will vote. If a citizen is infirm, is aged, or lacks transportation, the campaign identifies that person, sets a time, and then provides transportation to take that individual to the polls. Given that young voters are more likely to use cell phones, seniors are more reachable on landlines, particularly in the evening; however, that model is beginning to change as baby boomers become the newest generation of seniors.

ID calls are one of the most effective techniques to boost GOTV. According to research by Green and Gerber, phone bank contacts by volunteers will add about one vote for every thirty-five calls made.[13]

Door-to-Door

Despite being labor intensive, the most effective form of traditional voter contact is through door-to-door canvassing. The fact that voters meet face-to-face with representatives of local parties and candidates can make a difference. According to Green and Gerber, this methodology yields one vote for every fourteen contacts, which is not insubstantial.[14]

The sophistication of door-to-door canvassing reached new heights in 2002. The campaign committee for House Republicans, the NRCC (National Republican Congressional Committee), instituted the STOMP (Strategic Task Force to Organize and Mobilize People) program to get out the vote in congressional races. "Republicans from safe districts contributed staff and volunteers to work in competitive congressional races across the country."[15] This was the Republican seventy-two-hour GOTV program where dozens of experienced staff and campaign workers were shifted to key races to help incumbent Republican House and Senate candidates in tight election campaigns. The seventy-two-hour GOTV program has been the Republican base plan from 2002 to the present.

Each of the aforementioned tactics demonstrates the importance of candidate organization and field operations. In fact, the field division is the largest in any campaign because it involves dozens, or hundreds, or thousands of volunteers communicating candidate or party messages urging supporters to get out to vote. In the end, the old Tip O'Neill adage that "all politics is local" is manifest even in presidential campaigns because national organizations have to translate potential support into votes from macro-level strategies into micro-level performance. Despite this, parties have continued to refine and adapt their strategies in the modern campaign era, as campaigns move away from television, and as voters become more diverse consumers of new technologies.

Voter Mobilization in the Twenty-First Century

Campaigns are moving into a new era—customer-driven campaigns. Campaigns are now using a strategy developed from the corporate world called customer relationship management (CRM). CRM enables campaigns to blend traditional strategies of voter contact with new techniques. New techniques employ microtargeting (which will be discussed later on), multiple points of contact with voters (or customers), and multiple methods to get voters to the polls. In other words, the entire process focuses on the needs of each voter. The Obama campaign used this "bottoms up" approach in its GOTV effort in 2008. In this model, the individual volunteer contacts the voter through personal interaction. Patrick Ruffini, a Republican consultant, criticized his own party's GOTV efforts in 2008: "Obama volunteers are expected to do a lot more than volunteers on other campaigns, which is basically to park your butt in a headquarters and make lots of calls."[16]

Voters have increasing control of the media content that enables them to manipulate or alter information. Furthermore, as television viewing decreases and voters are spending more time online, campaigns have to develop new techniques to entice voters to come to their websites. In terms of voter mobilization, this means creating a virtual community where voters participate in the online campaign. Blogs, e-mail, web campaign events, and webinars represent some of the activities in which individuals participate.

Campaigns have to develop more personalized and stylized messages to interest voters who are barraged with visual cues at the click of a mouse. Statistical methods have become more precise in predicting turnout. The new age of voter mobilization strategy is vested in merging consumer or lifestyle information with traditional targeting models. Major campaigns and political parties now have the ability to target individual homes based on profile information available through public files or obtained through purchasing lists; this is known as *microtargeting*. Finally, new technology helps expedite the process of locating, contacting, and getting out voters. The amount of personal information becoming available to private industry and, thus, to campaigns and parties has raised fears about privacy issues because the parameters to determine what personal information should or should not be available for political campaigns are unclear.

Merging Traditional Models of Voter Mobilization With New Variables

The traditional models of GOTV operations have incorporated utilizing voting behavior histories and issue polling to mobilize interested citizens to vote. However, new elements have been utilized in the targeting process to make voter mobilization more precise and effective. Such techniques look at voters as customers and consumers to understand their lifestyle. Voters' lifestyle enables the campaign to engage them and get them out to vote on Election Day, as long as they are persuadable. Thus, today's world incorporates voting history + issue salience + consumer or lifestyle behavior.

According to TargetPoint, a Republican firm specializing in GOTV, "The control has switched from seller to buyer. Voters and consumers now have multiple sources for information and entertainment."[17] Thus, direct mail and personal contact alone will not suffice—the consumer (i.e., voter) must be reached by multiple sources of information, multiple times, in order for a campaign to get out the vote.

The 2004 Bush presidential campaign made a major investment in microtargeting. Its pioneering efforts have been adopted and refined by campaigns since 2004. According to an article in *Winning Campaigns* magazine, "Survey research that focuses on crosstabs such as income, gender, race . . . only provide a fraction of the story. . . . By using hundreds of data points, comprised of voter information, life cycle information, life style information, financial data, consumer behavior, geographic data, and political attitudes and preferences," voters can be placed into clusters or "segments" that provide precision methods of reaching them.[18] This approach was utilized successfully by the George W. Bush reelection campaign to get out its base vote in 2004.

The Bush campaign team realized early on that Democrats had a natural base advantage heading into the 2004 election. They reasoned that the Gore vote plus Ralph Nader's gave Democrats a 51 percent majority. Moreover, the Bush campaign also knew that the president's popularity was sliding downward to the critical 50 percent approval range, due largely to an increasingly unpopular war in Iraq. Matthew Dowd, who was the campaign's pollster and strategist, believed that Republicans "had to find and activate new GOP voters," and that meant new strategies. Dowd had one in mind: targeting people based on their lifestyles rather than just their voting histories and policy views.[19]

The Bush campaign assembled profiles of nearly 5,000 voters and "grouped (them) into thirty-four segments."[20] For example, in Michigan, segments included "Archie in the Bunker," "Religious Independents," and "Wageable Weak Democrats." Each potential GOP segment was valued in terms of its size and commitment to George W. Bush. Moreover, the Bush team was able to accurately predict (80–90 percent) how likely that segment was to vote for President Bush.[21]

Therefore, the Bush campaign was able to locate and get out the vote successfully of Republican voter segments that might be in strong or weak Democratic precincts. However, lifestyle/microtargeting enabled the Bush reelection campaign to locate, target and to mobilize to vote supporters. No campaign had done this on such a large scale in the past. Voter participation also went up in Democratic areas, but lifestyle targeting made a dramatic difference for Republicans in 2004. By 2008, Democrats had employed similar targeting yielding a base vote of 7 million more individuals—with large increases among young and African American voters.

In 2010, however, it appeared that there was a resurgence in traditional GOTV activity. Tea Party supporters had either galvanized the Republican base as in Kentucky (for senate candidate Rand Paul) or motivated the Democratic base as in Nevada (for incumbent senator Harry Reid). The back-to-basics GOTV program was best exemplified by the Tea Party in Kentucky. One branch of the Tea Party, known as FreedomWorks, used hundreds of volunteers each weekend to do door-to-door canvassing for Senate candidate Rand Paul (R). The group was without the convenience of sophisticated microtargeting information on iPhones and BlackBerrys. Instead, FreedomWorks supporters were encouraged by group activities that built cohesion such as sign waves, placing yard signs, leaving door hangers, and so forth. The concept of "fun" was used to describe such activities for volunteers. Tea Partiers were more "Republican, white, male, married and older than 45."[22] It also characterized the activists. This contrasted with a much larger cohort of younger volunteers who worked for the Obama campaign—and who were more technologically savvy.

Technology and GOTV

Modern technology has brought critical information into the hands of field organizations. Voting history, issue preferences, and lifestyle/consumer information are now available in PDAs and BlackBerrys for precinct workers. A volunteer working in the 2012 New Hampshire primary for either Barack Obama or Mitt Romney can be in a neighborhood in Manchester's fourth ward and ascertain what voters need to be mobilized for support on Election Day. No one wants to be caught napping. In 1976, one of the leading Democratic candidates for president, Senator Birch Bayh (D-Ind.), asked his campaign for its GOTV plan on the weekend before the New Hampshire primary. No plan existed.[23]

Technology also must be tested well in advance of Election Day. The Bush reelection campaign planned its GOTV operation well in advance—and the president was not burdened by having a primary opponent. The Bush campaign tested its GOTV effort in a simulation in July 2004.[24] This enabled the campaign to determine what was working well and what needed fine-tuning. The Kerry campaign did not have such a luxury, given the campaign's early contentious primary season, which shortened its planning for its GOTV effort.

Heading into 2008 and beyond, websites played an increasingly critical role for field organizations. Senator Barack Obama's (D-Ill.) presidential campaign advertised "Camp Obama" on its website, which it used to recruit volunteers for his presidential campaign—the focus clearly on youth. The campaign offered training dates in Chicago during the weeks of June 11 and June 18, 2007, for potential interns and volunteers—each session ranged from two to four days. The idea was to build campaign communities for Obama across the country. Thus, the website served as a tool to build an effective campaign organization for voter contact (e.g., phone banks and door-to-door canvassing), thus melding the traditional approach with modern technology.[25]

The Cutting Edge of Change: Into the Future With Voter Mobilization

The tactics of voter mobilization by campaigns and parties have become more diverse as we head into the second decade of the twenty-first century. The tactics discussed below demonstrate how voter mobilization changes involve many more moving parts than they did just twenty years ago.

Social Media and Virtual Community Building Igniting GOTV Efforts

The development and use of social media on the Internet (called Web 2.0) marked a profound change for campaigns between 2004 and 2008. "Mr. Obama used the Internet to organize his supporters in a way that would have in the past required an army of paid volunteers and organizers," according to Democratic consultant Joe Trippi.[26]

The holistic approach to GOTV was embraced by the Obama campaign. The Internet was used not only for volunteers, but also to inform, persuade, motivate, and mobilize voters. The prime social media site the Obama campaign used was YouTube. Trippi stated that "the campaign's official stuff they created for YouTube was watched for 14.5 million hours," which was the equivalent of "$47 million" worth of television. The difference between social media and television media is that recipients, as Trippi noted, actively "choose" the information they wish to receive.[27]

Meetups enable "virtual" volunteers to share information and thoughts about a campaign through blogs and comments. Moreover, well-designed Meetups enable campaigns to generate volunteers who are willing to do the footwork for voter contact and mobilization. Meetups were pioneered by MoveOn.org, a liberal online grassroots organization that recruited over 3 million members in less than two years.[28] Meetups then were employed by the Howard Dean (D-Vt.) presidential campaign in 2004 not only to increase interest in the campaigns, but to raise money and recruit an army of 177,000 volunteers (more than three times what any other candidate had).[29]

Foursquare took the concept of Meetups to a whole new level in 2010. "Foursquare is a location-based mobile platform that makes cities easier to use. By 'checking in' via a smartphone app or SMS, users share their location with friends while collecting points and virtual badges." As of April 2011, Foursquare had 8 million users, many in their teens and twenties.[30]

To encourage voter turnout, Foursquare created an "I Voted" badge that would be unlocked when the voter "checked in" to vote at the polls on Election Day. There were 50,000 check-ins on Election Day. This was done in conjunction with Rock the Vote, Google, Twitter, the Voting Information Project, and the Pew Charitable Trusts, among others seeking to mobilize youth voter turnout. In the future, political parties and candidates will probably create their own version of Foursquare to create communities of voters to build and maintain a relationship. For example, with Foursquare, campaigns can create communities of voters who attend events where they can unlock badges. By building an online relationship, campaigns can maintain the interest and enthusiasm of the community of voters built through their Foursquare- or other community-based app. Campaigns can also create Foursquare apps for their volunteers and organizers doing door-to-door canvassing. By collecting badges, canvassers can compare with those in their campaign community to see how they are doing.[31]

Building Relationships

Expanding on the previous point, one of the developments in GOTV efforts over the last two election cycles (2008 and 2010) has been to build stronger relationships between voters and campaigns. This means that campaigns are coordinating new technology (such as social media and mobile technology) with traditional GOTV tactics (such as phone contacts and door-to-door canvassing). Failure to utilize all the tools at one's disposal carries an inherent risk. Republican consultant Patrick Ruffini points out that the 2008 McCain campaign failed in its GOTV effort because it was overly reliant on phone calls and not on door-to-door canvassing. In fact, technology has enabled campaigns to become more community-based and personal. The Obama campaign built its campaign through "Neighborhood Team Leaders" who "were in supervisory roles on the ground, not desk jockeys parceling out call sheets and walk lists," according to Ruffini.[32] Geographic information systems (providing online maps) coupled with microtargeting data enabled the Obama campaign to maximize bottom-up GOTV efforts, as well as the traditional top-down GOTV efforts provided by labor organizations and others aiding the Democratic Party. Bottom-up strategies are not cheap—they require a lot of manpower, research, and monitoring. However, in large-scale campaigns the Obama effort will be mimicked and refined over the next several election cycles.

Presidential Campaigns as Party Organizations

The Democratic and Republican nominees will likely raise between $500 million and $1.25 billion *each* in the 2012 election cycle. By 2016, that fundraising number could easily increase by 50 percent or more. Given that presidential candidates are eschewing the voluntary presidential funding system because they can raise much more on their own, presidential candidates are utilizing more of the available political capital that might otherwise be contributed to congressional races and statewide races for governor.

Given that neither major party nominee, in all likelihood, will take federal funding for the 2012 general election, that could mean even less money will flow to national party organizations and more to presidential campaigns. The result is that presidential campaigns are transitioning to full-service organizations, not only for their own campaigns, but for their party's candidates on the ballot (i.e., senator, governor, and representative). The substantial costs in terms of manpower and money will tie presidential and congressional candidates closer together. The implication is that the winning presidential candidate will be in a more powerful position to demand support for Senate and House members of their party. For the loser, defeat is a self-explanatory consequence.

Greater Citizen Diversity Makes GOTV More Complex

Over the next forty years, a majority of the U.S. population will become non-white and Latino according to demographer Leon Bouvier. That means that candidates will have to communicate not only bilingually but also multilingually to get out the vote. The 2000 campaign was the first to feature both presidential candidates—Gore and Bush—"record[ing] messages in Spanish."[33] As Latino, Eastern European, Southeast Asian, and Central Asian populations increase, campaigns will need more field organizers who are bi- or multilingual to canvas potential voters whose second language is English. As the population continues to shift to the Southwest from the North and Midwest, this will become critical over the next decade. States such as Arizona and Florida are becoming electoral behemoths where the largest growing segment of the population is Latino. Texas is gaining four congressional districts and Florida two new districts based on the 2010 reapportionment.

The New World: The Mobilization of Early, Absentee, and Mail Voting

Early and absentee voting is transforming elections because campaigns have to spend more upfront in the general election campaign compared to the past. Florida allows early (i.e., "in-person absentee") voting. Oregon and Washington state have all voting by mail, where ballots are mailed out before Election Day. Today, thirty-two states (including the District of Columbia) allow for early voting, while twenty-seven others allow for excuse absentee (no excuse is required when requesting an absentee ballot) or in-person absentee voting.[34] Given that there are fifty states plus the District of Columbia, there is substantial overlap among states that allow both early voting and any type of absentee voting. This creates uncertainty for campaign managers because the time for persuasion now comes in two waves—one before the early voting period and another near Election Day. Given that much of this is new, campaigns have no guidebook on how much to budget for each wave.

According to Curtis Gans for the Center for the Study of the American Electorate, "No-excuse absentee-ballot voters are middle-class, upper middle-class and upper-class voters who are lazy. They want their convenience."[35] If such voters are lazy, Gans implies, some may not vote. Thus, not only is the cost rising for campaigns regarding their GOTV contact and mobilization efforts, but the future may imply that such efforts will be less cost-effective and entail bigger budgets.

Reinvigorating Traditional Voter Contact the Key to Higher Future GOTV?

The cutting edge of campaigns would seem to reside in technology. After all, e-mail contacts, text messages, and social media contacts would seem to attract voting consumers. Moreover, the use of iPhones, tablets, BlackBerrys, and cell phones would enable campaigns to target potential voters with greater accuracy. The preliminary evidence, surprisingly, has not been that promising.

Research by Green and Gerber has demonstrated that most GOTV methods, either traditional or new methods, are not very cost-effective. The early results show that new approaches such as e-mail contacts and robocalls have no detectable effect on voter turnout.[36] Research is not yet available on the effectiveness of websites in terms of voter contact. As stated earlier, text messages utilized in the Spanish general election of 2004 did seem to have a discernable and positive effect on voter turnout. Perhaps the reason is that young voters are more apt to communicate via cell phones and text messages.

While technology has changed and, some would say, makes the world more impersonal, it is those personal touches that make the difference. As mentioned earlier, Gerber and Green did find that personal contact (door-to-door canvassing) is the only method that is highly effective (one voter per fourteen contacts). Second is professional telephone canvassers reading scripts (one voter per thirty contacts) or volunteers reading scripts (one vote per thirty-five contacts).[37] Again, campaigns are becoming more consumer oriented, and that means personal contact is as important as ever.

Conversely, that makes the quality of information available to field organizers even more important. Thus, the more information available to the campaign about individual voters, the better the message can be targeted to that person. Companies such as Acxiom keep massive files on consumers that grow in complexity as more personal information is available to retailers through purchases and online services. Acxiom Corporation has more than 20 billion consumer records and has reached over 200 million consumers in 124 million households through its database files in 2011.[38]

Information Supply Versus Privacy Concerns

The implications from the last section certainly can have daunting effects in terms of where to draw the line between the rights of individuals to have privacy and the desire of campaigns to get out the vote. The amount of individual identity information available through public databases is substantial. According to the Electronic Frontier Foundation (EFF), an organization established to protect privacy rights, the United States is moving more toward a national ID system. The EFF was concerned that the Real ID Act of 2005 would allow the government to "create a vast national database linking all of the ID records together (of driver's licenses). Once in place, uses of the IDs and database will inevitably expand to facilitate a wide range of tracking and surveillance activities." The EFF then goes on to state that "the Social Security number started innocuously enough, but it has become a prerequisite for a host of government services and been co-opted by private companies to create massive databases of personal information."[39] The application to campaigns is quite clear. Given that the United States is a highly mobile nation, the most recent data show that 14 percent of the population moves every year; thus, having standardized information to track driving registration would certainly enable campaigns and parties to track potential voters with greater ease.[40] In a February 2011 report, the National Conference of State Legislatures showed that twenty-six state legislatures have now taken at least partial steps opposing the Real ID law requirements for states.[41]

Cost

As national advertising becomes less appealing to presidential candidates, and as media convergence (television and the Internet) becomes a greater possibility, driving down cost, campaigns may delegate a higher portion of their resources to voter mobilization. Currently, about 50–70 percent of a campaign's budget is allocated to paid advertising. For example, a winning Senate campaign from a large state in 2012 may cost in excess of $25 million. A 5 percent change in allocation of resources from paid advertising to voter mobilization would increase the GOTV budget by $1.25 million or yield approximately 250,000 new voters (at $5 per vote).

Voter registration activities are performed, but by parties and independent organizations and not campaigns. In the future, presidential campaigns may subsume the GOTV effort by the parties in presidential election years, as previously noted; however, parties still raise money for voter education activities under the auspices of the Federal Election Campaign Act Amendments of 1979. This enables parties to raise money in the states (what are called nonfederal funds). Moreover, special campaign committees that can raise unlimited individual contributions (527 groups) will continue to register voters in targeted areas.

Photo ID and GOTV Efforts

New voter identification laws proposed in states such as North Carolina, Missouri, Ohio, and New Hampshire could affect how campaigns and parties run their GOTV operations in 2012. (A similar law was recently passed in Wisconsin.) These laws would require citizens to present a photo ID when voting on Election Day, ostensibly to prevent fraud. Republican state legislators have been pushing such laws saying that it would prevent fraudulent voting. Democrats oppose such laws contending that many low-income and minority individuals (who are more likely to vote for Democrats) do not have photo identifications such as driver's licenses. Already ten states have such laws. All of the states listed above were swing states in the 2008 presidential election—so that passage could have a profound effect on national elections in the future. Campaigns and party organizations would need to find a way to assess which current voters and which potential voters have photo identification. Second, would campaigns and parties also seek to help individuals procure such identification? That is an issue that may be explored in the near future.[42]

The Future of Voter Mobilization—Marrying the New to the Old

The future of voter mobilization will enhance even more direct interface between candidate and voter, without the filter of television; the key is for campaigns to get access to more databases of information to communicate by cell phone, tablet, PDA, and e-mail. Getting such lists will facilitate the different avenues and mediums for reaching each voter.

Just as important, the future of voter mobilization will coordinate technology with old-fashioned GOTV techniques. Campaigns strategizing how to use GOTV will have to plan more complex operations, even those running for congressional office. The Tea Party successes and near successes in 2010 demonstrated that traditional GOTV efforts, such as door-to-door campaigning and using door hangers, still work effectively. The future trends will increasingly marry the new with the old. While it may be an aberration, the Obama organizational effort for voter contact and mobilization in 2008 provided a model of planning GOTV operations in the future.

The campaign's idea was to build communities of support and action for Obama across the country. Thus, the website served as a tool to build an effective campaign organization for voter contact (e.g., phone banks and door-to-door canvassing), thus melding the traditional approach with modern technology.[43]

Second, as mentioned earlier, the Obama campaign used Neighborhood Team Leaders who had the autonomy and responsibility for organizing "8–12 precincts." These leaders would be responsible for "connecting with all of the Democratic and undecided voters within their 'turf.'" This bottom-up strategy infused the campaign with thousands of precinct leaders, many of whom had been graduates of Camp Obama.[44]

Since the Obama campaign, iPhone technology has taken a major leap forward aiding GOTV efforts. Republican Scott Brown's campaign to replace the late senator Ted Kennedy of Massachusetts is a perfect example. Brown's campaign provided walk lists for its canvassers, but "supplemented them with a clever web-based application" for iPhones. "By geo-locating users through native iPhone features the app could show volunteers the nearest house to visit . . . and talking points to use in the conversation." Responses were then entered "into a Google Docs spreadsheet." The micro level of analysis gave the Brown campaign an unparalleled level of precision for analysis.[45]

The role of e-mail has not changed appreciably since the first edition of this book. E-mail can be tailored for each voter—the first stage is contact and introduction; the second stage is persuasion; and the third stage is mobilization to vote. For example, one possibility is that candidates will be able to send videos via e-mail to potential supporters (targeted by the aforementioned methods), and this can be followed up by virtual zip code captains who can e-mail their neighbors—all through a handheld device, such as an iPhone. (Of course, this depends on whether campaigns can get actual addresses or zip codes that match e-mail addresses.) Moreover, virtual zip code captains can dialogue with potential voters—for persuasion, for mobilization, and, perhaps, to volunteer. The campaign coordinates the activities among the virtual captains and the actual precinct captains in that zip code to ensure there is no overlap or overcommunication with any potential voter.

Campaigns will continue using an increasing number of tactics to reach voters through different media—moreover, the actual number of GOTV contacts per person is, thus, likely to increase. Campaigns will have to learn, by trial and error, how not to burden voters with too much pressure or information that could have the opposite effect—deterring voter turnout.

Conclusion

Campaigns will play an increasingly large role in identifying and getting out voters—particularly in presidential election contests because nominees will be soaking up a disproportionate amount of the available money raised, which may diminish the role of political parties. In essence, the new voter mobilization may mean that the emphasis on party-driven GOTV operations may be geared more to the midterm congressional elections. As new technologies are developed, and as methods to identify, track, and predict the likelihood of voting for individuals become more specialized, the sophistication of congressional campaigns for the House in the future will make today's presidential campaigns look arcane. Understanding how to mobilize voters in the future means understanding what each potential voter wants.

Notes

1. William Shakespeare, The Tempest, Act II, Scene 1. The phrase comes from Antonio's speech: "Whereof what's past is prologue, what to come/In yours and my discharge."
2. John Berman, "Obama Supporters Without a Cause" (*ABC News*, November 8, 2008). Accessed on May 23, 2011, from abcnews.com.
3. Molly Ball, "Comeback: How Did Reid Do It?" (*Politico*, November 4, 2010). Accessed on May 23, 2011, from politico.com.
4. Aaron Deslatte, "GOP Leads Democrats in Early-Voting Turnout" (*Sun Sentinel*, October 26, 2010). Accessed on May 23, 2011, from orlandosentinel.com.
5. See Samuel Eldersveld, *Political Parties in American Society* (New York: Basic Books, 1982); Austin Ranney, *Political Parties: Democracy and the American Party System* (New York: Harcourt, Brace, 1956); and V. O. Key, *Southern Politics in State and Nation* (Knoxville: University of Tennessee Press, 1984).
6. Anthony Corrado, "Where Are We Now: The Current State of Camp. Finance Law," in *Campaign Finance Reform: A Sourcebook*, edited by Trevor Potter (Washington, DC: Brookings Institution Press, 1997), 8–9.
7. Information confirmed by Tim Crawford, New Models Consulting. Interview on August 8, 2007.
8. The 2004 senatorial (Kit Bond, Republican reelected) and presidential (Bush winner) races, the 2006 senatorial race (Claire McCaskill, the Democrat, defeating Republican Jim Talent), and the 2010 senatorial race (Roy Blunt, the Republican, defeating Robin Carnahan, the Democrat).

9. Thom File and Sarah Crissy, "Voting and Registration in the Election of November 2008" (report P20-562, U.S. Census Bureau, May 2010), 1–2.

10. Amy Gardner, "'89 Thesis A Different Side of McDonnell" (*The Washington Post*, August 30, 2009). Accessed on May 25, 2011, from washingtonpost.com. Creative Direct, "A Message from Jeanine McDonnell" (Direct Mailer). Accessed on May 25, 2011, from creativedirect.net; CBS News Exit Poll, Virginia Governor's Race, November 3, 2009 (gender breakdown in vote). Accessed on May 25, 2011, from cbsnews.com.

11. "President Obama Talks to Chicago Radio Station, Asks Voters to Have His Back" (November 2, 2010). Accessed on July 25, 2011, from huffingtonpost.com.

12. Walter D. Clinton, "Building Relationships With Voters," in *Winning Elections*, edited by Ronald Faucheaux (New York: M. Evans and Co., 2003), 567.

13. Donald Phillip Green and Alan G. Gerber, *Get Out the Vote!* (Washington, DC: Brookings Institution Press, 2004), 94.

14. Ibid.

15. Richard J. Semiatin, *Campaigns in the 21st Century: The Changing Mosaic of American Politics* (Boston: McGraw-Hill, 2005), 219.

16. Patrick Ruffini, "Obama Opens the GOTV Firehose" (October 13, 2008). Accessed on May 26, 2011, from thenextright.com.

17. See TargetPoint Consulting website at http://www.targetpointconsulting.com/Micro Targeting. Accessed on June 12, 2007.

18. Alex Lundry, "Microtargeting: Knowing The Voter Intimately" (*Winning Campaigns*, Volume 4, No.1, date unknown). Also much background information on how microtargeting is used, as described in this chapter, was confirmed by Alex Lundry and Mike Myers of TargetPoint Consulting, in an interview on July 9, 2007.

19. Douglas B. Sosnik, Matthew J. Dowd, and Ron Fournier, *Applebee's America* (New York: Simon and Schuster, 2006), 33.

20. Ibid, 36.

21. Ibid, 37.

22. Nan S., "GOTV in Northern Kentucky for Rand Paul Thursday and Friday" (September 28, 2010). Accessed on May 27, 2011, from teaparty.freedomworks.org; Kate Zernike and Megan Thee-Brenan, "Poll Finds Tea Party Backers Wealthier and More Educated" (*The New York Times*, April 14, 2010). Accessed on May 27, 2011, from newyorktimes.com.

23. Martin Schram, *Running for President: A Journal of the Carter Campaign* (New York: Pocket Books, 1977), 23.

24. Terry Nelson, PowerPoint presentation on the Bush 2004 campaign, American University, February 15, 2006.

25. From my.barackobama.com/page/s/campobama. Accessed on June 12, 2007.

26. Claire Cain Miller, "How Obama's Internet Campaign Changed Politics" (*The New York Times*, November 7, 2008). Accessed on June 1, 2011, from nytimes.com.

27. Ibid.

28. MoveOn.org reports on its website that the organization has 3.3 million members. Accessed on August 26, 2007.

29. Declan McCullagh, "Newsmaker: The Cyberbrains Behind Dean" (CNETnews, January 16, 2004). Accessed on August 26, 2007, from new.com.com.

30. "What Is Foursquare About?" Accessed on June 1, 2011, from foursquare.com/about.

31. See "Check In and Vote on Foursquare" (October 28, 2010), blog.fourquare.com; and "I Voted" (November 2010), elections.foursquare.com. Both accessed on June 1, 2011.

32. Ruffini, "Obama Opens the GOTV Firehose."

33. Semiatin, *Campaigns in the 21st Century*, 230. Includes reference to Bouvier.

34. "Absentee and Early Voting" (National Conference of State Legislatures, updated July 22, 2011). Accessed on July 25, 2011, from ncsl.org.

35. Carol Anne Clark Kelly, "Early Voting: Getting the Jump on Election Day" (NPR, November 4, 2006). Accessed on June 12, 2007, from npr.org. Includes voting data references.

36. Green and Gerber, *Get Out the Vote!* 94.

37. Ibid.

38. "Automotive Consumer Dynamics Methodology" (2011). Accessed on June 2, 2011, from acxiom.com.

39. "Repeal the Real ID Act" (EFF Action Center). Accessed on June 13, 2007, from eff .org.

40. "Geographic Mobility: 2004–2005" (Table, U.S. Census Bureau). Accessed on August 26, 2007, from census.gov.

41. "The Real ID" (Chart, February 2011). Accessed on June 2, 2011, from ncsl.org.

42. Tom Curry, "Voter ID Debate Could Change 2012 Landscape" (MSNBC, May 25, 2011). Accessed on May 25, 2011, from msnbc.com.

43. From my.barackobama.com/page/s/campobama. Accessed on June 12, 2007.

44. Ruffini, "Obama Opens the GOTV Firehose." Ruffini is quoting from Zack Exley's article in the second quote in the paragraph.

45. Colin Delany, "How Candidates Can Use the Internet to Win in 2010" (e-book, p. 10 for all quotes). Accessed on May 25, 2011, from epolitics.com. All references in the paragraph are from this source.

PART II

The Evolving Campaign—Adaptation by Political Institutions and Groups

CHAPTER 7

Political Parties — Beyond Revitalization

Tari Renner

THE REVITALIZATION OF AMERICAN POLITICAL PARTIES over the last generation has been well established in academic research as well as popular commentary.
The national parties have come a long way from their feeble position in the 1960s
when the leading book on their role was titled *Politics Without Power.*[1] Over the last
generation, the national party organizations have dramatically increased their role
in candidate recruitment, fundraising, targeting of campaigns, communication,
and get-out-the-vote (GOTV) operations. They have adapted to, and even thrived
in, an era of changing campaign technologies. The latter set of activities is often
referred to as the "Service Party Model." The strategic role of party organizations
has been broadened to provide a variety of services to candidates in the second
decade of the twenty-first century. Those services include state-of-the-art television
studios, mobile technology, and extensive online outreach programs.

Interest groups, political action committees (PACs), and independent expenditure movements may also contribute money, but parties confer nominations
with legal authority. Indeed, the entire electoral process is organized around them.
Practically speaking, with few exceptions, successful candidates for the highest
offices in the country need to obtain a nomination from one of the two major
political parties. In the general election, the party labels and communication processes clearly structure campaign conflict. They are indeed unique entities in our
nation's electoral process. This chapter discusses the evolving role of American
parties in political campaigns. The primary focus is upon elections at the federal
level. The chapter then goes on to examine political party organizational leadership, programs, fundraising, and campaign tactics. It concludes that the parties
will continue to be critical actors, but they will face a variety of challenges in the
future.

Party Revitalization and Ideological Polarization

The primary cause of party resurgence has been organic—that is, the natural product of the coalitional shifts in the party bases and the increasing ideological polarization between the two major parties. Since the emergence of the New Deal Coalition in the 1930s, Democrats have very gradually lost their most conservative wing (primarily white southerners) over civil rights and social/cultural issues. As this group left the Democrats and became behavioral Republicans, the Democrats moved left, and the GOP was pulled even further to the right. The latter phenomenon caused liberal and moderate Republicans in the North to become either Democrats or Independents. In the process, the country went from having two ideologically diverse parties and a clear Democratic majority to having two ideologically distinctive parties whose strength is nearly equal.

The increase in ideological polarization between the two parties clearly helps the intraparty unity of elected officials (sometimes called the party in government) and party identifiers (sometimes called the party in the electorate). It also helps internal organizational unity and fundraising. Contemporary donors are likely to be highly motivated by ideology and more likely to open their pocketbooks when they know that their contributions are going to candidates with similar views of politics.[2]

Ideological Purists and Pragmatists

The existence of a two-party system probably makes intraparty divisions inevitable between the most intense ideologues (sometimes called purists) and party pragmatists. The former are most likely to see politics in stark moral terms, and the latter are more likely to be practical and see things in shades of gray. The divisions between the two types of partisans emerged among the first American parties and continue to the present. This was evidenced by the role of the Tea Party in the 2010 elections, as we discuss later in this section. The differences appear in all three segments of parties—the formal party organization, the elected officeholders, and the rank-and-file party voters.

The ideological realignment since the New Deal Era has strengthened the purists in both major political parties. However, it is important to understand the differences between the internal position of the most liberal wing within the Democratic Party and that of the most conservative wing within the Republican Party. Today, the liberal Democratic purists have, of course, increased in size within their party, but they remain a very diverse coalition (on race, ethnicity, religion, and geography). They might include large numbers of African Americans; Latinos; white Christian, Jewish, or unaffiliated urbanites and suburbanites; gays and lesbians; and other groups. In contrast, conservative Republican purists are likely to be a much more homogeneous coalition. They are overwhelmingly white and very likely to be born again evangelical Christians whose conservatism is primarily grounded in social or cultural issues—especially abortion and gay rights. Consequently, they are generally more united and easier to communicate with and mobilize. This situation is often an advantage for Republicans but can also pose possible problems since internal disputes are liable to develop as stark bipolar contests between unified ideological purists and pragmatists.

The emergence of the so-called Tea Party in 2009 and 2010 produced some serious intraparty splits in GOP primaries that probably prevented the Republicans from picking up three Senate seats in Colorado, Delaware, and Nevada. The primary victories of Tea Party–backed candidates in red states such as Kentucky and Utah did little to harm Republican general election prospects. In Florida, however, Republican governor Charlie Crist was recruited by the National Republican Senatorial Campaign Committee (NRSCC) but eventually abandoned the GOP to run as an Independent when it became clear that he couldn't win his party's primary against conservative purist Marco Rubio. The Tea Party movement is unusual in that it has united economic and social conservatives in opposition to the Obama administration's economic and health care policies. In the future, the power of the GOP's most conservative wing may continue to be a serious obstacle to the pragmatists' attempts to appeal to an increasingly diverse electorate.

National Party Organizations: Structure

The Republican National Committee (RNC) and the Democratic National Committee (DNC) are the primary national umbrella organizations for each major party. They are the centers of national campaign activity and are constituted by the fifty state party organizations and those of U.S. territories such as the District of Columbia, Guam, and Puerto Rico. The national Republican Governors Association and the national Democratic Governors Association and the "Hill committees" are also member organizations.

The Hill committees represent the four congressional parties on Capitol Hill—House Democrats, House Republicans, Senate Democrats, and Senate Republicans. They include the Democratic Congressional Campaign Committee (DCCC), the National Republican Congressional Committee (NRCC), the Democratic Senatorial Campaign Committee (DSCC), and the National Republican Senatorial Committee (NRSC).

Political scientist Ronald Shaiko summarized how party organizations work: "Each organization has divisions that include finance (fundraising), administration (office operations and payroll), legal (interpreting campaign finance laws), political (candidate recruitment, training, advertising, tactical advice, and voter mobilization efforts), and communication (earned media, paid media, and new media), as well as an office of the chairman or chairwoman."[3]

The older national party organizations performed few functions or services during the era of traditional campaigning. Contemporary parties, however, have adapted to the new style of elections and have become central players in American campaigns. As a consequence, they have needed to form more complex national organizations to handle a wide variety of more specialized functions.

The Emergence and Institutionalization of the Service Party Model

The modern role of the national political party organizations as service providers has become institutionalized over the last generation. The national committees, the Hill committees, and, more recently, the national governors associations provide services such as maintaining voter lists, organizing GOTV operations, and providing advice and training to candidates. However, they also do a lot more. They help recruit and legitimize candidates and continue to raise increasing levels of campaign cash that they channel into the field in a variety of ways. Further, the national parties' decisions to support candidates at the beginning of the process and the targeting choices they make in the homestretch serve as cues to the entire community of donors (PACs as well as wealthy individual contributors).

Table 7.1 presents the expenditures for each of the national party organizations (and their respective totals) from 2004 through 2010. This represents their campaign expenditures over the last two presidential and midterm elections. The expenditures of the organizations have generally increased over time (recognizing that there are natural spikes during presidential years). In fact, the combined Democratic and Republican party totals reached nearly $1 billion each during the 2008 presidential election cycle.

The emergence of the contemporary service provider function dates back to the 1970s for Republicans and to the 1980s for Democrats. For the GOP, the Watergate scandal, massive Democratic gains in the 1974 midterm elections, and the loss of the White House in 1976 were all catalysts for change. New party leaders emerged in this environment to rebuild and renew their national organization. They began aggressive programs for improving fundraising and professionalizing their staff. By 1980, the GOP even had a long-term strategy to recruit and groom candidates at the state legislative and local levels to help build a Republican "farm team." The goal was to ensure that there was a deep pool of party candidates for the future. The Democrats were, at first, comparatively slow to adapt to this modern service role. However, their catalyst for action was similar to the GOP's—devastating electoral defeat. After the Democrats' landslide loss to Ronald Reagan in 1980, the party began to supply the same kinds of services the Republicans had been providing to their candidates. Today, both major parties have become *the* central players in the strategic recruitment, training, and funding of congressional campaigns.

TABLE 7.I   Total Receipts: National Party Organizations: 2004–2010

Party Organization	2004	2006	2008	2010
Democratic Party	$824,442,985	$602,059,730	$961,199,298	$814,974,337
DNC	404,391,553	130,821,232	260,111,657	224,457,439
DCCC	92,945,101	139,994,367	176,204,612	163,896,053
DSCC	88,659,299	121,376,959	162,791,453	129,543,443
Republican Party	$894,336,719	$748,204,787	$920,479,521	$586,594,377
RNC	392,413,393	243,007,131	427,558,768	196,336,723
NRCC	185,719,489	176,300,627	118,324,756	133,779,119
NRSC	78,980,487	88,812,386	94,424,743	84,513,719

Source: Center for Responsive Politics. Accessed on May 31, 2011, from www.opensecrets .org.

Note: Total receipts include all reported donations to all party committees. DNC = Democratic National Committee; DCCC = Democratic Congressional Campaign Committee; DSCC = Democratic Senatorial Campaign Committee; RNC = Republican National Committee; NRCC = National Republican Congressional Committee; NRSC = National Republican Senatorial Committee.

Party Leadership and Strategies

In the decade since the disputed 2000 presidential election, the Democratic National Committee has had fairly consistent leadership while that of the Republican National Committee appears to be a revolving door. The DNC has had only four chairs (Terry McAuliffe, Howard Dean, Tim Kaine, and Debbie Wasserman Schultz) while the RNC has had eight chairs (Jim Gilmore, Marc Racicot, Ed Gillespie, Ken Mehlman, Mel Martinez, Mike Duncan, Michael Steele, and Reince Priebus).

Party Leaders, Styles, and Vision

These leaders brought a variety of different styles and strategic visions to their positions. Howard Dean, for example, attempted to change his party's mindset and targeting decisions with his fifty-state strategy. He believed the Democrats needed to broaden their battlefield in order to win back both houses of Congress in 2006 and the White House in 2008. This approach often led to strategic differences between Dean and DCCC chair Rahm Emanuel as the latter tended to favor a more traditional focused approach to targeting campaign resources.

In addition to strategic views, national party leaders differ in personal styles, and these differences can be very important in the performance of their public relations function. Consider the brief tenure of RNC chair Michael Steele

(2009–2011). Steele developed a reputation for being outspoken and unconventional. This style, however, turned out to be a double-edged sword. In the fall of the 2010 midterm elections, Steele launched an unprecedented "Fire Pelosi Bus Tour" with the primary goal of publicizing his party campaign to win back the U.S. House. In a six-week trip from mid-September through late October, Steele held rallies in over a hundred cities across the forty-eight states in the continental United States. In these stops, Steele used his bombastic speaking style to fire up Republican activists across the country. While he was widely praised for such public efforts to rev up the base, Steele's blunt and off-the-cuff remarks to the media brought him much criticism and may have cost him his job. For example, he was forced to apologize after describing right-wing icon Rush Limbaugh's work as "incendiary" and "ugly."[4] These and other blunt public statements became an issue in Steele's unsuccessful bid to retain his post as RNC chair. One state party chair said he was opposing Steele's reelection because "I'm tired of all of the drama."[5] In an interview after losing his job to Reince Priebus, Steele himself concluded that he lost because they (the RNC) wanted someone with a different style.[6]

The Effectiveness of Party Leadership and Tactics on Outcomes

The effectiveness of party leadership and tactics upon electoral outcomes are clearly affected, and often limited, by changes in the broader political environment. For example, while Rahm Emanuel (as head of the DCCC) received great praise for his party's winning control of the House in 2006 (with a gain of thirty-three seats), there is no doubt that he was operating within a very favorable national political climate for his party (the president's popularity was at record low levels, the war in Iraq was increasingly unpopular, and the Republicans had been in power for six years). The same can be said of Chris Van Hollen, who chaired the DCCC in the 2008 elections as the Democrats' "Red to Blue" strategy continued. The president's popularity and the economy continued to decline, and the Democrats gained twenty-two additional House seats. However, the same cannot be said for Chris Van Hollen in 2010, when his party faced devastating electoral losses as the GOP gained sixty-three House seats. The same leadership produced very different results because of a dramatic change in the national political environment. On the Republican side, NRCC chair Pete Sessions won little praise after the 2008 House elections but seemed to be able to do no wrong in 2010. In most cases, the leadership may be able to improve its party's success at the margins but can hardly do much to alter the intensity of an electoral tsunami. Put another way, it is easy to perform well (and look good) if you're dealt three or four aces as a party leader. It is quite another thing to succeed when you're dealt deuces.

The Importance of Strategy

Party leaders may realize when they've been dealt a bad hand and adjust their strategy accordingly. For example, Senator Patty Murray (D-Wash.) knew she was facing a tough job when she became DSCC chair for the 2011–2012 election cycle. Regardless of whether the national partisan pendulum swung back toward the Democrats in 2012, her party was going to be defending twenty-three of the thirty-three Senate seats at stake. Murray sought to maximize her party's chances by pushing on two distinctive fronts. First of all, in order to prevent Democrats from playing a totally defensive game, she aggressively attempted to expand the competitive playing field by targeting possible pickups in the traditionally red states of Arizona, Indiana, and Texas. Second, Murray pressured all Democrats in the caucus to take a greater and more direct role in maintaining their Senate majority. This involved having "as many as 16 senators . . . dialing for dollars in what is known as 'power hour'—lunchtime at DSCC headquarters."[7] Murray's efforts further illustrate that party leadership styles clearly vary but that their impact upon electoral outcomes is only liable to be realized at the margins.

The same point can be made for specific party strategies or programs. Consider the different effects of the Republicans' Young Guns program in the last two elections. The program was proposed by Congressmen Eric Cantor (R-Va.), Kevin McCarthy (R-Calif.), and Paul Ryan (R-Wis.) and was adopted for the 2007–2008 cycle and continued into the 2009–2010 cycle where it was much more successful. Young Guns recruited challengers to Democratic incumbents and open-seat candidates. It required those candidates enrolled to meet rigorous benchmark targets over time to improve their fundraising, campaign organization, and online communication strategy. Candidates could proceed through the three levels in the Young Guns program depending upon their success in meeting the targets: On the Radar, Contender, and Young Gun (the highest level). The latter group were those who met the most rigorous benchmarks, were considered the strongest candidates, and, therefore, were the most likely to receive the RNCC's financial support during the homestretch of the election (through the party's independent expenditure campaigns).[8]

In 2008, only a handful of Democratic incumbents or open seats fell into GOP hands. In 2010, however, the Republicans greatly broadened the battlefield. A total of 92 candidates were granted the Young Gun status. This program combined with effective targeting of financial contributions helped Republicans field viable candidates in an unprecedented number of congressional districts and enabled them to take full advantage of the national tsunami favoring their party. Ultimately, the NRCC waged independent expenditure campaigns in sixty-six districts. Of that group, they won fifty-two.[9] This included the defeat of several veteran Democratic House committee chairs, including Budget chair John Spratt (D-S.C.), Armed

Services Chair Ike Skelton (D-Mo.), and Transportation and Infrastructure Chair James Oberstar (D-Minn.).

The central point here is that specific programs and strategic allocation of resources can permit parties to maximize their performance given the broader political environment. However, their impact is likely to be marginal since they can do little to alter that environment. In other words, as a party leader you can recruit great surfers and craft great surfboards, but you can't control the size or intensity of the partisan political waves of an election. Both parties have experienced their share of favorable and unfavorable tsunamis in the last three election cycles. Democrats had two strong ones in a row (2006 and 2008), and Republicans had the strongest in recent memory in 2010. The overall political environment, however, includes more than just the changing partisan tides. The most important resource in American elections is money, and the changing rules of the fundraising game have affected both of the major party organizations.

Changes in Campaign Finance: BCRA (2002) to *Citizens United v. FEC* (2010)

Recent legislation and Supreme Court cases have dramatically altered the process of financing American elections. To the national parties these changes may have seemed like a roller-coaster ride for planning strategies and fundraisers. In 2002, Congress passed the Bipartisan Campaign Reform Act (BCRA), which prohibited national or state party organizations from raising "soft money" that had no formal contribution limits. However, the evidence shows that the national parties continued to increase their fundraising despite the BCRA. They were forced to adapt their strategies and use the independent expenditure loophole to influence their targeted races. Referring back to Table 7.1, it is clear that the BCRA did little to prevent the continuing increases in the receipts for all of the party committees. This is consistent with Ronald Shaiko's observation four years ago: "Contrary to the conventional wisdom, not only have the parties adapted, but they are financially stronger than one might have anticipated following the law's enactment."[10]

However, the U.S. Supreme Court's 2010 decision in *Citizens United v. FEC* dealt the parties another potentially serious blow. A closely divided (5-4) Court struck down a portion of the BCRA that prohibited corporations and unions from broadcasting "electioneering communications" (ads broadcast that mention a candidate within thirty days of a primary or within sixty days of a general election). The majority opinion held that the legislative prohibition of all direct independent expenditures by corporations and unions was invalid. This decision effectively permits these organizations to spend unlimited amounts of money without disclosing the sources of the contributions.

The data in Table 7.1 demonstrate that the decision did not appear to harm the parties' overall fundraising. The total party campaign expenditures rose from the 2006 to the 2010 midterm elections (although paradoxically the Democrats raised more and the Republicans less in 2010 while the reverse was true in 2006). However, Michael Toner and Karen Trainer compared the national parties' proportion of total outside spending in the last two midterms. They found that the national parties' spending as a percent of all outside group campaign spending decreased dramatically from 2006 to 2010.[11] The overwhelming majority of outside campaign spending in the former year came from national political party committees (before the decision in *Citizens United*). Four years later, the national parties were outspent by the independent expenditure groups. Consequently, the parties' position relative to independent expenditure groups declined substantially since the last midterm. In the 2010 elections, the top five races with the highest levels of outside independent expenditures were all U.S. Senate contests—Colorado, Nevada, Arkansas, Pennsylvania, and Washington. The top five groups making outside independent expenditures in 2010 were the U.S. Chamber of Commerce, American Action Network, American Crossroads, Crossroads Grassroots Policy Strategies, and the Service Employees International Union.

It is possible that the *Citizens United* decision will continue to reduce the national parties' role in funding elections relative to outside groups in the future. One implication of this possible trend is that both parties and candidates may lose control over their campaign messages. Independent expenditure efforts may not precisely choreograph a central message in the manner in which the parties and candidates might desire. Further, the rise of independent group expenditures might increase the negativity of campaigns in the future. There is empirical evidence that campaign ads geared toward express advocacy are significantly more negative than candidate advertisements.[12]

National Party Organizations: Traditional and New Technologies

Political parties use the same campaign techniques as individual candidates and independent expenditure groups. Beyond the core differences in the organizations discussed earlier, the operations of national party organizations are continuous whereas most individual campaigns have a discrete beginning and conclusion. The parties' activities obviously flare up during election season, but there is no clear beginning and end. Indeed, a devastating election may immediately spur the defeated party to begin a program of renewal for the next election. Cases in point include the above-mentioned Red to Blue and Young Guns programs by the Democrats and Republicans, respectively.

The biggest tactical challenge national parties currently face is to keep on top of changes in campaign communication. The Internet and associated new technologies, for example, have clearly emerged as critical "new" modes of communication since the first campaign website was set up in 1994 by California senator Dianne Feinstein's reelection campaign. However, just as we appear to get a handle on the likely impact of these technologies, new developments emerge to further complicate, and provide new opportunities to revolutionize, modern campaigning. These changes include the Howard Dean campaign's raising of unprecedented amounts of money online in the 2004 presidential race, the emergence of YouTube in 2006 (especially in the Virginia Senate race), Facebook and text messaging in the 2008 Obama campaign, and Sarah Palin's pioneering of Twitter in 2009. In the section below, some of the most important methods of traditional and nontraditional communication are discussed.

Direct Mail and Microtargeting

The rise of new technologies does not mean that the old ones fade away. In fact, innovative new strategies are being used to improve many traditional means of communicating with voters and prospective supporters. Direct mail, for example, continues to thrive for both campaign fundraising and message communication and will likely remain critical in the immediate future. Why does direct mail still play such an important role? According to Karen Tucker, manager of transaction mail for the U.S. Postal Service, there are three core reasons. First of all, the vast majority of voters report that they read or at least review their mail. Second, direct mail is especially effective in affecting attitudes and providing knowledge because it "allows for the inclusion of longer messages than other mediums, which means mailers can clearly define a candidate's campaign platform or address a single issue head-on. And, since it's tangible, it can be a very handy reference tool for people who are voting by mail when they fill out their ballot at home. . . . Mail is a flexible form of communication that can support multiple goals."[13] Consequently, direct mail in campaigns may change but is unlikely to be replaced by the newer technologies.

Future changes will likely be aimed at improving the efficiency and effectiveness of their microtargeting techniques. Parties use political preference, voting history, lifestyle, and demographic information in their voter databases (called Voter Vault by the RNC and Catalist by the DNC) to tailor their fundraising or campaign messages to very specific groups of voters. This custom messaging is geared toward increasingly small segments of the electorate—micro audiences. The latest waves of microtargeting go well beyond voter history in an attempt to predict individual voter attitudes and behavior long before Election Day. This is accomplished through *voter modeling*—a term that came into vogue with President Barack Obama's 2008 campaign and has dominated strategy discussions since."[14] More recently, John Phillips of Aristotle, one of the most prominent data collection firms, developed something called "Relationship Viewer" to probe more deeply into available data. It attempts to make more accurate predictions of individuals based upon the connections between them and other people they interact with—friends, neighbors, and coworkers, for example. The overall trajectory of this phenomenon was summarized by Laura Quinn, CEO of Catalist, the Democratic data firm: "Campaigns were generalizing the message for large swaths of people. Now campaigns are specializing the message for smaller swaths of people."[15] These refinements will permit future campaign communication to become more efficient and effective.

GOTV the New Voter Mobilization

Newer technologies such as microtargeting and Internet social networking have helped improve the effectiveness of another traditional campaign operation—get-out-the-vote (GOTV). The voter modeling discussed above is also extremely useful in tailoring messages for GOTV. It can, for example, help in predicting what type of voters will be the most receptive to an absentee ballot or early voting program.[16] Further, David All, founder of TechRepublican.com, and Jerome Armstrong of WebStrong.com maintain that organizing early on the Internet and social networking can greatly improve the effectiveness of a campaign's GOTV.[17] They advocate "early engagement" that integrates GOTV with early social networking. "Things like forming a network of supporters, including groups, listserves and personal fundraising pages, will all serve to fully engage the supporters early on, instead of them sitting around for months waiting to get active." All and Armstrong conclude that in the future "the best run campaigns are going to be those that execute their traditional activities while fully integrating an online GOTV campaign."[18]

The political parties' online GOTV campaigns are likely to include Google Network Blasts, which have been used successfully by candidates such as Democrat Scott Murphy in his special election victory in New York's twentieth congressional district in 2009. The idea is "to completely blanket a geo-targeted area with online ads quickly." The Murphy campaign ran a GOTV message touting Barack Obama's endorsement in the most Democratic areas in the final day before and on Election Day. Shane D'Aprile concludes, "For Google, the network blast is among the newest political tools."[19]

In the future, some version of the traditional programs such as the Republican's STOMP (Strategic Task Force to Organize and Mobilize People, also known as the "seventy-two-hour program") are unlikely to totally disappear. Rather, they will change to integrate with newer technologies and begin much earlier. In light of new turnout models accounting for early and absentee voting, one observer concluded: "It's 720 hours now."[20] This means campaigns will need to start earlier in order to adapt to the reality that an increasing number of votes are no longer cast on Election Day. (The Republicans' emerging strategy on this is discussed later on in the chapter.)

Traditional Media and New Media

No greater evidence of the blending of old and new campaign strategies exists than in the use of both traditional and new media. The sources of traditional media—television and radio—are losing their influence relative to other sources of information gathering on the Internet. Further, television itself as a medium has changed. Viewers have gone beyond watching the three major networks of twenty years ago to hundreds or more today. As a result, the contemporary television media environment has become more fragmented, and voters are becoming harder to reach. Modern campaigns have adapted to these changes by using the same type of microtargeting strategies discussed above in direct mail and GOTV. Tim Kay, director of political strategy for National Cable Communications, reports on the detailed microtargeting practices of the 2008 North Carolina Obama campaign in the Charlotte and Raleigh metropolitan areas. "Using identifiers such as counties, towns and even zip codes, the Obama campaign took advantage of cable to target pockets of potential voters."[21] Kay concludes that "television is still very influential in deciding people's opinions on candidates."[22] His analysis of the Federal Election Commission (FEC) reports from 2008 confirms that campaigns still seem to think this is the case. The Obama campaign spent about $380 million, about half of the total receipts, on paid media communication. This included approximately $20 million on print advertising, $21 million for online communication, and $338 million for cable, network television, and radio. So, despite all of its innovative use of nontraditional communication, about 85 percent of the Obama campaign's spending was on traditional media.[23]

Most modern campaigns, of course, use a variety of both traditional and new media forms in an integrated strategy to communicate with voters. This pattern is unlikely to change in the immediate future. In fact, a campaign may use a controversial or unique television ad to leverage earned media coverage on its distinctiveness and encourage viewers to see it on YouTube or the campaign website (further reinforcing the message). Another innovation toward this end is the "viral video." In 2008, the Missouri Democratic Party waged a successful campaign of spreading viral videos through the Internet and earned media against Republican candidate Kenny Hulshof. They produced several controversial and timely videos designed to keep their opponent "off his game, off message and on the defensive without interfering with the (Jay) Nixon campaign's positive message of the attorney general's vision for Missouri."[24] The consultant who ran the effort, Isaac Wright, points out that television ads are "meant to catch a viewer's eye for a 30-second window of advertising during the viewer's program of choice. The length of a viral video is limited only by its ability to hold a viewer's attention."[25] Wright notes that the strategy "was to use the videos to drive earned media coverage, not only of the videos themselves, but also of selected issues in the campaign. Videos were posted repeatedly on newspaper websites and on political news blogs and even aired on the news . . . The news in turn drove news consuming voters online to watch more of the videos, spreading the message even further."[26] This example helps illustrate that there is no rigid dichotomy between traditional and new media communication techniques. Both forms are evolving simultaneously in modern campaigns.

Modern Online Operations: A Growing Service Function

Both the Democratic and Republican parties have been updating their online operations since 2008. The purposes are to be more attuned to constituents and to increase the options and opportunities to communicate with the party. In 2010, the Democratic National Committee announced it was "the first-ever political party, committee or candidate to release an application for the iPad, we are showing once again that the DNC . . . (is) on the cutting edge of technology." Furthermore, the DNC's Brandi Hoffine further elaborated that the purpose was to show "new and innovative ways to communicate with our massive grassroots network of voters, supporters and activists."[27]

Republicans have focused on building a stronger integrated online and voter mobilization effort by overhauling their programs, which have been in place for the better part of a decade. The RNC announced in the spring of 2011 that it was revamping its seventy-two-hour (get-out-the-vote) program and modernizing its Voter Vault file system to prepare for the 2012 election. In both cases, the parties have sought to stay current with modern technology that is particularly important in their communication efforts with Generation X and Millennial Generation voters who grew up after the Vietnam War and Watergate.[28]

Future Challenges: Redistricting and Demographic Change

The parties face a variety of challenges in the short and long term beyond the continual adapting to changing technology. For example, the 2010 Census reflects long-term changes in the electorate itself. These results are a double-edged sword for both major political parties. The Republicans expect to gain because of the new apportionment in congressional seats and electoral votes. The allocation of new congressional seats is especially important for Republicans in the redistricting process since they gained so massively in the 2010 midterm elections. They now control the majority of the nation's governorships and state legislatures, so they can expect important strategic advantages for the new districts drawn for the next decade.

The demographic change in the electorate, however, may complicate the Republicans' effort to take advantage of reapportionment and redistricting. Consider, for example, that all but one of the Bush–McCain states that are gaining congressional seats currently have minority populations of 36 percent or more. The one exception is Utah, which had the second highest percentage rate increase in racial minorities (64.8 percent) among the states. In short, the "red states" are gaining population primarily because they are becoming more racially diverse.

Party Organizations—Beyond Revival

It is common for political observers to refer to the current era as one of party revitalization since the organizations have reemerged from their nadir in the 1960s and 1970s. American parties have now moved beyond revitalization. They revitalized in the 1980s and 1990s by adapting to changing campaign technologies and increased ideological polarization. At this point, parties are firmly established as critical service providers and the central players in national elections. The two major national parties currently spend nearly a billion dollars each per election cycle. They have elaborate organizational structures that perform a wide variety of campaign functions. In short, their service provider role in modern election campaigns has been firmly institutionalized. Therefore, any immediate future changes in American parties are likely to be incremental rather than radical.

Greater Integrated Roles and Functions of Parties

One likely change is that divergent campaign roles and functions will become increasingly integrated. The techniques of microtargeting, for example, are used in a variety of different forms of campaign communication—direct mail, fundraising, GOTV, and both traditional and new media. As discussed earlier, future campaigns must successfully integrate these seemingly divergent techniques.

A similar trend toward the merging of so-called traditional and new media is almost certain to continue. In the twenty-first century, no one or two means of communication are sufficient to get a campaign message out to voters. Today, campaigns must use direct mail, microtargeted television, and radio ads along with Internet ads, Facebook, YouTube, websites, e-mails, text messaging, and Twitter. The diversification of communication forms will certainly continue in the near future along with an increase in the importance of mobile technology. These various forms must be used in concert in order to choreograph a consistent message. The merging of campaign media is further indicated by the decreased distinctiveness of the instruments of communication. Cell phones, laptop computers, and televisions are beginning to perform many of the same core functions. Indeed, we may eventually get to the point where the distinction between traditional and new media itself becomes a relic of the past.

The 2010 Census Alters Party Strategies

In the immediate future, both national parties will need to adapt to more than changing campaign technologies in order to thrive. The 2010 Census clearly indicates that the electorate itself has changed in ways that will affect the future election campaigns of both major political parties. Overall, the minority population increased from 30.9 to 36.3 percent of the population. There are now four majority-minority states in the Union—California, Hawaii, New Mexico, and Texas. Further, the minority populations in five states are rapidly approaching a majority—Arizona, Florida, Georgia, Maryland, and Nevada. The diversification has been most dramatic in the Southwest and was largely responsible for turning three Bush states in the region—Colorado, Nevada, and New Mexico—toward Obama in 2008 (all by margins exceeding the national average). These changes present new challenges to Republicans and potential opportunities to Democrats.

Minorities and the Party Calculus for Winning

Republicans will try to increase their vote share among racial minorities, or they will need unrealistically high percentages among whites to prevail in future elections. Consider the critical case of Texas, which currently has a 55 percent minority population. The electoral arithmetic in contests for either the presidency or Congress would be very difficult for the national Republicans if they lost their majority status in the Lone Star State. In the last two elections, the GOP won by similar margins at the top of the ticket. In 2008, McCain won 55 percent to 44 percent for Obama, and in 2010 Rick Perry won the governor's race 55 percent to 42 percent. These 11 and 13 percent pluralities might seem fairly comfortable at the surface. However, in the most recent Republican tsunami year, the 45 percent white minority cast 67 percent of the state's votes. Further, Republican governor Perry won those white voters 69 percent to 29 percent. These are thresholds that the Texas GOP will not likely be able to reproduce in the future. In order for the party to maintain competitiveness, much less its majority status, it will need to make substantial inroads among racial minorities. This will be a very difficult task to accomplish without alienating conservative ideological purists on issues such as poverty and immigration. Democrats, on the other hand, cannot expect to take minority voters for granted as they did with blue-collar voters, who migrated away from the party after fifty years during the 1980s.

Conclusion

In the future, American political parties will remain as important central service providers in election campaigns. They will likely continue to adapt to changes in the political environment, to changes in the demographic composition of the electorate, and to the ever-evolving technological means of campaign communication and fundraising (although the *Citizens United* decision may reduce their control over message content and impact relative to independent expenditure groups). The new campaign technologies seem to revolutionize rather than replace the older traditional means of communication. Successful campaigns of the future will continue to integrate the two. Indeed, the distinctions between old and new technologies may eventually become moot.

The ideological polarization between the parties is likely to continue throughout the early twenty-first century. There are very real ideological differences between the two major political parties that have developed over the last two generations, and these differences are not likely to change anytime soon. The consequences of increased inter-party ideological polarization include increases in intraparty unity and discipline among elected officeholders, increased cohesion within the organizations, and the facilitation of campaign fundraising from ideological donors. However, while many observers claim that it also leads to overheated and exaggerated partisan rhetoric, election campaign distortions are as American as apple pie.

The balance of power between our ideologically polarized parties will remain very tight in the near future since there is no majority party in the United States today. Both the Democrats and the Republicans are minority parties. They are also nearly equal in their proportion of party identifiers in the electorate. In the current political environment, we consider winning 53 percent of the vote to be a decisive wave election (that was approximately the percent won by the Republicans in 1994, the Democrats in 2006, Obama in 2008, and the Republicans in 2010). The 53 percent figures (either Democratic or Republican) may come close to constituting the outer boundaries within which contemporary party competition is fought. This means that a very small segment of the electorate will continue to hold the balance of power in the United States. Consequently, in the foreseeable future, political parties will continue to develop more sophisticated techniques to increase the precision and effectiveness of campaign communication in reaching these voters to win elections.

Notes

1. Cornelius P. Cotter and Bernard C. Hennessy, *Politics Without Power: The National Party Committees* (New York: Atherton, 1964).
2. For example, arch segregationist Strom Thurmond of South Carolina was elected to the U.S. Senate as a Democrat until he changed parties in 1964 over the Civil Rights

Act of 1964. Until then, Thurmond was a member of the Democratic caucus along with liberal party purists George McGovern of South Dakota and Ted Kennedy of Massachusetts.

3. Ronald G. Shaiko, "Political Parties—On the Path to Revitalization," in *Campaigns on the Cutting Edge*, edited by Richard J. Semiatin (Washington, DC: CQ Press, 2008), 106.

4. Michael Saul, "GOP Chairman Michael Steele and Pundit Rush Limbaugh in War of Words" (Daily News, March 3, 2009). Accessed on November 11, 2011, from http:// articles.nydailynews.com

5. Quoted in "Race for RNC Chairman Remains a Toss-Up as Steele Defends Tenure" (*The Hill*, December 26, 2010). Accessed on June 20, 2011, from TheHill.com.

6. The Situation Room, "Interview With Former RNC Chairman Michael Steele" (Real Clear Politics, January 19, 2011). Accessed November 11, 2011, from RealClearPolitics .com.

7. Susan Davis, "Keeping Control of the Senate 2012 May Be a Hill Too Steep for Democrats. But Patty Murray Is Trying" (*National Journal*, June 9, 2011). Accessed on November 11, 2011, from NationalJournal.com.

8. Aaron Blake, "NRCC Young Guns Run the Gamut as Party Eyes Possibility of Big Gains in '10" (*The Hill*, February 16, 2010). Accessed on November 11, 2011, from TheHill.com.

9. Sean J. Miller, "Strategists Second-Guess Dem Spending Strategy After Losses in House" (*The Hill*, November 9, 2010). Accessed on November 11, 2011, from TheHill .com.

10. Shaiko, "Political Parties," 110.

11. Michael E. Toner and Karen E. Trainer, "The Impact of the Federal Election Laws on the 2010 Midterm Election," in *Pendulum Swing*, edited by Larry J. Sabato (Boston: Longman, 2011), 131–155.

12. See Sandy L. Maisel and Darrel West, *Running on Empty? Political Discourse in Congressional Elections* (Lanham, MD: Rowman and Littlefield, 2004); and David B. Magleby and Marjorie Holt, *Outside Money, Soft Money and Issue Ads in Competitive* 1998 *Congressional Elections* (Provo, UT: Brigham Young University, 1999).

13. Karen Tucker, "Mail Power Is Your Power" (*Politics*, May 2010, Number 291), 58.

14. Jeremy P. Jacobs, "Buzzword: Modeling: Definition: Analysis of Voters Used to Win Elections" (*Politics*, October 2009, Number 284), 16.

15. Ibid, 18.

16. Ibid.

17. David All and Jerome Armstrong, "Why You Should Start Your Online GOTV Early" (*Politics*, October 2009, Number 284), 19.

18. Ibid.

19. Shane D'Aprile, "Should You Buy Into the Google Surge?" (*Politics*, October 2009, Number 284), 37.

20. Rich Beeson quoted in Erin Pike, "72 Hours Is So Five Years Ago" (*Politics*, October 2009, Number 284), 51.

21. Tim Kay, "Making the Case for TV Buys in the Internet Age" (*Politics*, July 2009, Number 281), 32.

22. Ibid, 33.

23. Data calculated from Tim Kay's presentation above.

24. Isaac Wright, "It's More Than Just Putting Ads Online" (*Politics*, November/December 2009, Number 285), 39.

25. Ibid, 40.

26. Ibid.

27. Gautham Nagesh, "DNC Unveils iPad App to Organize Grass Roots" (*The Hill*, June 24, 2010). Accessed on July 20, 2011, from TheHill.com.

28. David M. Drucker, "RNC Looks to Revamp Ground Game" (*Roll Call*, April 11, 2011). Accessed on July 20, 2011, from rollcall.com.

CHAPTER 8

Interest Groups and the Future of Campaigns

Nina Therese Kasniunas and Mark J. Rozell

CANDIDATES FOR PUBLIC OFFICE in the United States may differ in their rhetoric on many issues, but they all seem to agree on this point: Interest groups are entirely too powerful. In truth, candidates need interest groups more than ever—not only as easy targets of attack to win public approval, but also to facilitate campaigns. Interest groups have become the potent intervening force in political campaigns by influencing the choices of voters. In recent years, interest groups have often resembled political parties in their ability to inform, influence, and mobilize hundreds of thousands or even millions of voters to get to the polls.[1]

As we prepare for the 2012 elections, it is clear that groups will have a larger and more pervasive influence on campaigns than ever before. Since the publication of the first edition of this book in 2008, two major developments involving the roles of groups in campaigns have profoundly altered the nature of electoral politics. One is the rise of the so-called Tea Party movement and the other a Supreme Court decision so controversial and sweeping in its import that it precipitated an extraordinary rebuke from an incumbent president during his State of the Union address.

Although the Tea Party is more mass movement at the grass roots than a traditional interest group, it has some of the hallmarks of a formally organized group. Usually we would prefer to avoid the use of the upper case since strictly speaking, the Tea Party is nothing like a formal political party, and there is no such recognized organization with a letterhead and leadership hierarchy. But the movement has achieved such political traction and even has some major corporate and business sources of funding that the media commonly give it the more formal recognition usually reserved for the types of traditional groups we discuss in this chapter.

As the following chapter describes, modern technology has given citizens and organized groups more and better means than ever to influence the electoral process. Without the rise of such vehicles of mass communication as social networking and Twitter, the extraordinary quick rise of the Tea Party in the United States—and now major democratic revolutions abroad—would not be possible. The Tea Party is at the present the most prominent manifestation of the profound changes taking place in U.S. electoral politics—changes that are happening so rapidly that some entirely different group or groups likely will emerge by the third edition of this book, or even by the time this edition is printed.

The other major development that will continue to have an impact in the 2012 elections is the Supreme Court ruling in *Citizens United v. FEC* (08-205 [2010]). In a 5-4 split decision, the Court invalidated a ban on independent expenditures set in place by the Bipartisan Campaign Reform Act of 2002. This ruling extends the individual right of using unlimited expenditures to advocate one's cause to corporations and labor unions, undoubtedly further enhancing their electioneering power.

The effects of *Citizens United* were already felt in the 2010 midterm elections and will likely increase greatly in 2012. The floodgates have been opened, and the money has come pouring in. It is more difficult now to track who is spending money and is responsible for advertising, which is in many cases negative and sometimes false. Wealthy interests, whether corporate, labor, or of some other form, will have more opportunity to use their money in attempting to shape electoral outcomes. The amount of money raised and spent will undoubtedly continue to break records, raising the bar of how much money a candidate has to raise in order to remain competitive.

In this chapter, we examine the various ways in which interest groups are using traditional and new technologies to influence electoral campaigns. Our emphasis will largely be on the modern techniques of interest group mobilization and communication. Groups today employ a variety of techniques to pursue their electoral and policy goals. Some place a strong emphasis on building a community of supporters that they can activate when necessary, and others mostly raise money to contribute to candidates. When it comes to the technologies that interest groups employ, some groups are at the forefront, implementing the newest devices and techniques, while others lag far behind.

Traditional Approaches by Interest Groups in Campaigns

Interest groups become involved in electoral politics in a variety of ways. For example, groups try to identify voters who are sympathetic to certain issue positions and then provide resources to ensure that those people vote. Many groups purchase campaign broadcast ads in areas of the country where there are competitive elections.

The 2010 race for Colorado's Senate seat attracted much interest group spending. The conservative American Crossroads, for example, spent $5.9 million in independent expenditures against the incumbent Democrat Michael Bennet (D-Colo.) while the liberal NEA Advocacy Fund spent $1.9 million advocating against the election of Republican Ken Buck.[3] Some groups train activists in the techniques of campaigns. And some groups actively recruit and train candidates for public office. EMILY's List, a group that supports pro-choice Democratic women, does so with great success. These are among the many ways in which interest groups try to affect the outcomes of U.S. elections at all levels.

Groups' efforts to influence elections have become increasingly sophisticated. Groups with substantial resources make use of the latest technologies to communicate with large numbers of activists, supporters, and other potential voters. New technologies have made it possible for groups with fewer resources also to communicate with large numbers of people in campaigns.

Although new technologies are rapidly transforming the ways in which groups become involved in campaigns, most still rely on tried and tested techniques. If anything, technology is enabling more efficient use of those methods. Recently there has been a lot of media buzz about the important roles that social networking sites such as Facebook, Twitter, and YouTube are playing in the latest election cycles. The trend seen in the 2010 election season, which likely will continue into 2012, is to edit publicly available video footage in a way that negatively distorts a candidate's original statement. In the controversial "Taliban Dan" ad, Republican challenger Dan Webster is shown speaking a number of statements that were taken out of context. Those statements include "Wives, submit yourself to your husband" and "She should submit to me." As the candidate who ran the ad containing manipulated video clips, Democrat Alan Grayson received a lot of negative attention although that only prompted thousands more to seek out and watch the ad online.[4]

Recruiting and Training Candidates

Traditionally, by reaching out to potential candidates and offering encouragement and support, interest groups can also influence who decides to run for office. By offering training, groups can potentially influence who wins elections. Many groups find that the most reliable and loyal candidates are drawn from the ranks of their own organizations. The AFL-CIO, for example, decided that it can best promote its policy goals by recruiting its own members, rather than by recruiting and training candidates from outside the labor movement, who may agree with some—but not all—of the labor agenda. The organization thus has pursued a program of actively recruiting and training labor union members to run for public offices.

The National Women's Political Caucus (NWPC) has mounted a large-scale effort to recruit women to run for public office. The caucus holds training events to teach state and local activists how to identify potentially strong candidates and campaign managers. Thousands of women have participated in NWPC candidate training seminars, including Rep. Linda Sánchez (D-Calif.), who says that she got her start in politics by attending one of these events.[2] Many other groups hold training seminars for potential candidates and provide various other resources such as training manuals, video- and audiotapes, and access to pollsters and campaign consultants.

The decision to recruit and train candidates is based on two considerations: first, whether the person agrees with the policy goals of the organization, and second, whether the person has a realistic chance of winning. Groups want to expend their resources strategically and may turn away from an ambitious person who supports key policy stands but is not likely to win an election for whatever reason.

Endorsements and Hit Lists

Many organizations issue formal endorsements to signal to their members which candidates best represent their viewpoint. Endorsements are primarily means to convince group members to vote for the candidates who will be most friendly to the group's interests once elected. Not all groups issue endorsements. Some do not so as to maintain tax-exempt status. Others make a strategic decision not to alienate candidates who might win and become unfavorably inclined toward those who had endorsed their opponent.

The endorsement is not only a signal to group members as to which candidates win the "seal of approval," but it is also a means to persuade a larger public. Thus, an endorsement from the Sierra Club or the League of Conservation Voters would be a strong signal to voters as to which candidate in a campaign is more environmentally friendly. A National Rifle Association endorsement tells many voters which candidate is likely to uphold the interests of gun owners. Groups have to issue endorsements carefully and strategically, however, because they can backfire.

In addition to issuing positive endorsements, interest groups may single out candidates for defeat via what is commonly known as a "hit list." Perhaps the best known hit list is the "Dirty Dozen" named by the League of Conservation Voters (LCV). It is a list of those the league considers the twelve most environmentally unfriendly members of Congress. By using a catchy and memorable name for the list, the LCV succeeds in attracting media and public attention to the races where it has targeted candidates for defeat.

But groups can also target candidates for defeat without calling the roll of names a hit list. With the use of social networking media, in the 2012 elections interest groups are already quickly and cheaply sending out news feeds requesting donations to support the opponents of candidates targeted for defeat. For example, EMILY's List will add to its Facebook news feed an item listing the members in Congress who are most hostile to the pro-choice agenda requesting support for the challengers to these incumbents. It does this without the fanfare of announcing a "hit list" as does the League of Conservation Voters, yet the intent is the same.

Modern Techniques Employed by Interest Groups in Campaigns

Although groups use a variety of techniques to try to influence campaigns, technology is changing at a rapid pace and redefining how races are conducted. Groups that can offer resources to candidates, in an environment that is demanding more and more knowledge of how to exploit emerging trends, thus become more influential.

An Overview of Cutting-Edge Fundraising Techniques

A fundamental but extremely important strategy of interest groups in campaigns is raising and contributing money. Since the Federal Election Campaign Act (FECA) was enacted in the early 1970s, interest groups that want to contribute to a candidate or party have had to do so through a political action committee (PAC). PACs are simply organizations that exist to raise and contribute money in federal elections. Although some PACs are unconnected—they are not affiliated with another organization—most are the fundraising entity of a parent organization. For example, BankPAC is the PAC of the American Bankers Association. BluePAC is affiliated with the Blue Cross and Blue Shield Association. An example of an unconnected PAC is the Prostate Cancer Research PAC, which was formed as an organization in its own right, without ties to any other.

Interest groups have various reasons for wanting to make campaign contributions. Some contribute to try to affect the membership of Congress. They want to elect members of Congress who support the ideas, ideologies, and policy positions of their organization. This is the case with labor unions, which are among the most prolific fundraisers. Because labor unions follow this strategy, they strongly support Democratic candidates; few Republican candidates have platforms that are compatible with unionism. The round of state legislative action against collective bargaining rights witnessed in Wisconsin, Ohio, and Indiana in early 2011 underscores why the ideological composition of a legislative body is the primary goal of labor unions. Other interest groups make campaign contributions to the candidates they believe are most likely to win, to seek favor with them once they become elected officials. This explains why the National Association of Realtors contributed slightly more money to Democrats in the 2008 and 2010 elections, and slightly more to Republicans in the elections from 1996 to 2006; it uses incumbency as the cue for whom it will support.

Even if an interest group chooses not to engage in elections by making campaign contributions, it has an interest in raising money. No organization can maintain itself without financial resources; rents, salaries, and other bills need to be paid. Interest groups that are businesses, corporations, or other for-profit entities use a portion of their profits to cover the costs of their lobbying efforts. Some support themselves financially through foundation or government grants or through the generosity of patrons. But other groups, especially membership groups, solicit contributions from individuals. Such solicitation has traditionally been done through massive direct mailings. AARP, the National Rifle Association, and the Sierra Club all have raised millions of dollars through direct mailings. Purchasing the mailing lists for these appeals can be costlier, as is creating a professional, attractive brochure or packet. While direct mailings were cutting-edge technology in the 1980s, many groups still find it an effective way to communicate a message. Newt Gingrich formed American Solutions for Winning the Future in 2007. In the 2010 election cycle, it spent $13.5 million in direct mailings and telemarketing mostly on its "Drill Here. Drill Now" campaign.[5]

New Trends in Interest Group Websites

Most interest groups now maintain their own websites, which characterize their personality. Some, such as the National Rifle Association (NRA), have a lot of live-action video and movement, highlighting action and independence. Others, such as the Communications Workers of America Committee on Political Education (CWA-COPE), display a blog-style menu that invites group participation. Technology now makes it possible for a group to collect contributions securely through its website. An interest group site may feature a page that enables the visitor to contribute using a credit card or check. At the very least the webpage can provide the user with a downloadable contribution form, which can be printed and sent to the organization. In some sectors of membership groups, such as civil rights and human rights, environmental, and single-issue groups, almost every website allows the user to donate money. Having an interactive website allows the interest group to collect contact information, which is then used to communicate information during a campaign or solicit a contribution for the group's PAC, 527 group, or super PAC.

Few, if any, businesses have this donation option on their websites, even when they feature a "governmental affairs" page. Business websites are geared toward consumers and investors rather than political activists or employees, so an option for making political contributions would not be appropriate. Labor unions similarly do not make this option available, at least not through the public websites. It is likely that once the user enters the "members only site" the option is available. Even without enabling contributions to be made over the Internet, these same businesses and unions are notable contributors to campaigns. For example, Honeywell International contributed $3,654,700 in the 2010 midterm elections, and AT&T contributed $3,262,375. Representing labor, the International Brotherhood of Electrical Workers gave candidates $2,993,373, and the American Federation of State, County and Municipal Employees contributed $2,314,000.[6] Not giving website visitors the opportunity to contribute hasn't hampered their ability to raise significant amounts of money.

Pop-ups Advance the Interest Group Cause

The pop-up windows soliciting donations are used strategically. A candidate might reveal a policy position in a debate or at a campaign stop that might be opposed by an interest group's supporters. As soon as that controversial position is revealed, the interest group can create a pop-up window to educate the website visitor of the stance followed by a request for a campaign contribution. The publicized event may have prompted the individual to visit the website because he or she either wanted more information or wanted to do something about the issue at stake. Playing on the possible emotional state of the visitor, the pop-up immediately was in the face of the user, asking for money. In this way, the pop-ups are akin to direct mail sent to individual households, soliciting money by making an emotional appeal. Although direct mail is used on an ongoing basis by some groups, some appeals are timed to follow events that might raise concern about the issue the group represents, a strategy we also see being used with the pop-ups.

Another feature of many of the interest group websites is an option to sign up for e-mail alerts. The National Organization for Women (NOW) website, for example, features this option under the "Take Action" section and once clicked reveals the message, "Sign Up to Stay Informed about Feminist Issues!" The NRA simply has a prompt for "Email Signup" on its Institute for Legislative Action webpage. Most of these prompts are positioned to suggest that subscribers will receive informational updates about the issues of concern. However, as these are among the groups that frequently use direct mail to solicit contributions, it should be no surprise that some would then also use the e-mail lists to solicit contributions. EMILY's List frequently used its e-mail subscriber list to request contributions for the women candidates has supported.

E-mail Alerts

We collected e-mail updates from a number of these interest groups over several months. Analyzing their content reveals how most groups use this feature. The League of United Latin American Citizens sends its e-mail network policy updates a couple of times a week. Although the e-mails are primarily informational, a prompt that is part of the template says, "Donate." Defenders of Wildlife uses its network similarly to the way that the NRA and NOW use theirs. All of these groups have similar templates and thus afford the same opportunity to their users. Greenpeace sends out an e-mail alert that breaks the pattern. Prominently featured on the right side of its e-mail, in an eye-catching green color, is the list "3 Ways to Help." The first is, "Donate." The prominence and frequency with which one can find an option to donate, contribute, or give point to the utility of the website as a fundraising venue.

A few groups use e-mail for the sole purpose of fundraising. Common Cause had a campaign to raise $50,000 to support a bill making its way through Congress that would require election voting machines to create a paper record. The e-mail alert urged the reader to make a contribution to help reach the $50,000 mark.[7]

Although it seems as if an e-mail network would frequently be used to solicit contributions, most e-mail only includes a passive prompt in the background giving the option of making a donation online. Very few groups use the network solely to raise money, and even the ones that do more frequently send e-mails requesting some other type of political action. E-mails asking for money are used sparingly. During roughly the same period that we were monitoring these e-mails (both action alerts and the ones asking for money), a steady stream of direct mail was sent out explicitly seeking money. The Sierra Club, the American Civil Liberties Union (ACLU), Defenders of Wildlife, the National Wildlife Federation, People for the American Way, Greenpeace, and Beyond Pesticides are just a handful of senders of the almost-daily direct mailings we received. Not only have groups not yet abandoned the age-old practice of using direct mail, but they are fattening their lists with addresses that are provided when individuals subscribe to e-mail alerts.[8]

Interest Groups, Elections, and Mobile Technology

Eighty-five percent of Americans in 2011 owned a cell phone, and more than half of Americans use their cell phone to go online for information according to the Pew Research Center.[9] Not willing to neglect an opportunity to connect with supporters, interest groups are also harnessing mobile technology. Text messages direct supporters to online links where they can make a financial contribution much like website pop-up messaging does. All the interest group needs is a user's cell phone number.

Interest groups are also holding true to the saying "There's an app for that!" While this is an emerging avenue for interest groups, already the NRA and America Votes have free smartphone applications available. As the 2012 elections draw nearer, one can only imagine a number of applications to be developed by interest groups, for example displaying voter guides that individuals can use at the polls.

Informing via Webcasts, Podcasts, and Blogs

Another way in which groups attempt to shape the issue agenda of elections is by providing information directly to like-minded individuals. That way the groups can frame the issue so as to emphasize their own policy positions. Technology has transformed this technique by enabling rapid transmission of news, campaign updates, and policy updates via webcasts, podcasts, blogs, Twitter, and social media sites such as Facebook.

A webcast is a live video feed or broadcast over the Internet. Webcasts are scheduled for live airing much as television shows are. A group's leadership can schedule a webcast, advertise it to its membership and other interested individuals, and then be able to enter the homes of the many supporters watching. An added benefit of webcasts is that usually they are then stored as a video file, accessible on the website for multiple viewings after the initial broadcast.

Podcasts are audio files that are fed over the Internet in a format that can be downloaded and listened to on an MP3 player. Podcasting enables a radio type of broadcast that is freely available to any subscriber. The advantage of podcasting is that the organization can feature news that is of interest to its members. The organization gets to pick the subject of the podcast and frame issues that serve its own interests.

Many groups feature blogs to try to engage activists regularly on core issues in campaigns. Human Rights Campaign, for example, features on its website its "Backstory Blog" to update gay and lesbian activists on a variety of developing policy and campaign-related issues. Interest groups even help to inspire and coordinate individual bloggers who may follow a campaign closely and write about it regularly. Almost all groups have Twitter feeds for activists to receive frequent updates and alerts on issues and campaigns.

Social Networking Sites for Interest Groups

Increasingly, however, the medium of choice is Facebook. Facebook allows the interest group to post news updates, which are then included in the news feeds of the subscriber. When the subscriber logs onto her Facebook page, she will see the news item posted by the interest group.

Additionally, Facebook allows commentary to be posted by subscribers, which can build a sense of solidarity. Subscribers can receive the information passively, or they can engage with others who are also compelled to respond. When the comments affirm or reinforce one another, a sense of community develops. Lastly, Facebook can be used to build social networks, literally. Increasingly, groups are using Facebook to announce meet-ups and demonstrations. Recently, the Tea Party Patriots used Facebook to announce and encourage the attendance to the opening of *Atlas Shrugged* in movie theaters. Mass attendance of Tea Partiers could create a sense of solidarity, which would affirm and strengthen their ideology. Various locals of the American Federation of Teachers frequently post demonstration dates and times on their Facebook page. Demonstrations in state capitals involved in the debate over public bargaining were largely publicized and disseminated through Facebook.

Facebook also is continuing to introduce programming that is more useful and relevant for interest groups. The conservative 527 committee RightChange has created a Facebook page that features options to "Connect," which prompt the user to sign up for e-mail updates similar to the requests found on group websites. Additionally, RightChange has an option on its Facebook page that allows individuals to "Donate." RightChange's cutting-edge Facebook use hints at the possibility of Facebook pages replacing websites as the central information and solicitation portals for interest groups in the future.

The Blogosphere

Interest groups have long cultivated relationships with the media not only to become a trusted source of information for reporters but also to gain favorable coverage in reporting. As bloggers now comprise an important sector of the media, they receive a lot of attention from the various groups involved in campaigns and elections. A number of PACs will host events and conferences that feature candidates. For example, the American Conservative Union's CPAC (Conservative Political Action Committee) hosts conferences each presidential election cycle to showcase the Republican candidates. When CPAC announces such events, it specifically invites bloggers and allows them special access to candidates immediately following their speeches. Thus Newt Gingrich's stance on immigration received a lot of coverage in the blogosphere following a speech he made to CPAC on the issue.

Issue Advocacy and Independent Expenditures

The law limits how much money PACs can contribute to campaigns. The current campaign finance law stipulates that no more than $5,000 per election may be contributed to any candidate (in the 2012 election cycle). For those PACs and interest groups that raise tens of millions of dollars each election cycle, these are severe constraints. Interest groups have found ways to circumvent them, however, raising and spending money in ways that are influential in elections yet still legal.

The first way is by engaging in issue advocacy. *Issue advocacy* is the term used to identify any money that is spent advocating some specific issue or policy position. For example, Citizens Against Government Waste ran a one-minute campaign ad that depicts a Beijing, China, lecture hall in the year 2030. The visual presentation shows images of Ancient Greece, the Roman Empire, the British Empire, and the United States of America, while the professor lectures how none of these nations embraced the lesson that made them great. Their one failure: They attempted to tax and spend their way out of recession. Health care spending and public takeover of private industry are noted, and the professor laughs, saying that because China owned most of the American debt, Americans now work for China. The commercial ends with the message "Stop the spending that is bankrupting America." The ad implies the viewer should vote out of office those responsible for the runaway spending—the Democrats, without ever explicitly calling for the election or defeat of any one candidate or party.[10] Because they contain no explicit call for the election or defeat of a candidate, these types of ads technically are about issues, not the elections, and therefore are protected by the group's free speech rights. There is therefore no limit on the amount of money an interest group may spend on issue advocacy.

The Tea Party as an Interest Group

The Tea Party (with *Tea* standing for "taxed enough already") is a mostly conservative grassroots movement that first organized in 2009 as an opposition force to what its followers consider a big government agenda in the Obama administration. The president's effort to promote health care reform was perhaps the most powerful influence on the rise of the Tea Party. Due to the availability of new and inexpensive means of mass communication along with a willing constituency ready to be organized into action, what largely began in the living room of a disgruntled citizen grew into a major force that played a large role in upending the political landscape in the 2010 midterm elections.

Like traditional interest groups, Tea Party organizations often make endorsements, target opponents, issue pledges for candidates to sign, and mobilize supporters in campaigns, among many other activities. In Colorado in 2010, Republican gubernatorial candidate Scott McInnis refused to fill out a questionnaire from a Tea Party group, the Independence Caucus. Many conservative activists disapproved of his refusal, and McInnis struggled for much of the primary season to win their support, which ultimately went to his Republican opponent, Dan Maes.[11]

One of the goals of many Tea Party groups in 2010 was to urge voters to turn out on Election Day for conservative candidates. These groups often had little to no money for traditional political advertising or for expensive mailers or phone banking. But the motivated efforts of millions of Tea Party sympathizers at the local level were directed toward voter mobilization, often with rallies and peer-to-peer contacts. Some of the larger organizations in the movement, such as Tea Party Patriots, Tea Party Express, and FreedomWorks, sponsored large phone banks and bus tours, but the confederated nature of the Tea Party lent itself more to personal contacts. Interest groups can also try to mobilize potential voters who are not group members. This was certainly true of the Tea Party in 2010, as local groups sought to make their case to frustrated voters to support upstart conservative candidates, some of whom had little or no prior political experience.

Evidence of the growing importance of the Tea Party is the rise of efforts by other groups to counter its political influence. In 2010, the Tea Party movement inspired some progressive efforts, including a "One Nation Working Together" rally in Washington, DC, organized by a coalition of labor and liberal advocacy groups. Such countermobilizations are often less enduring than the effects of sustained efforts by movements and groups to politicize their followers and members.

The Impact of Citizens United v. FEC (2010)

As stated earlier, because of the Supreme Court ruling in *Citizens United v. FEC* (08-205 [2010]) there are no limitations on what type of group or entity may use independent expenditures. Neither are there limitations on spending or when these types of advertisements can be aired. The term *super PAC* has been created to identify those entities that engage solely in independent expenditures. Super PACs emerged in the 2010 elections with quite a presence. According to the Center for Responsive Politics, super PACs spent $65.1 million in the midterm elections. Conservative groups led by American Crossroads spent $35.4 million with liberal groups trailing behind with $28.4 million.[12] These numbers certainly have raised public skepticism about the veracity of claims made with this spending and about the potential influence these groups have over lawmakers.

The costs of waging an effective political campaign have continued to rise, and candidates can no longer afford to rely on contributions from individuals and political parties alone, if ever they did. Wanting to be able to shape the outcome of elections or at least have access to the winning candidate once seated, a number of corporations and labor unions are willing to fill the fundraising gap. But when corporate and labor expenditures reach tens of thousands of dollars, the American public grows uneasy, which is in part why Congress passed the Bipartisan Campaign Reform Act in the first place. Limiting contributions and improving the transparency of these expenditures were largely achieved with this act. But *Citizens United* changes everything. The ban on corporate and labor independent expenditures has been lifted, and the ability of the public to discern who is purchasing advertisements and other electioneering materials is mired. VoteVets.org, an organization that is difficult to track, ran an anti-Toomey ad in Pennsylvania. The ad depicts a number of soldiers expressing surprise and disgust that Pat Toomey voted against a $1,500 combat bonus, citing it as wasteful spending, yet did nothing to take away bonus pay from corporate CEOs. VoteVets.org spent $1.4 million in anti-Republican candidate advertising.[13]

527 Groups

Since the 2004 elections, a new type of interest group has emerged that engages exclusively in issue advocacy. The 527 committee is named after Section 527 of the Internal Revenue Code, which covers political organizations and traditionally has been used only by candidate or party committees. Engaging solely in issue and express advocacy, 527 committees or groups do not have to register with the Federal Election Commission. These groups, many which are also known as SuperPACs, have been raising and spending unprecedented amounts of money. For example, in the 2010 election, the top five 527 committees spent a combined $74.8 million. These groups have gained notoriety in a short time partly because of the controversial advocacy they engage in. One such 527 SuperPAC, American Crossroads, which supports conservative candidates, raised $28 million in 2010 alone (and spent much more), with 91 percent of that money coming in the form of large contributions from billionaires.[14]

In sum, interest groups that are able to raise large amounts of money do not allow the contribution limits of the current campaign finance laws to hamper their spending. To get around the restrictions, they engage in issue advocacy and funnel their money toward independent expenditures. Whether they buy airtime for their commercials or buy advertising space in major newspapers, they are finding ways to reach voters during elections.

The Future of Groups in Campaigns: From Candidate-Centered to Group-Centered Politics

For years, scholars have written about the evolution of the American electoral process from a party-centered to a candidate-centered system. According to the conventional analysis, political party organizations were once the focal points of campaigns. The parties controlled the process of candidate selection, and they had real influence on platforms and policies. Then beginning in the 1960s and 1970s, with a series of reforms, the parties started to lose their grip on nominations, platforms, and policies. Instead, candidates themselves began to seek nominations through popular primaries and often ignored the party apparatus. Party platforms became merely symbolic, and elected officials came to feel that they owed nothing to their party on policy. Campaigns thus became focused on candidates, and parties were, according to some, relegated to mere labels.

Although parties have always been stronger than the candidate-centered-politics thesis suggests, there is no doubt that campaigns have evolved to allow for more independence from the parties on the part of political candidates. That trend is being fostered in part by the ever-increasing role of interest groups. Candidates today do not need to rely so heavily on party organizations as in the past because they can benefit from the electoral activities of supportive groups to advertise a message and mobilize voters. After the Supreme Court decision in *Federal Election Commission v. Wisconsin Right to Life* (09-969 [2007]), which overturned the ban on issue advocacy, and *Citizens United v. FEC* (08-205 [2010]), which eliminated restrictions on independent expenditures, interest groups are likely to play a stronger independent role in the future. Although interest groups may not supplant parties, it is likely that as we approach the 2012 elections the power of such groups will rival the power of political parties.

Not only are interest groups becoming more like parties, but they are also merging all their fundamental activities together—legislative, electoral, and grassroots advocacy. Technology allows them to combine all the roles so that the distinct roles of each are becoming less so (even though campaign finance laws require some separation).

Further, the U.S. electoral system has evolved again, from candidate-centered to increasingly group-centered politics. Groups are more involved than ever before in electoral politics, and often their activities do more to influence campaign discourse than do the parties and the candidates themselves. This development raises an important question to ponder: How is democratic accountability affected when the voices of those whose names appear on the ballot are overwhelmed by the steady and ever-louder stream of noise from organized groups? In the past, interest groups fostered strong links to candidates and political parties and thus had a positive role in enhancing accountability to citizens. Interest groups have actually strengthened political parties in the past and helped define the issue agendas of candidates more clearly for the public. For example, labor interest groups such as the AFL-CIO have traditionally been known for their links to the Democratic Party, while the U.S. Chamber of Commerce has been known for its relationship with the Republican Party.

Today not only is the symbiosis between interest groups and parties weakening, but so are the links between interest groups and candidates. Interest groups are becoming more independent as electoral entrepreneurs, advancing their own agendas and asserting themselves in election contests even when the candidates do not welcome their activities.

New Technologies Enhance the Power of Interest Groups in Campaigns

What, then, is the future of interest groups in campaigns? It is likely that groups will be increasingly active and influential as they exploit new technologies and means of communication. As one group leader put it, "The speed, scale, and precision with which issue groups can target candidates for communications from their membership and supporter base" will continue to advance. Viral communications techniques can "geometrically multiply the power of the membership base."[15] Whereas in the past groups focused on communication to mobilize a finite membership base to political action, in the future they will look not only to mobilize their base but to use it to create much broader and more diffuse political pressure in campaigns. The emphasis will be on pushing issue agendas out into the public, rather than on forming bonds with candidates and party organizations as in the past.

Groups are also experimenting with ways to connect to potential voters through popular social networking sites on the Internet. As the Sierra Club's Greg Haegele put it, the potential payoff for groups could be substantial, if they can find ways to tap into social networks without undermining the very thing that attracts people to the sites in the first place—social bonds. Influencing potential voters, especially young people, to think of political activism and group politics as part of a social bond is a special challenge, but one with strong potential for groups to exploit. Young voters used to adopt the party affiliation of their parents and hold onto those political bonds for a lifetime. As voters have become increasingly independent of the parties, they have also sought out alternative sources of political identification and networking. Groups will need to look for ways to attract the attention of these potential voters and convince them that certain issues are more paramount than others.[16]

Internet fundraising and organizing have been increasingly successful in recent election cycles, as particular issues or even candidates have attracted voter enthusiasm. For groups this means that it will be more difficult in the future to rely on traditional means of building a steady core of dues-paying members; they will have to exert more effort to attract the attention of issues-conscious citizens. Haegele, for example, may have found convincing many environmentally conscious people to join the Sierra Club and write a check every year a greater challenge than did his predecessors. But he had available to him many more technologies to promote environmental issues before the public and to influence voters and candidates to place those issues at the forefront of campaigns.

Interest groups provide a feedback loop for consuming and producing information. Known as *prosumerism,* this is a marketing approach now used by corporations such as General Electric and Sony.[17] *Prosumerism* is a term invented by Alvin Toffler in his book *The Third Wave.*[18] The prosumer is an individual or group that is both a producer and a consumer of information. Thus, interest groups use their websites as receptacles for their members in the virtual world. They produce information, establish blogs for feedback, and enable their members to feel involved. The cyclical dynamic enables the interest group organization and its individual members to contribute and consume information. Alan Locke, publisher of *Winning Campaigns* magazine, argues that websites attract the interested and the "faithful."[19]

Interest groups can use websites as effectively as, if not better than, parties or candidates because they have an ideological constituency that will normally traffic to their site. In the next decade, interest groups will likely become more adept at mobilizing their existing base to participate in the elections process. Moreover, if interest groups can harness that advance to substantially increase their fundraising, then their potency and reach will increase as well.

Conclusion

Despite all of the work that groups do to advertise issues and promote the fortunes of sympathetic candidates, campaigns will continue to lambaste "the politics of special interests." Whether they are Democrats, Republicans, or Independents, candidates find that attacking interest groups has populist appeal. But interest groups are healthier than ever today because sophisticated techniques to reach constituents—such as e-mail, blogs, podcasting, and online videos, as well as traditional snail mail—enable them to remain in continual contact with their members. This is critical not only for fundraising but for mobilization to get out the vote. Although interest groups may never be a popular feature of the electoral environment, they will continue to be at the forefront of campaigns in U.S. politics.

Notes

1. Mark J. Rozell, Clyde Wilcox, and Michael Franz, *Interest Groups in American Campaigns: The New Face of Electioneering*, 3rd ed. (New York: Oxford University Press, 2012); Richard J. Semiatin and Mark J. Rozell, "Interest Groups in Congressional Elections," in *The Interest Group Connection*, 2nd ed., edited by Paul Herrnson, Ronald Shaiko, and Clyde Wilcox (Washington, DC: CQ Press, 2005), 75–88.
2. National Women's Political Caucus, "National Women's Political Caucus Training Program." Accessed on July 16, 2007, from www.nwpc.org/ht/d/sp/i/47229/pid/47229.
3. Nancy, Walzman, "Swing State Confidential: Colorado—the Wild West." Sunlight Foundation, November 5, 2010. Accessed on December 28, 2011 from Http://sunlight foundation.com/blog/taxonomy/term/swing-state-confidential.
4. "Taliban Dan" (ad) produced by Grayson for Congress, uploaded on September 25, 2010. Accessed on December 28, 2011 from http://wwww.youtube.com/watch?bwdyf9skqQ.

5. "American Solutions Winning the Future: Expenditures, 2010 Cycle." Center for Responsive Politics. Accessed on December 28, 2011 from http://opensecrets. org/527s/527cmtedetail_expends.

6. Campaign contribution data come from the website maintained by the Center for Responsive Politics, www.opensecrets.org. They compile in a user-friendly format data that are publicly available through the Federal Election Commission.

7. See Common Cause Research Center for background on "Taking Elections off the Block," (May 2010) for content on e-mail. Accessed on December 28, 2011 from http://www.commoncause.org/site/pp.asp?c=dkLNK!MQIwG&b=4773601.

8. Although the individual is signing up for an e-mail alert, the interest group typically asks for a name and home address in addition to the e-mail address. This technique not only helps individuals add to their own mailing lists, but the lists are also sold to other groups for profit.

9. According to the survey report released on February 3, 2011, called "Generations and Gadgets" (http://pewresearch.org/pubs/1879/gadgets-generations-cell-phones-laptops-desktop-comupter) and also the survey report released by Pew Research on July 7, 2010, titled "Mobile Access 2010" (http://www.pewinternet.org/Reports/2010/Mobile-Access-2010.aspx). Both surveys and reports were written by the Pew Research Center (both accessed on July 14, 2011).

10. "Chinese professor" (ad). Citizens Against Government Waste, uploaded on October 20, 2010. Accessed on December 28, 2011 from http://www.youtube.com/watch?v=OTSQozWP_rM.

11. Kathleen Baker, "McInnis Declines to Fill Out Independence Caucus Questionnaire" (2010). Accessed on July 12, 2011, from http://www.examiner.com/conservative-in-denver/mcinnis-declines-to-fill-out-independence-caucus-questionnaire.

12 "2010 Outside Spending, by Groups." Center for Responsive Politics. Accessed on December 28, 2011 from http://opensecrets.org/outsidespending/summ.php?cycle=2000.

13. "Trained," ad by Vote Vets. Uploaded on October 12, 2010, to YouTube.com. Spending data from $1.4 million come from data compiled by the Center for Responsive Politics at OpenSecrets.org based on data released by the FEC, August 28, 2011. YouTube and OpenSecrets websites both accessed on September 1, 2011.

14. Dann Eggen and T. W. Farnam, "Pair of Conservative Groups Raised $70 Million in Midterm Campaign" (*Washington Post*, December 2, 2010). Accessed on July 12, 2011, from http://www.washingtonpost.com/wp-dyn/content/article/2010/12/02/AR2010120205667.html?wprss=rss_politics; Kenneth P. Vogel, "American Crossroads Now Targets House Races" (*Politico*, September 20, 2010). Accessed on July 12, 2011, from http://www.politico.com/news/stories/0910/42433.html.

15. Greg Haegele, Sierra Club, personal interview by e-mail, July 5, 2007.

16. Haegele interview.

17. R. Vincent Park, vice president, Edge Communications, interview by phone, June 20, 2007.

18. Alvin Toffler, *The Third Wave* (New York: Bantam, 1984).

19. Alan Locke, editor, *Winning Campaigns*, personal interview, July 12, 2007.

CHAPTER 9

Campaign Press Coverage — Instantaneous

Joseph Graf and Jeremy D. Mayer

AT 9 A.M. LOCAL TIME, June 10, 2011, the state of Alaska released five boxes with 24,000 printed e-mails sent while Sarah Palin was governor from 2006 to 2009. The e-mails were released after requests from media outlets under Alaska's open records law, a typical and even mundane exercise undertaken by political journalists. They use such laws to pry loose documents from the government. There was also nothing unusual about these e-mails being released long after Senator John McCain tapped Palin as his presidential running mate in 2008, and nearly two years after she left office in Alaska. This is all fairly typical.

What was extraordinary was the extent of the coverage, the speed at which it took place, the fascination with the *event* of the release, and the little attention paid to the documents themselves. The six boxes carted into a hallway before television cameras *were* the news. At least three networks broadcast live, and counted down the hours to the release. More than thirty-five reporters were on the scene. On-air reporters worked their way through one live standup after another all afternoon, trying to project interest in a few e-mails about Sarah Palin's workout schedule, her comments about the news, or notes to her family. Whatever was inside those boxes was almost beside the point. The news *was* the release. Once the boxes arrived, journalists seemed unsure what to do next. It was impossible to sift through 24,000 pages live, on the air, so once the lights dimmed everyone flew home.

Jon Stewart lampooned the broadcast media mercilessly on his late-night *Daily Show*. Blogs and discussion boards lit up with commentary. The media's curious fascination with technology was on display. *The New York Times* took the unusual step of asking readers "to help us identify interesting and newsworthy e-mails, people and events that we may want to highlight."[1] Palin supporters organized to analyze the e-mails themselves. Stewart's lampoon became the next day's news, and by the end of the week he had appeared on *Fox News Sunday* with Chris Wallace. The story had come full circle.

American campaigns are getting faster and paradoxically longer at the same time. Sound bites that played on the news for sixty seconds in 1968 have been reduced to seven seconds in the modern era, and the presidential campaign begins nearly two years before the election. The rhythm of media coverage determines the pace of the modern campaign at all levels of politics. The speed of coverage makes for more volatile campaigns where the dynamic of a race can be altered by a video on YouTube. Political attacks, which used to take weeks or at least days to hit the airwaves and make an impact on the voters, now reach citizens at the click of a button. Speed is the most obvious but far from the only change that the Internet is making upon the way campaigns appear to the American public—and the Internet is now an indispensable part of news coverage. Given the declining ratings for national news networks and the even more rapid decline in newspaper circulation, campaign news has begun to go online all the time. That is why the emergence of online media is the focus of our attention in this chapter.

It is only natural to expect that the Internet will radically alter the way the media cover campaigns. After all, the rise of television to media dominance fundamentally changed election coverage. Television reduced the importance of issues and raised the profile of personalities and private scandals from the rise of John Kennedy to the Bill Clinton–Monica Lewinsky scandal. The Internet will have even more decentralizing effects on campaigns and media power. This process has already begun, as campaigns put more emphasis on online media. The age of the Internet also raises fundamental questions about the divisions between citizens, reporters, and political actors. The clear lines that separated those groups are blurring, and no longer are reporters the primary conduits between politicians and the public. The evolution of our media also allows new opportunities for "narrowcasting" in which discrete messages are targeted at specific groups, thus bypassing the media, and allowing rapid responses to emerging media story lines.

This chapter traces the role of the press in covering campaigns, and then discusses the plight of traditional media and its implications. Finally, we discuss the trends in how the Internet is shaping press coverage, and how traditional journalistic standards of review are missing. We call this "filterlessness," and its cutting-edge change is irrevocably changing press coverage because separating facts from rumors becomes muddled. New media have increased the reactiveness of politics, as we shall see.

Origins and Development of American Press Coverage

The major form of political discourse for most of American history was newspapers. When America was deciding how to govern itself after the revolution, men like James Madison and Alexander Hamilton wrote newspaper articles advocating the new Constitution. (Today we know these articles as *The Federalist Papers.*) The national campaigns for and against ratifying the Constitution were fought in the pages of the nation's newspapers.

The First Century: Strong Linkages Between Parties and Newspapers

But during the nation's first century, newspapers had a relationship to campaigns that would surprise most of today's readers. Most papers were openly supportive of one party or the other. A survey of 359 newspapers published in 1810 could find only 33 that had no party affiliation.[2] The modern idea of a separation between the "news" section and the opinion page was also unknown. It was easy to tell by simply looking at the headlines of the day which party a newspaper supported. Indeed, many newspapers put the name of the party into their titles. For this reason, larger cities during the nineteenth century would have a minimum of two newspapers, one for each party. So tight was the relationship between parties and newspapers that often the local party would meet at the offices of the local newspaper, since parties lacked infrastructure at that time. Reporters were expected to follow the party line in their coverage. The printing presses of supportive newspapers also were used to print party pamphlets, and even presidents picked one newspaper, called a "house organ," to publish their views and to benefit from government contracts.[3] Several times during America's early history mobs of supporters of one party attacked the newspaper controlled by the other party.[4] This "partisan press" era persisted well into the twentieth century in many American cities, where the newspaper was a key to political machines run by local parties.

Linkages Weaken Between Parties and Newspapers

At the national level, however, the strong linkage between parties and newspapers in campaigns began to weaken in the late nineteenth century with the rise of the mass media. Newspaper empires like those built by William Randolph Hearst and Joseph Pulitzer were designed to appeal to readers across party lines; they could not be so directly tied to the interests of a single party. At the same time, standards of professional journalistic ethics began to emerge. More and more, journalists were expected to at least attempt to be objective as they covered political campaigns, and to avoid conflicts of interest.[5] During political campaigns, newspapers became more like referees in a boxing match, rather than the cheering supporters they had been in the partisan press era. There were notable exceptions, and certainly journalists, editors, and publishers were not perfect in their adherence to objectivity. But the norm was to at least appear to be fair, which was a significant change from the nineteenth century. Journalism also became a true profession during the early twentieth century, as the first schools of journalism were founded. In the past, those covering American campaigns were often working-class writers without college degrees or family wealth. Journalism, previously not a prestigious occupation, was becoming desirable and even occasionally well paid.

Emerging Mass Media

During the early years of the twentieth century, radio networks emerged across the United States and the world. Yet radio never became the dominant medium for campaign coverage or political advertising. During the era of radio's greatest popularity, the major newspapers were still more important in setting the nation's agenda. However, radio's rapid rise signaled that newspapers were vulnerable to electronic media. Television emerged after World War II and eventually replaced the papers as the dominant means of political communication. The moment when American presidential campaigns moved into the television age is commonly identified as the first televised debate in 1960 between John F. Kennedy and Richard Nixon. Those listening on the radio believed the debate to have been a tie. Those watching on television believed the far more charismatic Kennedy had won.[6] Historians have since come to question whether this was true, but politicians and journalists believed in the power of television, and American political campaigns would never be the same. It had of course been an advantage in politics to be reasonably attractive. Yet prior to television, we had elected men who were widely acknowledged to be homely-looking, such as Abraham Lincoln, or morbidly obese, such as William Howard Taft. Television has forced politicians at all levels of American campaigns to pay more attention to their looks than ever before. In 2007, presidential candidates Republican Mitt Romney of Massachusetts and Democrat John Edwards of North Carolina were criticized for spending thousands of dollars of campaign money on makeup artists or hairstylists. Sarah Palin underwent some of the same criticism after she was named McCain's vice presidential running mate in 2008. But looking as good as possible on television is a vital part of every modern American campaign since Kennedy-Nixon.

The Power of Television

The impact of television on campaigns has been vast, and goes beyond makeup and hairstylists. It focused attention on image and sound, and less on logic and thought. Television contributed directly to the decline of issues and the rise of personality and individual character as a decisive factor in American elections.[7] And television may be more powerful in its campaign coverage than print media ever was because it can have a dramatic effect on voter choice in presidential primaries.[8] This is not only through directly making a candidate look competent or incompetent, corrupt or honest, charismatic or dull. The media also help set expectations, which can make winners of losers and losers of winners. A candidate expected to overwhelmingly win a primary, such as Senator Edmund Muskie (D-Maine) in the New Hampshire primary of 1972, is declared the loser for failing to win by a sufficient amount. A candidate could be anointed by the media (and himself) as the "comeback kid" even though he finished second, as Governor Bill Clinton did in New Hampshire in 1992. When Senator John McCain exceeded expectations to win the New Hampshire primary in January 2008, his fundraising surged. Expectations leading up to the straw polls before the Iowa caucuses mean candidates jockey to set expectations more than a year before the 2012 election. The point in some primaries was not to win or to avoid losing but simply to surpass expectations set by the media.

Fundamentally, television put the media at the heart of political power in the United States by supplanting means of communication that favored political institutions such as parties, and by separating these institutions from their own elected officials.

An Era of Transformation: The Decline of Mainstream Media

The emergence of a powerful broadcast media has often been correlated with the decline of the newspaper industry. The number of daily papers in the United States declined from over 1,900 in 1940 to slightly over 1,400 by 2000, according to the Project for Excellence in Journalism. Interestingly, the total circulation of newspapers did not begin to decline until 1990. Furthermore, the rise of national newspapers, such as *USA Today*, helped compensate for the loss of papers from rural, suburban, and urban markets.[9] Campaign coverage was consolidated in fewer newspapers. Large corporations such as Hearst and News Corporation (which bought *The Wall Street Journal* in 2007) have been accused of homogenizing news coverage. According to Federal Communications Commission (FCC) commissioner Jonathan Adelstein, "It raises a real question as whether or not there is independence between ownership and the journalists."[10]

This is true not only for newspapers, but for broadcast television. Corporations hire consultants to improve the image of local and national news. *ABC News* anchor Charles Gibson points out the problem: "News directors who rely on consultants wind up producing newscasts that look like every other newscast around, and if they read the minute-by-minutes and program merely what they think people want to watch . . . they're not directing anything, they're being directed."[11] The focus becomes less on reporting the news than on image. This profoundly increases the personality-driven aspect of campaigns.

Finally, the rise of cable television drove down the network news ratings of ABC, CBS, and NBC. In the thirty years from 1980 to 2010, the three networks lost more than half their audience.[12] Competition from new media has also driven down the audiences for evening network newscasts. More citizens are turning away from the filter of television news as online audiences increase dramatically, and in many of those cases, the only filter is the viewer.

Newsrooms are also in the midst of enormous upheaval. Advertising revenues have dropped precipitously. Craigslist and eBay have eviscerated the classified ad sections of newspapers, which were historically the most profitable advertising. Media writer Eric Alterman calls the atmosphere at newspapers "a palpable sense of doom."[13] While some of the lost audience has moved online, online advertising rates make up only a fraction of the lost revenue. In response, many media properties, especially newspapers, have laid off thousands of journalists since about 2006. Some organizations have been dramatically cut. *ABC News* laid off one quarter of its staff in 2010; the BBC did the same in 2011. One estimate is that from 1990 to 2008 a quarter of all newspaper jobs were lost.[14] Fewer journalists means they are less able to fulfill their role as watchdogs on power. One of the first areas media outlets cut in a budget crisis is foreign reporting. One trade magazine found the international press corps was cut from 307 in 2003 to 234 in 2007, as reported in a 2011 study.[15] There has been a similar decline in the number of journalists covering state legislatures and governors,[16] and far fewer journalists cover federal departments and agencies, like the Federal Bureau of Investigation, the Federal Aviation Administration, or the Department of Commerce. Not a single newspaper reporter works in the newsroom of the Department of Agriculture, one of the largest government employers.[17] Newspaper analyst John Morton argues that the cutbacks have diminished the journalism produced by newspapers. "What the industry partly sacrificed with its cost-cutting is the one attribute that has protected it against all previous competitive threats—the overall quality of its journalism," he wrote.[18]

These changes are particularly evident in Washington reporting and campaign coverage, but they are not all bad. The number of mainstream political journalists has declined in the past twenty-five years, but more important the nature of the Washington press corps has changed. Whereas there are fewer mainstream journalists—who might have worked for outlets such as *Newsweek, The Washington Post,* or *ABC News*—there are many more journalists working for newsletters, blogs, and websites. The Cox Newspapers chain, publisher of seventeen newspapers, closed its Washington bureau in 2009. But new outlets are emerging. Talking Points Memo, a news and politics blog, had one full-time reporter assigned to the presidential campaign in 2008 and plans to expand to fifteen for 2012.

Politico, an online magazine about politics, tripled its staff from 2008 to 2011 and has become an important source of political news, in some cases setting the national agenda.[19] *Politico* was founded by former *Washington Post* writers John Harris and Jim VandeHei in 2007. The newspaper appears in both print and online editions and has become a reliable mainstay of political coverage. In the 2008 election, *Politico*'s online traffic reached 11 million "unique visitors per month," making it one of the most highly trafficked news websites during the election year. Because *Politico* was created by journalists not pushing an ideological agenda, it has credibility in the Washington, DC, political community.[20]

The number of foreign correspondents based in Washington has also increased, illustrating a surge in coverage of Washington by international media outlets. Arab satellite channel Al Jazeera opened an office in Washington in 2001 and had 105 staff members accredited to cover Congress in 2009, almost as big a staff as that of *CBS News*, which has a proud history of political news coverage that began with the company's founding in 1927.[21]

The type of work agreements and what is expected from journalists has also changed. There has been a rise in "atypical work," or journalists employed casually, or on a freelance or contract basis, in the United States and overseas.[22] These kinds of workers are generally lower paid and without the protection of full employment or labor unions. Online content is more likely to be produced by these workers, and some major media political blogs are produced by atypical workers. The new model of working in a converged newsroom is called "individualization," where journalists are expected to be more flexible, more varied in their skill set, and more mobile.[23] Most political journalists are expected to blog, send Twitter messages, maintain a presence on social networks, and perhaps even take photographs or video. In the past those roles were more strictly prescribed to photographers or videographers. In broadcasting this has led to increased use of "one-man bands" or "backpack journalism."[24] A single journalist with a video camera much lighter than just ten years ago can take high-quality footage, edit the footage on a portable computer, and produce a complete package alone, far from the office. The impact of these changes can be seen in some far-flung correspondents and in immediate self-produced coverage of political campaigns. *NBC Nightly News* employs Mara Schiavocampo, a one-woman news team who travels the world for the network capturing news video for its website.[25] This model of news coverage is expanding.

Cutting-Edge Cost Effects on Political Campaign Coverage

The Costs of the Digital Divide: Mass Media and End Users

The Internet changes the financial equation, creating a "digital divide" among end users—those who can fully consume information and news on the Internet versus those with limited or no access. The digital divide describes the gulf between those who have frequent easy access to the Internet and those who, for reasons of finance, occupation, or even demographic characteristics like gender, race, and age, do not have equal access. The divide used to be primarily between those who did or did not own a computer. Now, given how important Internet video has become, it is sometimes characterized as a divide between those who can afford broadband access and those who are still dialing up. Two-thirds of American adults have broadband access at home, but the other third realistically cannot conveniently access online video at home.[26] Broadband access means access to online video, and campaigns and political coverage are using more and more. For example, news organizations now utilize broadband to broadcast live political events, such as presidential debates and even campaign announcements. This is just the beginning.

The Advantage of Online News Production: Costs Driven Down

It is on the production side that the Internet is having a greater impact, particularly for the new wave of media bloggers. Bloggers such as Andrew Sullivan and Matt Drudge have remarkably low overheads. Printed newspapers are limited because every inch of space has a fixed cost. However, on the Internet there is limitless space. As a result Sullivan and Drudge, and lesser known Internet journalists and bloggers, have had a tremendous impact on American politics, for better or worse. Matt Drudge was relatively unknown when he first reported important scoops in the Monica Lewinsky scandal on his website. Reporters face competition from anyone with a laptop and Internet access, and that can matter in a campaign. Many of these political bloggers in 2008 fashioned themselves as outsiders, and indeed may not have the training or experience of mainstream political reporters. *The Huffington Post* generated a great deal of campaign coverage from bloggers who were not formally trained journalists and often unpaid. An independent blogger, Nate Silver of fivethirtyeight.com, became required reading to decipher 2008 campaign polling. Finally, some of those independent bloggers have been "captured" in a way by the mainstream media; Sullivan now blogs for the online magazine *The Daily Beast* and writes columns for *Newsweek* magazine. "The 2008 campaign made it clear that the old model, in which journalists interpret campaign events for the masses, is kaput," wrote journalist John McQuaid, "and that the new model is more chaotic and interactive."[27]

Part I—On the Edge of Change: Politics at the Speed of Light

Perhaps the greatest change the Internet has introduced into American campaign coverage is the pace at which politics is conducted. The twenty-four-hour news cycle was much discussed when cable television first rose to prominence, since it suggested that campaigns and government institutions would no longer have a full day to plan reactions and make decisions. The Internet has sped this up even further. On just one day in the campaign, September 17, 2000, the Bush and Gore campaigns for president sent fifty-six e-mails to their press e-mail lists (consisting of 2,000 and 1,200 names, respectively). Most of these concerned a sixteen-page "Blueprint for the Middle Class" issued by the Republican nominee. The Democrat's "pre-buttal" was twenty-four pages long. The fifty-six e-mails spun and respun around the topic of which candidate had the better economic plan for the United States.[28]

Lessons From the 2000–2008 Campaigns

If a reporter gets something that occurs at a public event wrong, an average citizen can challenge the media account directly. Some of the most famous mistakes in campaign coverage might have been caught earlier if they had happened in the age of Internet dominance. For example, in 2000, two national reporters badly misquoted Vice President Al Gore as claiming he had been the first to bring the Love Canal chemical disaster to the nation's attention. What Gore actually said was factually correct, but the reporters' inaccurate account fit into the Republican portrayal of Gore as a serial liar and exaggerator. The false story about Gore battered his reputation for weeks.[29]

Only four years later, a larger error was more quickly corrected. In 2004, *CBS News* ran a major story on documents that allegedly showed that President George W. Bush had refused a direct order to appear for duty during his service in the Texas Air National Guard during the Vietnam War era. While the public had long known that Bush used family connections to get into the Guard during a time when it was a popular way for wealthy men to avoid the war, the documents revitalized the issue of Bush's wartime conduct, and his later failure to fulfill the terms of his enlistment. Very quickly, thanks to conservative bloggers, questions emerged about the documents' authenticity. Experts and amateurs pointed out factual and stylistic problems with the documents. In a massive humiliation for *CBS News* and the main reporter on the story, Dan Rather, the network was forced to admit that the documents were probably forgeries. Rather, long accused by conservatives of having a liberal bias, faced difficult questions about how he had accepted as legitimate anti-Bush documents rejected by other mainstream media outlets as highly questionable. Without the Internet's amazing ability to link people rapidly, citizens would have lacked the ability to quickly challenge the *CBS News* story.

Both stories demonstrate the synergistic power between traditional media and the Internet today. Stories are reported rapidly, often without fact-checking, as more media compete in the marketplace. Not only does it have implications for what the press does, but it forces campaigns to react. Damage control is now a twenty-four–seven operation for major political national campaigns, and they have to rapidly respond to news events. Failure to do so can have profound implications. John Kerry (D-Mass.) discovered this in the summer of 2004 when he failed to respond to charges of the "Swift Boat Veterans for Truth," who questioned whether he truly was a Vietnam war hero. The Swift Boat Veterans advertisement was widely reported on the Internet, in major newspapers, and on national newscasts. Kerry was slow to respond, and that gave greater credibility to the charges. Eventually an *ABC News Nightline* investigation in Vietnam, with eyewitnesses, gave a more accurate story, but it was October, and the damage had already been done.[30]

Perhaps the richest example of what the Internet has wrought is the false, ongoing e-mail campaign that President Obama is a follower of Islam. The Obama campaign carried on a long-running rearguard action against this e-mail campaign that began at least as early as January 2007. The origination appears to be someone posting what he or she claims is an e-mail received detailing information about Obama's ties to Islam. The original source is never clear. True believers pass the e-mail to others, never clear about where it began. "The labor of generating an e-mail smear is divided and distributed amongst parties whose identities are secret even to each other," according to political scholar Danielle Allen. Someone makes a comment that is the original claim, and then those claims are reposted and forwarded by another group of people. "No one coordinates the roles."[31] This was the Swift Boat campaign on steroids, and the rumors have never entirely ended. The truth about these claims does not penetrate the closed online communities where these ideas are fostered and flourish,[32] and in some cases the myth has been helped by leaders who encouraged rumors about it.[33] It seems inevitable that these rumors will reappear in the 2012 campaign, and this, too, is a new aspect of political campaigns made possible by the Internet.

Part II—On the Edge of Change: Citizen Groups as Campaign Reporters

Citizen groups have emerged as the new press in the twenty-first century. Unlike the mainstream media, citizen groups lack the reporting standards of *The New York Times* or *ABC News*. Their agenda is to promote and persuade, rather than report facts. As a result, they often lack standards to filter their stories and check them for veracity. This has profound consequences for campaigns because such groups serve as a third force in national politics and campaigns.

Citizen Groups: An Unfiltered Challenge to Mainstream Media Covering Campaigns

The Internet, in addition to speeding up campaigns and media coverage, also makes it easy for a citizen activist to start up a webpage, create a blog, or post a comment on an existing webpage or blog. This poses serious problems for mainstream media outlets because they have competition for "news" and information. The grassroots fervor and involvement that voters experience on websites like Daily

Kos and Free Republic means that major media companies are confounded in how to approach and compete with these groups for viewers. These viewers favor news from a distinct point of view, and this may encourage other websites and even mainstream news sources to cater to these audiences.

At the Daily Kos, the largest left-wing political website in terms of number of unique daily visitors, anonymous posters can become famous quickly if they write well, post frequently, and battle the right with panache. Similarly, the slightly less interactive and more filtered Free Republic is the leading spot on the web where conservatives can (once they register and become trusted) interact with each other. Both Daily Kos and Free Republic have been involved in rallying voters for mass demonstrations and fundraising. In fact, the Daily Kos has commissioned polls over the last five years, seeking to generate its own news and gain greater journalistic credibility.

While there is organized funding and expert political advice behind the Tea Party movement, much of its energy was fostered on independent political blogs. A decentralized network of dozens, maybe hundreds, of these blogs organizes supporters and passes along information. The reason is that the Tea Party does not have a nucleus, but rather is a loose confederation of hundreds of groups under the Tea Party banner.[34]

Over the Edge: When Online Groups Become Campaign News

MoveOn.org, the nation's largest political Internet grassroots organization, decided in 2004 to hold a national contest, called "Bush in 30 Seconds." MoveOn's Voter Fund invited submissions of thirty-second anti-Bush ads. The concept was brilliant—harness the diffused and wild creativity of Americans, and some ten or twenty unknown writers and directors will come up with ads that are better than those professional political consultants come up with. The judging process, in which MoveOn members would watch videos and vote for their favorites, boosted the visibility of the site. The contest was a huge success in terms of number of submissions, number of page views, the amount of money raised, and the stunning quality of the top thirty or so ads.

But 2 ads out of 1,500 on the site had images of Bush speaking juxtaposed with images of Adolf Hitler ranting. Although MoveOn.org eventually removed the offensive ads, the comparison attracted national media attention. The clips were prominently displayed on right-wing websites as examples of "MoveOn" ads. The fact that MoveOn merely provided a forum for these ads, and did not create, or sponsor, or in any way fund these ads, was irrelevant.[35] In 2010, MoveOn.org ran a high-tech online ad that was aimed at voter turnout. The ad, called "Back From the Future," shows a young woman broadcasting from a bunker in 2057 with the message that if young people did not vote in large numbers, the future would become apocalyptic. The ad ends with her and a compatriot saying "save the future" by voting on Election Day.[36]

Part III—On the Edge of Change: Campaigns as Reporters— Opponent Surveillance Expands in the Twenty-First Century

In the nineteenth century, many men ran for president while seldom leaving their homes. These "front porch" campaigns were possible in an era of print discourse. The level of media scrutiny of the daily lives of the candidates was minimal. In the twenty-first century, candidates find themselves trailed by opposition partisans, taping every moment of their campaigns and even their daily lives, hoping to find a gaffe, an unflattering or ridiculous image, or, best of all, some hint of scandal. These are known as trackers. The best known tracker is S. R. Sidarth, who captured Senator George Allen's (R-Va.) "macaca" slur during the 2006 Virginia Senate election campaign. The slur, aimed at Sidarth's ethnicity, backfired and helped lead to Allen's defeat. Technology enables campaigns to do their own reporting cheaply; and they take advantage to get an edge over their opponent through surveillance.

Campaign Surveillance: The Difference Between the Present and the Past

The rise of the Internet combined with miniaturization of video technology has changed what is considered "fair game" for campaign coverage. Ten years ago, when Larry Sabato wrote *Feeding Frenzy* about how the media have taken over the presidential campaign, he wrote of the media's endless appetite for scandal and negative information and images.[37] But the Internet has made the surveillance of candidates even more constant and damaging.

The contrast between today and 1968 is illustrative. On the campaign trail in 1968, film was shot of various candidates at most rallies, usually by the networks. Film cameras were large and bulky, and quite expensive. Typically, to get quality images required not only access to the equipment but training. And a news organization would have to rush the actual film to a studio for developing, and then processing, and, later in that day or the next day, broadcasting. Today, an amateur with a $400 digital video camera can capture better images than the best professional footage of 1968. They do not need processing and can be posted on YouTube or another free video distribution service within minutes. This change is not just the way of the Internet; it is also the miniaturization revolution in electronics, making video cameras and editing equipment smaller and affordable.

Campaigns have always sought ways to make their opponents look bad. The 1960 campaign of John F. Kennedy used myriad ways to get under the skin of Richard Nixon, the Republican opponent. Dick Tuck, the mischievous genius of the low blow in that race, came up with a tactic to make Nixon look like a loser in the presidential debate, regardless of how it turned out. The morning after Nixon's first presidential campaign debate with John F. Kennedy, Tuck asked an elderly woman to wear a Nixon button, hug the candidate, and say loudly, "Don't worry, son. He beat you last night, but you'll win next time."[38] The picture was captured nationally. The Internet changes the speed and impact of such dirty tricks. The Tuck trick was a minor moment in a long campaign. Today, a clip on YouTube can mean the end of a Senate career.

Surveillance and Future National Campaigns

Constant surveillance of candidates will increase the emphasis on personality, appearance, and character, and further lessen the importance of parties, platforms, and issues. In the print media era, the nation elected leaders who were poor speakers (Jefferson), remarkably awkward in personal interactions (Nixon), extremely tight-lipped (Coolidge), close to dying (Roosevelt in 1944), prone to drunkenness (Grant), and recklessly promiscuous (Kennedy). Most of those men could not be elected in the television era (Kennedy was at the turning point between print and television). Could any be elected in the Internet age? In 2010, former presidential candidate John Edwards (D-N.C.) admitted he had fathered a child out of wedlock after the story was broken by the *National Enquirer,* effectively ending his political career.

The more access we have to the personalities and personal conduct of our leaders, the greater the likelihood we might vote on such ephemera as appearance and personality. This is the picture portrayed in recent election cycles, and beyond this election, there is nothing to suggest anything different.

Part IV—On the Edge of Change: Campaign News Coverage in the Hands of Citizens

The Internet is an interactive medium, and unlike television, a passive medium, the Internet requires that the user be involved. Thus, the Internet may also weaken the media's control over what citizens learn about politics. If they wish to be, citizens can become more independent of the power of media than at any time in human history. Compare a daily newspaper to a thirty-minute evening news broadcast to a CNN website. The 40,000 words of text available in the newspaper represent the editors' view of current events that day. A reader has some degree of independence; a committed Republican could choose not to read any upbeat reports about President Obama, while a committed Democrat might choose not to read any positive stories about Republican presidential candidates. This "selective perception" by the viewer is reinforced by the Internet because that person interacts and manipulates the medium to his or her own satisfaction, which is the opposite of mainstream mass media.

Political Campaigns and Social Network News

The political campaigns of 2012 and beyond will focus enormous efforts with social networks. In a world of "selective perception" and limitless information, users need trusted sources of information. The information and recommendations people send to their friends and family on social networks fill this need, and campaigns know it. The Obama campaign of 2008 had an enormous campaign presence on Facebook and even created its own social network on the campaign website. These networks are fostered by the campaigns. In some respects this gives local activists the power to start their own discussions and, in effect, wage their own minicampaigns for the candidates of their choice, sending messages, persuading others, and raising money.

Ordinary citizens become agents of political change and may play a larger role in the campaign. On the other hand, the campaigns are working hard to empower these activists, but also focus the online discussion as best they can. Social networks and social media pose this problem for communicators of all types. These networks can empower communicators—advertisers, journalists, and political campaigns—but also cause them to lose control of their message to some degree. Campaigns willing to give up some control can take greater advantage of social networks; campaigns that insist on controlling the message may not. The Obama campaign walked this fine line in 2008. The campaign's dedicated use of social networks and its direct appeals to supporters gave it a real sense of involvement. The campaign released many of its announcements to its supporters first, not to journalists through press conferences. Supporters who received an e-mail or a text with real news were brought into the fold of the campaign. At the same time, the campaign controlled its message. This sort of balance between empowering supporters and controlling the campaign may be the template for 2012.

Anonymous Campaign Reports: Narrowcasting News Without a Gatekeeper

Another possibility that the Internet raises is a new type of anonymous campaign messaging that masquerades as news. Narrowcasting enables the producer to send information to an end user who has logged on or registered at a website. In the past, the media could receive an anonymous or confidential tip on the campaign trail, as one side hoped to put a rumor or negative story into the coverage. In 1920, Franklin Roosevelt, running for vice president, hoped to get reporters to cover the allegations that Warren Harding, the Republican nominee for president, had black parentage.[39] Such negative campaigning is as old as democracy. But typically, in order to widely distribute such messages, some elements within the mainstream media would have to agree to cover it. The Reverend Jerry Falwell produced a videotape called "The Clinton Chronicles" that he mailed to thousands of his supporters in the 1990s. "The Clinton Chronicles" falsely alleged that Bill Clinton was involved in a string of drug-related homicides in Arkansas. The mainstream media did not pick up the story because it was without factual basis, so it remained off the radar for most voters.[40]

Today, a campaign can put wild anonymous rumors into circulation with much greater ease and get attention. In 2007, an activist associated with the Mitt Romney campaign posted a website called PhoneyFred.org saying Republican rival Fred Thompson was "Once a Pro-Choice Skirt Chaser, (and) Now Standard Bearer of the Religious Right?" This was presented as fact. Moreover, it noted that Thompson had once lobbied for Planned Parenthood.[41] The inference was that Thompson dated attractive women and was pro-choice, and therefore no friend of the religious right. The distinction between news and rumor gets blurred even further because campaigns have to react immediately. The result is that narrowcasting messages often end up being broadcast to large audiences as news, and that can throw a campaign off-message for days. Narrowcasting is an expanding forum for political coverage, and it is taking many different forms. E-mails, direct mail, and websites can all be narrowly broadcast to very specific audiences and carry a narrowly tailored message. The Obama White House issues daily e-mails and online video to its supporters, giving the president's perspective on events—White House coverage without the journalist middleman. The National Rifle Association operates its own daily news channel online with its specific take on the day's events.

Mobile News Technology and Campaigns

As mainstream media adapt to new technologies, mobile users will be able to access CNN, Fox News, and MSNBC, for example, to get their news. That will put more pressure on news organizations to produce news headlines at a faster rate because handheld devices facilitate frequent access by users. Campaign coverage, as well as all news, may become more focused on headline news coverage because the shorthand fits easily on the screen. Already on mainstream media, we see tickers on the bottom of the screen (such as CNN and Fox News) to make all news accessible in shorthand to viewers. The danger is that news coverage will become even more superficial and the seven-second sound bite from candidates even more important.

Conclusion

The Internet will produce greater changes in campaign coverage than the rise of television. In the Internet era, mainstream media elites will lose some power over political communication, but *The New York Times* will not disappear anytime soon. Yet those empowered by the rise of the Internet are unlikely to be politicians and party leaders, but rather a mix of new media figures and citizen activists. Bloggers and leaders of nonparty organizations like MoveOn.org and Free Republic are the ones who will thrive in this new media environment. In this sense, the Internet has opened up American politics to a new set of players without discarding the old power structure.

There is value to having many independent media outlets with reporters who strive for objectivity and produce in-depth stories on important issues such as Social Security and military preparedness. Despite their lack of professional training or adequate resources, many bloggers and independent websites produce important campaign news coverage. At the same time, ten thousand bloggers mostly repeating the talking points of their respective parties cannot adequately replace one top national journalist investigating a vital national question in a rigorous and unbiased fashion. As we have seen, the foment in journalism at the moment means this sort of work is less and less likely. The Internet makes traditional media outlets less profitable by stealing viewers and readers, thus forcing many newspapers and broadcast outlets to fire just the reporters we need. The new political journalism that has arisen online in the last five years is extraordinarily valuable, but at the same time we have lost a great deal.

The second challenge for media coverage is what Neil Postman called "infotainment." If we all get to select exactly how much campaign news we will receive, and the depth of that coverage, it may be that too many Americans will choose shallow, biased sources of news on the Internet.[42] As political commentator H. L. Mencken said in the early twentieth century: "For every complex problem, there is a solution that is simple, neat and wrong."[43] But the voices arguing for nuanced and difficult solutions to complex problems may be softer now than at any time in the past, thanks in part to the vitriolic and biased way in which Internet media often treat political campaigns, and the popularity of such coverage among viewers selecting freely from a plethora of websites. The mainstream media are not disappearing, but the Internet is having a profound effect on the superficiality of campaign news coverage, promoting a greater emphasis on personality, rumor, and infotainment. New technology propels campaign coverage at the speed of light. We may long for the days when the television news at least gave the voters seven-second sound bites by the presidential candidates.

Notes

1. Mike Baker, "Palin Emails Let Old Media Test New Media Methods" (Associated Press, June 13, 2011). Accessed on November 16, 2011, from http://www.cleveland.com/business/index.ssf/2011/06/palin_emails_let_old_media_tes.html; Derek Willis, "Help Us Review the Sarah Palin E-Mail Records" (*The New York Times*, June 9, 2011). Accessed on June 14, 2011, from http://thecaucus.blogs.nytimes.com/2011/06/09/help-us-investigate-the-sarah-palin-e-mail-records/?scp=1&sq=derek%20willis%20and%20sarah%20palin&st=cse.

2. Jeffrey L. Pasley, *The Tyranny of Printers: Newspaper Politics in the Early American Republic* (Charlottesville: University Press of Virginia, 2001), 201.

3. John Tebbel, *The Compact History of the American Newspaper* (New York: Hawthorne, 1963), 87.

4. Tebbel, *The Compact History of the American Newspaper*, 67–68.

5. Michael Schudson, *Discovering the News: A Social History of American Newspapers* (New York: Basic Books, 1981).

6. Jeremy D. Mayer, *American Media Politics in Transition* (New York: McGraw-Hill, 2007).

7. Scott Keeter, "The Illusion of Intimacy Television and the Role of Candidate Personal Qualities in Voter Choice" (*Public Opinion Quarterly*, Vol. 51, No. 3, 1987), 344–358.

8. Thomas E. Patterson, *Out of Order* (New York: Vintage Press, 1994).

9. "The State of the News Media 2004" (Project on Excellence in Journalism). Accessed on September 13, 2007, from stateofthenewsmedia.org.

10. Rick Karr, Interview with FCC Commissioner Jonathan Adelstein (*NOW with Bill Moyers*, PBS, April 3, 2003). Accessed on September 14, 2007, from pbs.org/now/politics/bigmedia.html.

11. Charles Gibson, Paul White Award Speech, RTNDA convention, Las Vegas, NV, on April 24, 2006. Accessed on September 14, 2007, from journalism.org.

12. Reported in "State of the News Media 2011" (Project on Excellence in Journalism). Accessed on July 6, 2011, from stateofthenewsmedia.org.

13. Eric Alterman, "Out of Print: The Death and Life of the American Newspaper" (*The New Yorker*, March 31, 2008). Accessed on June 18, 2011, from http://www.newyorker.com/reporting/2008/03/31/080331fa_fact_alterman.

14. Sarah Lyall, "BBC, Facing Budget Cuts, Will Trim World Service and Lay Off 650" (*The New York Times*, January 26, 2011). Accessed on November 17, 2011, from http://www.nytimes.com/2011/01/27/world/europe/27bbc.html; Brian Stelter, "Job Cuts at ABC Leave Workers Stunned and Downcast" (*The New York Times*, April 30, 2010). Accessed on November 17, 2011, from http://www.nytimes.com/2010/05/01/business/media/01abc.html.

15. Priya Kumar, "Foreign Correspondents: Who Covers What" (*American Journalism Review*, 2011). Accessed on June 22, 2011, from http://www.ajr.org/Article.asp?id=4997.

16. Jennifer Dorroh, "Statehouse Exodus" (*American Journalism Review*, 2009). Accessed on June 22, 2011, from http://www.ajr.org/Article.asp?id=4721.

17. Jodi Enda, "Capital Flight" (*American Journalism Review*, 2010). Accessed on August 6, 2011, from http://www.ajr.org/article.asp?id=4877.

18. John Morton, "Costly Mistakes" (*American Journalism Review*, 2011). Accessed on June 12, 2011, from http://www.ajr.org/Article.asp?id=4994.

19. Jeremy W. Peters, "Political Blogs Are Ready to Flood Campaign Trail" (*The New York Times*, January 29, 2011). Accessed on August 4, 2011, from http://www.nytimes.com/2011/01/30/business/media/30blogs.html.

20. Michael Wolff, "Politico's Washington Coup" (August 2009). Accessed on August 8, 2011, from vanityfair.com.

21. Project for Excellence in Journalism, *The New Washington Press Corps: As Mainstream Media Decline, Niche and Foreign Outlets Grow* (Washington, DC, 2009).

22. Emma Walters, Christopher Warren, and Mike Dobbie, *The Changing Nature of Work: A Global Survey and Case Study of Atypical Work in the Media Industry* (Brussels: The International Federation of Journalists, 2006). See also Mark Deuze and Timothy Marjoribanks, "Newswork" (*Journalism,* Vol. 10, No. 5, 2009), 555–561.

23. Mark Deuze, "Understanding Journalism as Newswork: How It Changes, and How It Remains the Same" (*Westminster Papers in Communication and Culture,* Vol. 5, No. 2, 2008).

24. See, for example, the Backpack Journalism Project at American University (http://www.american.edu/soc/backpack/).

25. Edward J. Delaney, "Profile of a Backpacker: Inside Mara Schiavocampo's Toolkit" (Nieman Journalism Lab, January 12, 2009). Accessed on August 7, 2011, from http://www.niemanlab.org/2009/01/mara-schiavocampo-backpack-journalist/.

26. Pew Internet and American Life Project, *Home Broadband 2010* (Washington, DC: Author, 2010).

27. John McQuaid, "The Netroots: Bloggers and the 2008 Presidential Campaign" (*Nieman Reports,* 2009). Accessed on August 2, 2011, from http://www.nieman.harvard.edu/reports/article/101910/The-Netroots-Bloggers-and-the-2008-Presidential-Campaign.aspx.

28. Bob Davis and Jeanne Cummings, "Hot Buttons: A Barrage of E-Mail Helps Candidates Hit Media Fast and Often" (*The Wall Street Journal,* September 21, 2000), A1.

29. Evgenia Peretz, "Going After Gore" (*Vanity Fair,* October 2007). (Issue available online before official release date.) Accessed on September 12, 2007, from vanityfair.com.

30. Andrew Morse, "What Happened in Kerry's Vietnam Battles?" (*ABC News,* October 14, 2004). Accessed on September 13, 2007, from abcnews.go.com.

31. Matthew Mosk, "An Attack That Came out of the Ether; Scholar Looks for First Link in E-Mail Chain About Obama" (*The Washington Post,* June 28, 2008). Accessed on November 17, 2011, from http://www.washingtonpost.com/wp-dyn/content/article/2008/06/27/AR2008062703781.html.

32. Cass R. Sunstein, *Republic.com* (Princeton, NJ: Princeton University Press, 2001).

33. John Dickerson, "Why Won't Any Republicans Condemn the 'Obama Is a Muslim' Myth?" (CBS News Political Hotsheet, 2010). Accessed on August 9, 2011, from http://www.cbsnews.com/8301-503544_162-20014532-503544.html.

34. Hans Noel, "Ten Things Political Scientists Know That You Don't" (*The Forum,* Vol. 8, No. 3, 2010). Accessed on August 2, 2011, from http://www.bepress.com/forum/vol8/iss3/art12.

35. See Ari Shapiro, "Using Hitler to Make a Point" (NPR, July 4, 2004). Accessed on September 13, 2007, from npr.org.

36. "Back From the Future" (MoveOn.org, October 25, 2010). Accessed on August 8, 2011, from YouTube.com.

37. Larry J. Sabato, *Feeding Frenzy: Attack Journalism and American Politics* (Baltimore: Lanahan, 2000).

38. Tom Miller, "Tricky Dick" (*The New Yorker,* August 30, 2004). Accessed on November 17, 2011, from http://www.newyorker.com/archive/2004/08/30/040830ta_talk_miller.

39. Jeremy D. Mayer, *Running on Race: Racial Politics in Presidential Campaigns 1960–2000* (New York: Random House, 2002).

40. "Loathed by Liberals, Falwell Was Force Among Right-Wing" (CNN, May 15, 2007). Accessed on September 14, 2007, from cnn.com.

41. Glen Johnson, "Romney Denies OKing Anti-Thompson Website" (Associated Press, September 11, 2007). Accessed November 17, 2011, from http://www.usatoday.com/news/politics/2007-09-11-1019414238_x.htm.

42. Neil Postman, *Amusing Ourselves to Death: Public Discourse in the Age of Show Business* (New York: Penguin Books, 1986).

43. The quote is Mencken, but the original source of the quote (newspaper article, book, or other medium) is not known.

CHAPTER 10

Campaign Finance Reform in the Post–*Citizens United* Era

Peter L. Francia, Wesley Joe, and Clyde Wilcox

THE 2008 PRESIDENTIAL ELECTION was the most expensive in history, and it is likely that campaign spending by candidates, political parties, and outside groups will again reach new heights in 2012. Early speculation has incumbent president Barack Obama raising as much as $1 billion for his nomination and general election campaigns.[1] A handful of Republican candidates have also begun to raise large sums of money for their campaign committees, and have received considerable financial backing and support from "independent" groups.[2] Many of the independent organizations that will be active in 2012 are well-established groups, such as the National Rifle Association, the Sierra Club, the Chamber of Commerce, and the AFL-CIO. Other groups will be newly established, and it will be difficult and, in some cases, impossible to know who is funding them despite a complex set of existing campaign finance laws and rules that developed nearly four decades ago.[3]

These statutes and regulations restrict how much individuals can give to candidates, parties, and certain types of interest groups, and regulate how individuals can spend various types of funds. Tax rules also govern the types of money that different kinds of groups can raise and how each kind can use that money to assist campaigns. Often the laws and regulations make subtle, sometimes murky, distinctions between different types of contributions and spending.

One example of this complexity would be the limits on what individual citizens can do with their money in an election. On grounds that individuals cannot corrupt themselves, the Supreme Court has prohibited any limits on the amounts of money that candidates can give to their own campaigns for office, although there are limits on the amounts that individuals can contribute to others, including family members who run for office. An individual can give larger, but limited, sums to political parties and to political action committees (PACs) sponsored by interest groups. However, an individual can give unlimited amounts to some committees and nonprofit organizations,[4] which can run ads that attack a candidate, pass out voter guides, and register voters. These distinctions are the result not of carefully planned regulations, but rather of episodic rulemaking and judicial action.

To elucidate the complexities of the campaign finance system and the factors that will shape its future, this chapter covers several important issues. First, we review the framework of the Federal Election Campaign Act and discuss the events and circumstances that led to its eventual unraveling. Second, we discuss the Bipartisan Campaign Reform Act and consider its initial successes and failures. Third, we analyze the Roberts Court decision on campaign finance, including the 2010 *Citizens United* decision. Fourth, we review some new and prominent proposals for campaign finance reform and speculate about their prospects of ever becoming law.

The Evolution and Framework of Campaign Finance Reform

The 1974 comprehensive amendments to the Federal Election Campaign Act (FECA) of 1971 established the fundamental framework for the modern campaign finance system. The law set out four main elements: (1) to set limits on contributions and expenditures from individuals, parties, and interest groups; (2) to establish disclosure requirements for contributions and spending; (3) to complete a public financing system for presidential candidates; and (4) to create an enforcement agency, the Federal Election Commission, to regulate the new campaign finance system. All significant actors in national campaigns were required to form committees, which would raise and spend money according to FECA rules and file regular reports. Interest groups formed PACs, which could raise money in limited amounts from members and use it in election campaigns. Candidates were to form campaign committees, which would report all contributions and spending.

Although initially successful, the FECA regulatory system gradually unraveled by the late 1990s. Campaign professionals discovered ways to channel unregulated donations, termed "soft money," to party committees. This practice was immensely attractive to party leaders because they could raise as much from a few interest groups in an evening as they could from tens of thousands of individuals over several months. In 1992, the national political party committees together collected $86 million in soft money. By 2000, that total had swelled to $495 million—a sixfold increase in just eight years.[5] In 1997, Republicans in Congress held hearings about soft money fundraising by the Clinton White House,[6] at the same time that Republican leaders were busily raising large sums of their own soft money.

Reformers, including members of Congress, criticized the growth of soft money on several grounds. First, because these contributions were often very large, they had the capacity to influence the actions of Congress. If a PAC gave a candidate $5,000 before an election, it was unlikely that the PAC could expect any favors from that candidate if the candidate won. But, interest groups could channel hundreds of thousands of dollars through political parties into the same election, and that amount was substantial enough that many members believed that it affected legislation.

Second, the process of raising soft money became increasingly unseemly. Both political parties held soft money fundraising events the day before major markups of legislation. Interest groups complained that they had no choice but to contribute if they wanted a voice in the negotiations. A number of prominent business leaders criticized soft money fundraisers as a form of extortion, but only a few were willing to make a public pledge not to contribute.[7]

Finally, some argued that soft money distorted the equality of the political process. Those who can afford to give hundreds of thousands are an elite group that already enjoys numerous advantages in politics. These large soft money contributions, which average citizens could not afford to give, amplified the voices of the wealthiest Americans.

Large sums of money spent on "issue advocacy" advertisements, which avoid the restrictions specified in FECA because they do not explicitly endorse a candidate, also caught the eye of reformers. Critics charged that issue ads were not transparent because it was difficult, and often impossible, to trace who was funding them. During the 1996 election, for example, Democrat Bill Yellowtail of Montana watched his lead in the polls disappear to Republican Rick Hill when an issue ad alleged that Yellowtail physically abused his wife and failed to pay child support. The group that paid for the ad went by the innocuous name "Citizens for Reform."[8] Ads such as these often dominated local elections in the late 1990s and early twenty-first century, and in some cases were more common than the ads paid for by the candidates themselves.

The Bipartisan Campaign Reform Act

Nearly thirty years after the passage of FECA, Congress passed the Bipartisan Campaign Reform Act (BCRA) in 2002. Unlike FECA, the new law did not try to create a comprehensive campaign finance regulatory system, but instead sought to patch the biggest problems that had developed over time. BCRA banned large soft money contributions to political parties and barred politicians from soliciting soft money for interest groups. The law also required state and local parties to fund any federal activities with "hard money" (contributions subject to federal limits) as opposed to "soft money" (contributions not subject to federal limits), although there are limited exceptions for voter registration and get-out-the-vote activities. State and local parties may pay for voter registration and get-out-the-vote efforts with soft money (known as "Levin Amendment" funds) up to $10,000 per source (if allowed under state law). Money raised for Levin Amendment funds must also meet a number of requirements.[9]

The law still allowed large contributions to various interest groups, which could run issue ads. There were, however, limits on the ads, as well as new standards for identifying campaign ads. Under the new law, "campaign ads" included those that mentioned a candidate by name or appeared on television or radio during the period of intense campaigning before the election. PACs could still fund these ads as independent expenditures, but they could only do so with funds raised through regulated contributions. Other political advocacy committees could run issue ads, but not during the final days of the election.

BCRA contained one other important set of provisions. It doubled the amount that individuals could give to candidates for federal office, increased the amount that they could give to political parties, and left in place the limits on how much they could give to PACs. These provisions were intended to make it easier for candidates, and to a lesser extent parties, to raise hard money once the ban on soft money took effect.

An eclectic coalition of interest groups immediately challenged BCRA before the U.S. Supreme Court. The plaintiffs ranged from progressive groups such as the AFL-CIO to conservative groups such as the National Rifle Association. Despite the challenge, the Court upheld the core elements of the law in *McConnell v. Federal Election Commission*, 540 U.S. 93 (2003).

The Initial Impact of BCRA, 2004–2006

In the first two elections that followed BCRA, the law had some of the effects hoped for by its supporters. For example, national parties were able to continue to raise significant amounts of money, and in increasing sums from small donors.[10] Indeed, national party committees were able to raise more in hard money alone in 2004 than they raised in hard and soft money combined in 2000 (see Table 10.1). Party receipts did decline slightly in the 2006 midterm election compared with the totals posted in the 2002 midterm election; however, the amounts remained comparable. Party independent expenditures also increased for Democratic Party committees from $2.3 million in 2000 to $176.5 million in 2004, and for Republican Party committees from $1.6 million in 2000 to $88 million in 2004.[11] Perhaps most significant of all, between 2000 and 2004, the amount parties raised in contributions of $200 or less surged from $226 million to $449 million.[12] The national parties raised considerably more money from small donors in 2006 than in 2002 as well.

Yet BCRA did not completely end large contributions by wealthy donors and interest groups. In 2003, many Democratic strategists worried that their party could not raise enough to compete with George W. Bush, and many wealthy party

TABLE 10.1. Party Receipts in Presidential Elections Immediately Before and After BCRA, 2000–2006

	BCRA Era (Hard Money Only) 2006 election	BCRA Era (Hard Money Only) 2004 election	Pre-BCRA Era (Hard + Soft Money) 2002 election	Pre-BCRA Era (Hard + Soft Money) 2000 election
DNC	$130.8	$404.4	$162.1	$260.6
DSCC	$121.4	$88.7	$143.4	$104.2
DCCC	$139.9	$93.2	$102.9	$105.1
Total	*$392.1*	*$586.3*	*$408.4*	*$469.9*
RNC	$243.0	$392.4	$277.9	$379.0
NRSC	$88.8	$79.0	$124.6	$96.1
NRCC	$179.6	$185.7	$179.6	$144.6
Total	*$511.4*	*$657.1*	*$582.1*	*$619.7*

Note: Dollar amounts in millions. DNC = Democratic National Committee, DSCC = Democratic Senatorial Campaign Committee, DCCC = Democratic Congressional Campaign Committee, RNC = Republican National Committee, NRSC = National Republican Senatorial Committee, NRCC = National Republican Congressional Committee (NRCC).

Source: Federal Election Commission, http://www.fec.gov/press/press2009/05282009Party/20090528Party.shtml.

patrons increased their giving to political advocacy groups. A number of large committees such as America Coming Together (which spent more than $78 million in the 2004 election), the Media Fund, and others raised large sums and helped coordinate a pro-Democratic campaign in the media and door-to-door.[13] Billionaire George Soros gave tens of millions to political advocacy groups in 2004 and nearly $4 million to similar groups in 2006.[14] Nearly three-fourths of the funds that political advocacy groups raised came in contributions of $100,000 or more in 2006.[15] In short, BCRA did not eliminate the ability of wealthy interests to invest in campaigns.

By the end of the 2006 election, reformers hoped to address BCRA's shortcomings. The push for reform gained momentum after a highly publicized scandal sent "superlobbyist" Jack Abramoff to federal prison for fraud, tax evasion, and conspiracy to bribe public officials. Yet, the prospects for reform became more complicated when two new conservative members, John Roberts (whom Congress also confirmed as chief justice) and Samuel Alito, joined the Court in 2005 and 2006, respectively. The new Roberts Court's decisions would dramatically alter campaign finance law and affect how candidates and organizations raised money for campaigns.

Rulings From the Roberts Court on BCRA—2007–2010

The first major campaign finance case brought before the new Roberts Court came in 2007 with *Federal Election Commission v. Wisconsin Right to Life, Inc.*, 551 U.S. 449. The Court significantly altered BCRA by striking down the law's electioneering communications restrictions (which banned the use of corporate and union treasury funds to fund advertising that featured the name or likeness of a clearly identified candidate for federal office in the final thirty days of the primary election and the final sixty days of the general election). The effect of this ruling according to one scholar was that the Court "essentially eviscerated the McCain-Feingold provisions and green-lit the efforts of nearly any group to fund pro-candidate ads close to elections."[16]

A year later, the Roberts Court again took aim at BCRA in *Davis v. FEC*, 554 U.S. 724 (2008). In this ruling, the Court struck down a provision in the law that increased the contribution limits for opponents of wealthy self-financed candidates. The Court ruled that the provision was "discriminatory" in singling out wealthy candidates and added that there was no "legitimate government objective" to level the playing field for candidates facing a wealthy self-financed opponent.[17]

Yet the most significant ruling of all came in 2010 when the Court reached a decision in *Citizens United v. FEC*, 558 U.S. 08-205. The case involved the nonprofit corporation Citizens United, which produced a critical film about presidential candidate Hillary Clinton and sought to use its general treasury funds to finance the film's distribution. In its ruling, the U.S. Supreme Court overturned *Austin v. Michigan Chamber of Commerce*, 494 U.S. 652 (1990) and part of *McConnell v. FEC* by ruling that the prohibition on corporations from using their general treasury funds to finance express advocacy communications (i.e., independent expenditures) or electioneering communications violated the First Amendment of the Constitution.

Similar to the rationale in *Buckley v. Valeo*, the majority in *Citizens United v. FEC* ruled that money spent independent of a candidate's campaign was not necessarily corruptive. According to Justice Kennedy, "Independent expenditures, including those made by corporations, do not give rise to corruption or the appearance of corruption."[18] Absent the establishment of corruption, the majority reasoned that the law's restrictions on free speech sufficiently burdened the First Amendment. As Kennedy explained, "If the First Amendment has any force, it prohibits Congress from fining or jailing citizens, or associations of citizens, for simply engaging in political speech."[19]

Put in plainer terms, *Citizens United* had the effect of allowing corporations to spend money that independently (i.e., groups do not coordinate their activities with a candidate's campaign) and expressly advocated for the election or defeat of a candidate (i.e., language such as "vote for" or "vote against") beyond their PACs.

For the first time in the modern campaign finance era, corporations would be able to use general treasury funds for independent expenditures in federal elections.[20] The decision would have far-reaching significance for elections and political campaigns in 2010 and beyond.

The Impact of the Roberts Court's Decisions on the 2008 and 2010 Elections

The various rulings of the Roberts Court had some broad effects on elections in 2008 and 2010. In the aftermath of the *Wisconsin Right to Life* decision, electioneering communications from outside independent groups increased to $119.3 million in 2008 from $100.2 million in the previous presidential election of 2004.[21] (As such, outside groups have even a stronger impact affecting campaigns, as mentioned in the interest groups chapter by Kasniunas and Rozell.) Likewise, following the *Citizens United* ruling, outside money poured into the 2010 election. Independent groups not affiliated or connected with a candidate or party spent more than $300 million in the 2010 election.[22] Independent expenditures, in particular, increased significantly in the 2010 election. Interest groups spent $210.9 million on independent expenditures in 2010 compared to $156.8 million in 2008 and $37.4 million in the previous midterm election of 2006. To put the 2010 independent expenditure totals into even greater perspective, the $210.9 million was nearly three times the combined total of the $75.1 million spent on independent expenditures by interest groups in every midterm election from 1990 through 2006. Additional analysis of the 2010 election reveals that 67 percent of total independent expenditures in 2010 came from "groups freed by *Citizens United*."[23] With more money available to use for independent expenditures in the aftermath of *Citizens United*, the 2010 figures confirm that corporations and labor unions (which could also draw money from their treasury funds) took eager advantage of the ruling. They spent $210 million, which was triple what they had spent in the last midterm election in 2006.[24]

The increases in independent expenditures are also the product of another decision, *SpeechNow.org v. FEC*, 599 F.3d 686, 694-95 (D.C. Cir. 2010), although the case received considerably less attention than *Citizens United*. In *SpeechNow.org v. FEC*, the District of Columbia Circuit Court of Appeals ruled that federal political action committees that made independent expenditures and did not contribute to any candidates or political parties could raise unlimited sums of money. The result of this ruling was a new group of "independent expenditure committees" that became known as "super PACs." These super PACs also contributed to the rise in independent expenditures in the 2010 election, accounting for more than $65 million of the more than $210 million spent in 2010 on independent expenditures.[25]

The Growth of SuperPACs

Super PACs not only have contributed to the rise in independent expenditures, but also have increased the voices of wealthy donors. Reports surfaced in 2011 that American Crossroads, formed by former George W. Bush adviser Karl Rove, received more than 90 percent of its money for the year from just three billionaires.[26] Democrats, likewise, have moved to create what one operative called their own "soft money Death Star."[27] Of note, the House Majority PAC, which is targeting Republican freshmen who supported Congressman Paul Ryan's (R–Wisc.) controversial Medicare proposal in the 2012 election, has raised half of its money from a small number of billionaires, wealthy donors, and corporations.[28]

The increased money that outside groups and their big-money patrons funneled into elections that followed the rulings of the Roberts Court, however, only tells part of the story. Deregulation of the campaign finance system also had effects on campaigns themselves. The new campaign finance environment altered aspects of candidate strategy and activities as well as party campaign efforts.

The Effects of Campaign Finance Deregulation on Campaign Activities

With more outside money allowed into the electoral process, the Court's various rulings have increased the ability of interest groups to set the political agenda through advertising blitzes. Candidates and their campaigns, as a result, are under increased pressure to raise money to prevent ceding control of the issue agenda to outside groups. As one campaign finance expert explained, "[As the candidate] you want to have control of your message, you want to call the shots and be able to spend the money where you want to spend it."[29]

While outside groups have the potential to undercut a candidate's message,[30] they also provide cover for candidates who may need to attack an opponent to gain traction with voters. Instead of the campaign attacking the opponent directly, outside groups can do this instead, allowing the candidate to deny "going negative" while still reaping the advantage that the attack might generate. As one expert noted, "They [outside groups] can say things the campaign wants to keep a distance from."[31] This strategy can appeal to independent and swing voters who may turn against a candidate who makes what appears to be an unfair or overtly partisan attack against an opponent.

Fundraising Practices Have Changed

The deregulated campaign finance system also has altered campaign fundraising practices. Although the *Citizens United* ruling upheld the constitutionality of disclosure requirements, an FEC ruling in 2007 played a significant role in weakening disclosure. Nonprofit groups, according to the FEC, only have to disclose donations that are specifically earmarked and designated for use on election ads. This ruling in combination with the *Citizens United* ruling helped make nonprofit groups an especially attractive vehicle for wealthy donors who fear the possibility of political reprisals. One lobbyist remarked that nonprofit groups now hold "the keys to the political kingdom because they allow [wealthy donors] anonymity."[32] Indeed, early reports from 2010 suggest that the percentage of reports filed with the FEC that list the sources of the group's money dropped considerably from 71 percent in 2004 to just 15 percent in 2010.[33]

Perhaps the most notorious example of the breakdown of the campaign finance system's disclosure requirements came in 2011. W Spann LLC, a mystery company with no corporate records about the owner of the firm, its address, or type of business, funneled $1 million into the super PAC Restore Our Future. Only months after it formed, W Spann dissolved, creating what one campaign finance expert called a "roadmap for how [donors] can hide their identities."[34]

Adding to the intrigue is that the super PAC Restore Our Future is a group created by former political aides to presidential candidate Mitt Romney. Romney himself spoke at a private dinner event in New York City for the group's donors in the summer of 2011.[35] While Restore Our Future claims to be an independent group, the group's close association with one of the leading presidential contenders in 2012 highlights how blurred the lines have become on coordination between candidates and "outside" groups in the new deregulated world of campaign finance.

National Party Committees Adapt to Change

Party committees, similar to candidates' campaign organizations, have found ways to sidestep coordination prohibitions as well. During the 2010 election, for example, the National Republican Congressional Committee (NRCC) took the novel approach of publicly disclosing its ad buy strategy. This gave cues to conservative and pro-Republican outside groups about where to direct their spending.[36] These outside groups also coordinated among themselves, sharing target lists and television-time ad buy data—a practice borrowed from Democratic-group efforts in 2006 and 2008. The political director of the Chamber of Commerce, Bill Miller, explained that NRCC's information and coordination with other outside groups allowed the Chamber to "see where the holes are and figure out who is filling what holes."[37]

In summary, the effects of recent rulings from the Roberts Court have been to turn the clock back to the pre-Watergate era or even much earlier for campaigns. As former FEC chairman Trevor Potter explained, "Well, it would be overstating it, but it would still be in the right ballpark to say it's going to look a lot like the 1904 campaign, which was the last one before there were federal laws regulating money in politics. You're going to find a lot of money being spent. I think you're going to find people who don't want to disclose donors being able to hide the money. So you'll find secret money."[38] Taken together, the primary goals of the modern campaign finance system under FECA and the BCRA reforms—to limit money in federal elections and to improve disclosure—now appear to have been largely undone by the rulings of the Roberts Court.

Prospects for Legislative Reform: An Overview

As BCRA unravels, it is doubtful that comprehensive reform will find its way onto the congressional agenda, let alone pass, at least in the near term. According to former representative. Christopher Shays (R-Conn.), a chief sponsor of BCRA in the House, "[The] bottom line is that right now the country is facing such huge challenges with the wars—three of them—and almost a financial meltdown that campaign finance reform is not high on legislative agendas. . . . And frankly, it wouldn't be high on mine."[39] The current partisan composition of Congress is another obstacle. In a recent, largely party-line vote, for example, the House voted to abolish instead of repair the moribund presidential public financing system.[40] Any reform policies that might emerge in the near term at the federal level will probably fall short of the scale of even BCRA, perhaps taking the form of measures that address relatively narrow targeted areas, such as the disclosure regime; or perhaps the executive branch may unilaterally attempt to adopt minor, targeted repairs.

In the longer term, the current five-justice conservative majority of the U.S. Supreme Court continues to narrow the range of options that it will accept as constitutional, pushing reformers toward policy responses that (1) do not conflict with that majority's claims about the First Amendment to the U.S. Constitution and (2), as a practical matter, move toward a laissez-faire, market-oriented vision of campaign finance policy instead of an approach that emphasizes regulation. Although the Court has framed its deregulatory moves in terms of free speech, the cumulative effect of the recent decisions has been to push reformers toward such a vision. Hence some reforms, such as disclosure, survive because they are consistent with laissez-faire, market-oriented principles.

Legislative reforms that conflict with laissez-faire principles, however, are less likely to stand. To be sure, the majority opinions in the recent cases do not explicitly seek to impose a laissez-faire political ideology that, for example, equates citizen participation with the exercise of "consumer sovereignty." But recent shifts in proposals for broader campaign finance reform strongly suggest that future BCRA-scale legislation will follow the kind of laissez-faire direction that has prevailed in so many other areas of public policy over the past few decades.

During the Reagan administration, which appointed or employed every member of the U.S. Supreme Court's current conservative majority, the White House and its interest group allies pushed policy reforms (e.g., school vouchers, transferable pollution rights, enterprise zones for urban renewal, and the privatization of providing public services) that favored more laissez-faire approaches, such as deregulation and the manipulation of incentives, over the "command and control" approaches that prevailed in the Great Society era (but began to lose favor even among some Democrats in the 1970s).[41] The initial Roberts Court era reform efforts indicate that future large-scale proposals may well look more market-oriented and less like "Great Society" approaches that attempt to "level the playing field" by relying heavily on regulating the activity of affluent political actors. Indeed, a group of scholar-reformers who worked with Congress on the design of BCRA recently argued for "a new agenda" for reform.[42] While acknowledging the importance of contribution limits, their new agenda would emphasize the use of incentives (e.g., matching funds and tax credits) to increase small donor participation.

Nearer-Term Prospects: Damage Control for the Disclosure Regime

U.S. Supreme Court Justice Louis Brandeis wrote, "Publicity is justly commended as a remedy for social and industrial diseases. Sunlight is said to be the best of disinfectants; electric light the most efficient policeman."[43] Voters can only hold policy makers responsible for any special policies or favors they provide donors if they have access to information about who has given to whom. Thus, disclosure is a necessary condition for accountability in campaign financing.[44]

As noted earlier, however, recent developments in campaign finance leave the disclosure system incomplete. While there is full disclosure to the FEC of contributions to candidates, political parties, and PACs, it is the IRS that tracks contributions to 527 committees, which results in less complete and timely disclosure. Moreover, there are no disclosure provisions for contributions to various section nonprofit organizations, leaving a major gap in the ability to trace money in elections. Independent groups allied with both major political parties are raising vast sums of money using legal entities that enable them to circumvent campaign finance disclosure requirements.

Shortly after the Court issued the *Citizens United* decision, Democrats pressed to strengthen disclosure requirements in nearly every policy-making venue that can impose them. In 2010, Sen. Charles Schumer (D-N.Y.) and Rep. Chris Van Hollen (D-Md.) introduced legislation (S. 3628; H.R. 5175) that would have required corporations, labor unions, and other nonparty groups to disclose the identities of individuals who financed their spending on advertising. The "Democracy Is Strengthened by Casting Light On Spending in Elections" ("DISCLOSE") Act passed the U.S. House of Representatives by a largely party-line vote (most Democrats supported the measure) but was stopped in the Senate by a Republican filibuster.[45] Similarly, Democratic members of the FEC attempted to use administrative rules to require greater disclosure of sources of independent expenditures and electioneering communications. Twice in 2011, however, the commission could not even agree to get through the first stages of the rulemaking process. Finally, the White House drafted an executive order that would require federal contractors to disclose their contributions to political groups that claim exemption from campaign finance disclosure requirements. At the time of this writing, the order remains in draft form.

Nevertheless, many Republicans have historically supported, or at least tolerated, disclosure requirements, and there are plausible scenarios in which a more narrowly tailored disclosure bill could pass. For example, a coalition of incumbents could become more concerned about losing control over their own campaigns than some other considerations that weigh against more comprehensive disclosure laws. Additionally, some Republican opposition to the DISCLOSE Act may owe to the fact that the party enjoyed an advantage in undisclosed funds in the 2010 election cycle.[46] If that should change, some opposition might yield. Legislators might be able to agree on legislation that is narrower than the DISCLOSE Act was. The Schumer–Van Hollen proposal included provisions that went beyond requiring disclosure, such as a requirement that ads paid for by corporations include an image of the chief executive officer, and prohibiting corporations that receive large federal government contracts from making independent expenditures or electioneering communications.

Long-Term Prospects: Changes in Public Financing Options

The collapse of the presidential public finance system has not discouraged some members of Congress and public interest group allies from continuing to press for a system of public financing for congressional elections. Public financing remains a primary feature of the broadest proposals for campaign finance reform. Advocates of public funding of congressional elections cite a variety of reasons for promoting such programs. Many justifications arise from the broad goal of increasing the competitiveness of congressional elections.[47]

In the 2010 November general election, for example, nearly two dozen congressional candidates ran without opposition from a major political party, presenting voters with no effective choice in the election. Proponents claim that a system of public funding could reduce the need to raise a large sum of money as a barrier to running for office. Those who do not easily have access to money, but are otherwise candidate material, might be able to establish their credibility as candidates and attract the support needed to wage a campaign. Such programs could also increase the diversity of the pool of potential candidates by enabling women, members of some minority groups, and others who often lack access to networks of wealthy prospective donors to run for office more easily.[48] Until very recently, public financing proposals ran the gamut. They included full public funding of major-party candidates in the general election, more limited proposals to provide some subsidies to candidates at the start of their campaign or after they meet a certain threshold, and plans that give incentives to individuals to contribute to candidates (e.g., through tax credits).

Fair Elections Now Act

Following the recent U.S. Supreme Court decisions, the proposals have begun to shift in a more laissez-faire, free market–oriented direction. This turn is evident in changes that sponsors in the 111th Congress (2009–2011) introduced in what is perhaps the most prominent legislative proposal for large-scale reform, the Fair Elections Now Act (FENA). In the 110th Congress, Senate assistant majority leader Dick Durbin (D-Ill.) (and fellow Illinois senator Barack Obama, among others) introduced a version of the bill (S. 1285) that drew heavily from the "clean elections" systems that Arizona, Maine, and Connecticut had adopted. As in Arizona, FENA would have created a voluntary system that supported the campaigns of qualifying candidates with, among other things, a combination of flat grants, media broadcast vouchers, and supplemental "fair fight funds" that would be made available if a participating candidate confronted unusually high spending in support of a non-participating opponent. Congressional candidates could choose to finance their campaigns with public money if they could demonstrate sufficient public support for their candidacy. Candidates could raise some private funds at the earliest stage of the campaign. These contributions could not, however, exceed $100 from a particular individual. Ultimately, to qualify for public funding a candidate would have to raise a specified number of "qualifying contributions" from residents of the candidate's state.

Similar to Arizona's state election public financing system, which served as a model for FENA, the FENA-qualifying contributions would be limited to $5. By raising many of these small contributions, a candidate would demonstrate his or her campaign's viability, thereby reducing the possibility that public funds would go to marginal candidates. Candidates receiving public funds would then have to agree to refuse private contributions to the campaign and to abide by voluntary limits on campaign expenditures. Rep. John Tierney (D-Mass.), who had annually introduced similar legislation for nearly the entire preceding decade, sponsored a companion measure, the Clean Money, Clean Elections Act of 2007 (H.R. 1614), in the U.S. House.

Following a series of federal court decisions that struck at various portions of BCRA and state campaign finance laws, Durbin and his allies revised FENA for the 111th Congress (S. 752; H.R. 1826). The direction of the revisions is instructive. The new version still awards a large, flat grant of funding to candidates who volunteer to participate in the system. New provisions, however, move the legislation in a more laissez-faire, market-oriented policy direction: Spending limits are eliminated as long as candidates agree to rely on small private donors and public funds. Small donors are defined as those who give no more than an aggregate of $100 to the candidate's campaign. The legislation also provides a $4-to-$1 public matching fund subsidy to a limited proportion of the funds that participating candidates raised from small donors.

Proponents of FENA's new emphasis on small donors believe that the potential of small donor fundraising is dramatic, particularly when coupled with matching funds. Consider the example of President Obama, whose presidential campaign spent more than any in history. In 2008, Barack Obama received nearly 69.5 million votes in the November general election. If half of the people who voted for Obama in November 2008 donated $20 to his general election campaign, or if 20 percent of his voters gave $50, he would have raised nearly $700 million from small donors. If a third of those who voted for Obama in November 2008 gave $10 to his campaign and he received a $2-to-$1 match, the campaign would have raised $695 million from extremely small donations and a matching fund program that is far more modest than the $4-to-$1 match that is proposed in the latest version of the FENA (S. 750; H.R. 1404). Obama raised $747.8 million from *all* sources to fund both his prenomination and general election campaigns. All of the contributions would have been completely fungible; no donor would enjoy a lobbying advantage by virtue of donating to the Obama campaign.

The Pro-Reform Prospect

In the near term, public funding proposals face nearly insurmountable obstacles. As noted earlier, the congressional agenda is extremely crowded. Even if Congress actively considered FENA, the dire fiscal context probably renders public financing a nonstarter. Although some citizen activist groups may be attempting to build public support for public financing, public opinion on the subject remains volatile and highly sensitive to the wording of survey questions.[49] A majority of Americans typically support the idea of replacing private financing with public funding. However, public support plunges when a survey words a question in a way that emphasizes the use of tax revenue to finance elections and de-emphasizes the objectives of public funding programs. Consequently, one can easily imagine that if the Durbin bill were to approach possible enactment, it might not survive a "public education" campaign aimed at its defeat. Moreover, even if citizens generally favor such a proposal in principle, will they spur Congress to put it on the active legislative agenda? If the Abramoff-era scandals have failed to engender sufficient public pressure for this reform, one wonders what it would take to mobilize sufficient public demand.

Market-Oriented Alternatives for Campaign Finance

A very different proposal, coming mostly from libertarians and conservative Republicans, is to scrap contribution limits entirely in favor of a regime that depends entirely on disclosure. Former California representative John Doolittle (R) sponsored a bill, the Citizen Legislature and Political Freedom Act, to reform the campaign finance system in that manner. In November 1999, he introduced H.R. 1922, to remove all limits on political contributions and end public funding of presidential campaigns. The bill would also strengthen disclosure, requiring more timely and thorough reporting of soft money donations.

The argument for deregulation is sometimes based on principled arguments about free speech, and sometimes based on the ineffectiveness of limits.[50] As Doolittle himself argued, "The goal of effective campaign finance reform is to encourage political speech rather than limit it. It is to promote competition, freedom, and a more informed electorate. . . . Today's system hurts voters in our republic by forcing more contributors and political activists to operate outside of the system where they are unaccountable and, consequently, more irresponsible."[51] Doolittle's legislation, however, received only tepid support in the 106th Congress and stands little chance of passage in the foreseeable future.

More recent legislative attempts to deregulate the campaign finance system have focused on specific areas. For example, in the 110th Congress, Sen. Bob Corker (R-Tenn.) and Rep. Zach Wamp (R-Tenn.) offered legislation that would have allowed political party organizations to spend unlimited amounts in coordination with candidates for federal elective office. That measure did not receive much attention. Wamp is no longer a member of Congress, so the proposal currently lacks a sponsor in the House.

Interestingly, however, some reformers have embraced a related proposal. A joint task force consisting of members of the Campaign Finance Institute, the American Enterprise Institute, and the Brookings Institution proposed allowing unlimited coordinated spending of party funds that are collected from small donors, defined as individuals who give an aggregate of $200 or less.[52] Under such an arrangement, parties would have an incentive to become aggressive recruiters of small donors, thereby diluting the importance of large contributions. A similar proposal appears in the 112th Congress's version of the Fair Elections Now Act. Although there is no realistic expectation that legislation will pass in the near term, this provision might achieve some bipartisan support if it came up untied to a public financing bill.

State-Level Initiatives

Despite the obstacles at the federal level, it would be a mistake to conclude that proponents of public financing are engaged in a quixotic quest. During the past decade they have succeeded in establishing such programs in Maine (1996), Vermont (1997), Arizona (1998), Connecticut (2005), and some major U.S. cities. A 2004 pilot program to fund state legislative elections in New Jersey with taxpayer subsidies has produced mixed results, but the state will continue to experiment with public financing. In 2007, governors Bill Richardson (D-N.M.) and Christine Gregoire (D-Wash.) endorsed public financing of elections in their respective states. More recently, New York governor Andrew Cuomo's 2011 "State of the State" address declared that "we need public financing of campaigns."[53] Certainly, one can imagine a long-term scenario in which more states ultimately embrace public financing, and that state legislators who embrace such systems eventually move on to Congress and bolster support for a comparable federal-level system. If, at the same time, the systems garner favorable reviews from citizens, public support for comparable federal legislation could harden. Still, that is a long way off at best, and even the current systems must survive and/or adapt to further opposition in the courts.

Conclusion

In the 1970s, Congress established a regulatory framework that built on earlier rules and that was designed so that different elements worked together. Contribution limits reduced the supply of campaign money somewhat and decreased the voice of the wealthiest donors, while spending limits were designed to decrease the demand for campaign funds. Public financing was available to help candidates reach voters, and all campaign activity was to be made transparent by a national agency.

Today little of this framework remains operational. Contribution limits still regulate the size of contributions directly to candidates, but wealthy individuals and corporations can channel unlimited amounts into committees that openly support the same candidates. Spending limits are gone, public financing is irrelevant to national campaigns, and a sizable (but unknowable) portion of activity is not transparent to voters.

The future of campaigns thus seems headed backward in time to the pre-Watergate era in which campaign finance was largely unregulated and disclosure was all but nonexistent. Wealthy donors, corporations, and, perhaps to a lesser extent, labor unions will surely take advantage of this unregulated environment, amplifying their influence in the political process. This environment, however, has brought with it campaign finance scandals in the past. It is possible that this will happen again after the 2012 campaign, but what is different today than in the past is that it is not clear whether the Court would uphold Congress's legislative response to public pressure for reform in wake of a major scandal.

Notes

1. Patricia Zengerle, "Billion-Dollar Obama to Run Moneyed Campaign" (MSNBC, April 4, 2011). Accessed August 11, 2011, from http://www.msnbc.msn.com/id/42415155/ns/politics-decision_2012/t/billion-dollar-obama-run-moneyed-campaign.

2. See Michael Isikoff, "Firm Gives $1 Million to Pro-Romney Group, Then Dissolves" (MSNBC, August 4, 2011). Accessed August 4, 2011, from http://www.msnbc.msn.com/id/44011308/ns/politics-decision_2012.

3. Ibid.

4. These organizations are known as "527" and "501(c)" organizations, which are labels that refer to the internal revenue codes that govern their tax status. Unlike a traditional PAC, some 527 groups do not contribute to candidates for federal office, but rather are established for the specific purpose of engaging in political advocacy. 501(c)s are tax-exempt organizations that, like some 527s, cannot contribute to campaigns, but can engage in some political activities, such as voter mobilization and education, provided that political activity is nonpartisan for 501(c)(3) organizations or does not become their primary purpose for 501(c)(4) organizations. There are "super" PACs as well that can raise funds without restrictions provided that these groups also do not make campaign contributions and that they spend their money in federal elections independent of candidates and political parties.

5. "Campaign Finance eGuide" (Campaign Finance Institute). Accessed July 15, 2011, from www.cfinst.org/legacy/eguide/basics.html.

6. For more information, see John F. Harris, "Clinton Defends Fundraising" (*The Washington Post,* September 23, 1997), A01.

7. Bradley A. Smith, "Faulty Assumptions and Undemocratic Consequences of Campaign Finance Reform" (*Yale Law Journal,* Vol. 105, No. 4, 1996), 1049–1091.

8. Viveca Novak and Michael Weisskopf, "The Secret G.O.P. Campaign" (*Time,* November 3, 1997). Accessed July 15, 2011, from www.time.com/time/magazine/article/0,9171,987280,00.html.

9. Levin Amendment funds must meet the following conditions: (1) Federal officeholders and national parties may not receive Levin Amendment funds; (2) all receipts and disbursements of Levin Amendment funds must be disclosed; (3) party committees in two or more states, or two or more party committees in the same state, are prohibited from jointly raising Levin Amendment funds; (4) a state party committee cannot raise the money for use in other states; (5) Levin Amendment funds cannot be used for federal candidate-specific or generic advertising; (6) Levin Amendment activities must be funded consistent with FEC hard money or soft money allocation rules; (7) the state or local party must raise its own matching hard money; and (8) Levin Amendment funds cannot be transferred between party committees.

10. Peter L. Francia, Wesley Y. Joe, and Clyde Wilcox, "Campaign Finance Reform: Present and Future," in *Campaigns on the Cutting Edge*, edited by Richard J. Semiatin (Washington, DC: CQ Press, 2008).

11. Robin Kolodny and Diana Dwyre, "A New Rule Book: Party Money after BCRA," in *Financing the 2004 Election*, edited by David B. Magleby, Anthony Corrado, and Kelly D. Patterson (Washington, DC: Brookings Institution Press, 2006), 198.

12. Anthony Corrado, "Parties Playing a Major Role in Election '06" (Campaign Finance Institute). Accessed June 30, 2011, from www.cfinst.org/books_reports/pdf/Parties_Corrado_102606.pdf.

13. Stephen R. Weissman and Ruth Hassan, "BCRA and the 527 Groups," in *The Election After Reform: Money, Politics, and the Bipartisan Campaign Reform Act*, edited by Michael J. Malbin (Lanham, MD: Rowman and Littlefield, 2006), 81.

14. Stephen R. Weissman and Kara D. Ryan, "Soft Money in the 2006 Election and the Outlook or 2008" (Campaign Finance Institute). Accessed June 30, 2011, from www.cfinst.org/books_reports/pdf/NP_Softmoney_06-08.pdf.

15. Ibid.

16. Michael M. Franz, "The *Citizens United* Election? Or Same as It Ever Was?" (*The Forum*, Vol. 8, 2010), Article 7.

17. *Davis v. Federal Election Commission*, 554 U.S. 724 (2008).

18. *Citizens United v. Federal Election Commission*, 558 U.S. 08-205 (2010). Justice Kennedy's quotation in *Citizens United v. Federal Election Commission* was accessed from http://www.law.cornell.edu/supct/html/08-205.ZO.html.

19. Ibid.

20. The *Citizens United v. Federal Election Commission* decision did not directly rule on whether unions can use their general treasury funds on election-related independent expenditures in federal elections; however, there is near-unanimous legal agreement that the court's logic would apply to labor.

21. Center for Responsive Politics, "Outside Money." Accessed June 30, 2011, fromwww.opensecrets.org/outsidespending/index.php.

22. Tom Curry, "Big-Bucks Presidential Fundraising Still Vital in Citizens United Era" (MSNBC, August 3, 2011). Accessed on November 17, 2011, from http://firstread.msnbc.msn.com/_news/2011/08/03/7242125-big-bucks-presidential-fundraisers-still-vital-in-citizens-united-era.

23. Spencer MacColl, "Citizens United Decision Profoundly Affects Political Landscape" (May 5, 2011). Accessed on November 17, 2011, from http://www.opensecrets.org/news/2011/05/citizens-united-decision-profoundly-affects-political-landscape.html.

24. Center for Responsive Politics, "Outside Spending." Accessed on June 10, 2011, from opensecrets.org/outsidespending/index.php.

25. Ibid.

26. Michael Isikoff, "Billionaires Give Big to New 'Super PACs'" (MSNBC, June 26, 2011). Accessed on November 17, 2011, from http://www.msnbc.msn.com/id/43541131/ns/politics-decision_2012/t/billionaires-give-big-new-super-pacs/?ns=politics-decision_2012&t=billionaires-give-big-new-super-pacs.

27. Matt Bai, "This Donation Cycle Catches G.O.P. in the Upswing" (*The New York Times*, October 20, 2010). Accessed November 17, 2011, from http://www.nytimes.com/2010/10/21/us/politics/21bai.html.

28. Michael Isikoff, "Billionaires Give Big to New 'Super PACs.'"

29. Curry, "Big-Bucks Presidential Fundraising Still Vital in Citizens United Era."

30. David B. Magleby, "Conclusions and Implications," in *Outside Money: Soft Money and Issue Advocacy in the 1998 Congressional Elections*, edited by David B. Magleby (Lanham, MD: Rowman and Littlefield, 2000).

31. Curry, "Big-Bucks Presidential Fundraising Still Vital in Citizens United Era."

32. Peter H. Stone, "Center for Public Integrity: Campaign Cash: The Independent Fundraising Gold Rush Since 'Citizens United' Ruling" (Democracy 21, October 4, 2010). Accessed June 30, 2011, from www.democracy21.org/index.asp?Type=B_PR&SEC=%7BAC81D4FF-0476-4E28-B9B1-7619D271A334%7D&DE=%7B037D17B6-F488-4FF6-A849-D519900C50A0%7D.

33. T. W. Farnam, "Disclosure of 'Issue Ad' Funding is on the Wane" (*The Washington Post*, September 16, 2010). Accessed June 30, 2010, from www.washingtonpost.com/wp-dyn/content/article/2010/09/15/AR2010091507172.html.

34. Isikoff, "Firm Gives $1 Million to Pro-Romney Group, Then Dissolves."

35. Ibid.

36. Jeanne Cummings, "Republican Groups Coordinated Firepower" (*Politico*, November 3, 2010). Accessed on November 17, 2011, from http://www.politico.com/news/stories/1110/44651.html.

37. Ibid.

38. Kathy Kiely, "Rules Be Damned" (*National Journal*, July 14, 2011). Accessed on August 10, 2011, from http://www.nationaljournal.com/magazine/former-fec-chairman-trevor-potter-on-campaign-finance-20110714 .

39. T. W. Farnam, "Not All Public Campaign Finance Will Raise Supreme Court Ire" (*The Washington Post*, June 29, 2011). Accessed on July 1, 2011, from http://www.washingtonpost.com/politics/not-all-public-campaign-financing-will-raise-supreme-court-ire/2011/06/29/AGNdIQrH_story.html.

40. Jonathan D. Salant, "U.S. House Votes to End Campaign Finance System, Senate Unlikely to Agree" (Bloomberg, January 27, 2011). Accessed on July 1, 2011, from http://www.bloomberg.com/news/2011-01-27/u-s-house-votes-to-end-campaign-finance-system-senate-unlikely-to-agree.html.

41. Charles Schultze, *The Public Use of Private Interest* (Washington, DC: Brookings Institution, 1977).

42. Campaign Finance Institute, *Reform in an Age of Networked Campaigns* (Washington, DC: Author, 2010).

43. Brandeis University, see www.brandeis.edu/investigate/sunlight (accessed September 1, 2007).

44. Herbert E. Alexander, Janet M. Box-Steffensmeier, Anthony J. Corrado, Ruth S. Jones, Jonathan S. Krasno, Michael J. Malbin, Gary Moncrief, Frank J. Sorauf, and John R. Wright, *New Realities, New Thinking* (Los Angeles: Citizen's Research Foundation, 1997), 9.

45. Ben Pershing, "House Passes Campaign Finance Bill: Disclose Act would Curb Corporate Political Spending on Elections" (*The Washington Post*, June 25, 2010), A2. See also Dan Eggen, "Bill on Political Ad Disclosure Falls Short in Senate" (*The Washington Post*, July 28, 2010), A3.

46. Paul Blumenthal, "The Citizens United Effect: 40 Percent of Outside Money Made Possible by Supreme Court Ruling" (Sunlight Foundation, November 4, 2010). Accessed on November 17, 2011, from http://sunlightfoundation.com/blog/2010/11/04/the-citizens-united-effect-40-percent-of-outside-money-made-possible-by-supreme-court-ruling/.

47. Kenneth R. Mayer, Timothy Werner, and Amanda Williams, "Do Public Funding Programs Enhance Electoral Competition?" paper presented at the Fourth Annual Conference on State Politics and Policy Laboratories of Democracy: Public Policy in the American States, Kent State University, April 30–May 1, 2004.

48. Timothy Werner and Kenneth R. Mayer, "The Impact of Public Election Funding on Women Candidates: Comparative Evidence from State Elections," paper presented at the 2005 annual meeting of the Midwest Political Science Association, Chicago, April 7–10, 2005.

49. Stephen R. Weissman and Ruth A. Hassan, *Public Opinion Polls Concerning Public Financing of Federal Elections 1972–2000: A Critical Analysis and Proposed Future Directions* (Washington, DC: Campaign Finance Institute, 2005). Accessed on November 17, 2011, from www.cfinst.org/president/pdf/PublicFunding_Surveys.pdf.

50. Bradley A. Smith, *Unfree Speech: The Folly of Campaign Finance Reform* (Princeton, NJ: Princeton University Press, 2001); see also John Curtis Samples, *Welfare for Politicians? Taxpayer Financing of Campaigns* (Washington, DC: Cato Institute, 2005).

51. John Doolittle, "The Case for Campaign Finance Reform" (Hoover Institution). Accessed on August 11, 2011, from http://media.hoover.org/sites/default/files/documents/0817996729_307.pdf.

52. Michael Malbin, "Reform in an Age of Networked Campaigns" (Campaign Finance Institute, January 14, 2010). Accessed August 11, 2011, fromhttp://www.cfinst.org/press/PReleases/10-01-14/Reform_in_an_Age_of_Networked_Campaigns.aspx.

53. As quoted in Katrina Vanden Heuvel, "Cuomo's Reform Moment" (*The Nation*, January 24, 2011). Accessed on August 13, 2011, from thenation.com/blog.

CHAPTER 11

Redistricting — The Shift Toward South and West Continues

Jeffrey Crouch

AUGUSTE COMTE, a philosopher in nineteenth-century France, supposedly once said that "demography is destiny."[1] Comte's quote is just as relevant today. In 2012, the apportionment of congressional seats following the 2010 Census will reflect the continuing shift of Americans from the Northeast and Midwest to the South and West that began in the late 1940s when Americans became more mobile as car ownership increased dramatically.[2] The implication of this shift seems simple: The Democratic base shrinks while Republicans add to their numbers. The reality may portend something different for the future, however. The following chapter will consider key principles of redistricting and examine what it is, why it is important, how it is undertaken, and by whom. It will provide an overview of congressional redistricting processes already under way in the larger states, and will conclude with a discussion of future redistricting trends. *Redistricting can have a powerful impact, determining which party controls the House of Representatives for an entire decade, because it involves reapportioning the congressional districts in each state, where some gain seats and some lose seats based on population gain or loss.*

How Redistricting Works

For hundreds of years, boundaries have divided the polity into districts, and voters have then determined which candidates to pick to send to Washington, DC, as their representatives. Decisions on how to draw those boundary lines have affected politics in a number of ways, and several political scientists and legal scholars have examined redistricting and the issues of history and race it has raised in recent decades.[3] The topic is popular for good reason: Who is in office can have a dramatic impact on the policies and concerns that are discussed in Congress (or not discussed). And, of course, congressional careers can take off or stall depending on which voters within a state are able to vote for or against a particular candidate.

Redistricting occurs when the responsible entity within a state (often a state legislature or a commission) draws new district lines, usually following a decennial census.[4] *Gerrymandering* is the term that describes how the district lines may be redrawn to further a partisan goal. In 1812, Massachusetts governor Elbridge Gerry backed a redistricting plan that helped his party and also looked like a salamander. The term, a combination of *Gerry* and *salamander,* stuck.[5]

Redistricting is a separate process from *reapportionment,* which is a nationwide reallocation of congressional seats following the census to accommodate changes in the relative populations of the states.[6] If a state gains or loses residents within that ten-year span compared to the forty-nine other states, the congressional districts within that state may need to be redrawn to ensure that everyone in the state is represented in Congress. In the past, Congress would simply add seats to keep up with population growth, but because of legislation passed in 1911 and 1929, the number of representatives in the House is set at 435.[7]

The cap on the number of congressional representatives means that the 2010 census will trigger changes (gains or losses) in congressional seats for eighteen states. The state with the largest gain (four seats) is Texas. Florida will receive two new seats, while Arizona, Georgia, Nevada, South Carolina, Utah, and Washington will each pick up one seat. On the other side of the ledger, New York and Ohio will lose two seats apiece, and each of the following states will lose one seat: Illinois, Iowa, Louisiana, Massachusetts, Michigan, Missouri, New Jersey, and Pennsylvania.[8] Excluding districts from states with only one district, or those with lines being reconfigured by a commission, Republicans will dominate the creation of new districts, taking charge of over 200 from the 340 districts eligible to be reworked by state legislatures this time around.[9] Whether Republicans will be able to gain significant seats, or merely shore up what they currently hold, is one of the more intriguing questions about the most recent round of redistricting. As of June 2011, final answers are many months, perhaps even years, down the road.

Redistricting and Minority Rights

Redistricting, or lack thereof, can have real consequences, both at the ballot box and for public policy. Before the "redistricting revolution" of the early 1960s, states rarely bothered to redraw congressional district lines following the census. While the old lines stayed in place, population growth patterns gradually led to a situation where one citizen's vote could count for considerably more than another's depending on where each lived. Sometimes (pre-"revolution") African Americans were disadvantaged by states simply opting not to change district lines to reflect population changes. Urban areas began to see significant population growth from black southern transplants, but boundary lines were not changed to accommodate the new status quo. Consequently, the vote of (white) citizens in a hypothetical rural district of 20,000 residents carried considerably more heft than those of citizens in a hypothetical urban district of 40,000 residents. This gave the rural voter an advantage over the urban voter when selecting a representative.[10] Tennessee was a primary example where this occurred.

Packing, Cracking, Stacking, and Tacking Districts

If a skilled mapmaker is trusted to make redistricting decisions, she may use her knowledge strategically to unite or split groups of voters with similar or different interests, depending on her goals. One technique, called "cracking," splits members of a majority group into two or more districts in order to lessen that group's voting impact. Another tactic, "packing," occurs when the mapmaker tries to squeeze as many members of a particular group as possible into a single district, thereby weakening the group's strength in other districts. A third example of strategic line drawing is "stacking," where, in a multimember district, a group that is large enough to be a majority in a single-member district loses time and again to another group. The idea behind these three tactics is to help a group—often a political party—to win as many districts with as few votes as possible, thus avoiding "wasted" votes, while redistributing any excess votes to other districts where they can help that group's candidates. Finally, the person drawing district lines will sometimes carefully bring a small area or even a single individual into a district, a strategy that can add or "tack" a potential political officeholder's home to a district that he or she may one day campaign to represent. Packing, cracking, multimember districts, and Jim Crow laws helped prevent African Americans from being elected to office for decades.[11]

The Civil Rights Revolution and Redistricting

Gradually, however, conditions improved for minority voters and candidates, thanks to a series of court cases and a very important federal law that has helped to level the playing field for both. In 1962, the Supreme Court triggered the "reapportionment revolution" with its decision in *Baker v. Carr*, 369 U.S. 186 (1962), in which the Court agreed for the first time to consider reapportionment questions that had, until that point, been refused as "political questions."[12] As scholars Gary W. Cox and Jonathan N. Katz point out, the 1960s redistricting court opinions recognized that most of the nation's congressional districts were, to a degree, unequal in size. This led to "the most comprehensive remaking of the electoral map that the nation had ever seen."[13] Redistricting according to court-enforced requirements helped equalize the number of residents from one district to the next within a state, and helped even out the relative value of urban and rural votes.

The Voting Rights Act of 1965 was another big step by the federal government in the direction of allowing black citizens to vote for their candidates of choice without having to overcome unnecessary obstacles.[14] Section 2 and Section 5 are particularly important in redistricting cases. Section 5 requires jurisdictions in areas with a history of discrimination to obtain "pre-clearance" of their proposed maps from the U.S. Department of Justice. The idea is to prevent changes that could hurt minority voters' opportunities to participate.[15]

More important, Section 2 prevents line drawers from undertaking "vote dilution," or drawing districts intended to reduce the influence of minority votes. According to the decision in *Thornburg v. Gingles,* 478 U.S. 30 (1986), a minority group can defeat an allegedly discriminatory redistricting plan in court under Section 2 if, considering the minority group's size, proximity, and cohesiveness— among other factors—the power of its votes has been unfairly lessened. As a remedy, the court may order that a new, "majority-minority" district be drawn, a move that will usually lead to the election of the minority group's favored candidate.[16]

Can Districts Be Drawn for Political Reasons?

New maps calling for more equal districts helped drive toward a "dramatic increase" in blacks serving in public office in the South, as noted by scholar Charles Bullock.[17] In the early 1990s, Republicans in President George H. W. Bush's Department of Justice worked with black leaders to create majority-minority districts, an innovation that helped to elect African Americans to Congress while at the same time helping Republicans. This was because white conservative voters became more receptive to Republican arguments at a time when white Democrats in the South began to rely more heavily on black votes to get and stay in office. A consequence of this maneuvering is that some districts were "bleached," with black voters taken from one district and instead added to another, making the first district whiter than it was before. According to scholar David Lublin, majority-minority districts had a greater effect on the South than on the North because it was easier to replace liberal white voters outside the South. The courts have struggled with how (if at all) to account for district lines influenced by race. North Carolina's remarkably strange-looking twelfth district triggered the *Shaw v. Reno* 509 U.S. 630 (1993) case, in which the Supreme Court held that race cannot be the main criterion for drawing a district. (The district traversed a narrow corridor around Interstate 85 from the Winston-Salem area down to Charlotte.) However, the Court decided that drawing districts based on *party* considerations was fine, even though African Americans would vote overwhelmingly for Democrats.[18]

By 2001, the goal of Democratic leaders had changed from creating "majority-minority" districts to protecting Democratic incumbents (regardless of color), and that required sending black voters into districts to help white Democrats win. Black leaders in the South agreed because they were afraid of Democrats losing seats to Republicans, did not wish to concede seats held by African Americans, and were encouraged by the increasing willingness of white voters to vote for black candidates. Research has shown that black candidates can still get elected even with fewer black votes. In Texas and other southern states, the new strategy was to keep black-held seats and protect white Democrats by not asking for as many black voters in the majority-minority districts as before. Indeed, the Georgia Legislative Black Caucus supported a plan to help white Democrats and protect black chairs of committees by taking some black voters out of majority-minority districts and using them to bolster Democratic numbers elsewhere.[19]

Modern Techniques to Implement Redistricting

Using computers to redistrict is not a new idea. In 1961, William Vickrey was one of the earliest to propose using algorithms to create districts, an innovation that would likely have required a computer to implement. The first redistricting-focused computer software was developed by Stuart Nagel a few years later. Fast forward a couple of decades, and computers had become more common. By the time of the 1991 redistricting, computers were "practically universal" in mapping, but required state-of-the-art machines and continuous technical assistance, according to scholars Micah Altman, Karin MacDonald, and Michael McDonald. Ten years later, they observe, the software was "substantially faster and cheaper," and less computing power was needed to run it. The geographic information system (GIS) software designed to assist mappers in putting together districts became easier to use and more affordable, and more interested parties could operate it without requiring technical expertise. GIS software was a revelation: In the past, mapmakers had to use actual, physical maps, which limited the number of alternative plans they could produce in the time they had available to produce the maps. In doing so, they could only zero in as far as the precinct level (1,000–2,000 voters). Currently, the software allows mapmakers to get down to census block level, which, as Charles Bullock notes, "contains less area than an electoral precinct." Now, mapmakers can draw precise lines that allow them to create nearly perfectly equal districts. Still, no matter how sophisticated computers and software become, someone has to program them, and there is no way for anyone to reconcile all of the competing interests. Thus, the most that computers can really do to improve redistricting is help arrange a rough prioritization that addresses the most important issues, though probably not all of them.[20]

Who Gets to Draw District Lines?

Responsibility for drawing lines varies greatly by state. Some states never have a problem, as they have just one congressional district in the first place. Those seven states are Alaska, Delaware, Montana, North Dakota, South Dakota, Vermont, and Wyoming. Most states entrust their state legislatures with drawing congressional district lines for federal elections. The advantage to this approach is that state legislators are very familiar with their states, and they are accountable to the public at the ballot box for any mischief. For the thirty-seven states where the state legislatures are responsible for sketching boundary lines for federal elections, politics often comes into play. Party control matters: Where one party controls both houses of the state legislatures and holds the governorship, it is more likely that the map they approve will help their electoral prospects. Where there is split party control, the default solution is often to just preserve incumbents of both parties. In cases where a tough decision requires a colleague to "take one for the team," newer members without an extensive network or seniority tend to bear the brunt of redistricting changes.[21]

The remaining six states, Arizona, California, Hawaii, Idaho, New Jersey, and Washington, all rely upon "commissions" to assist with drawing the lines, in some cases attempting to remove political calculations from the equation. For example, the largest state, California, recently opted for a bipartisan citizens' commission to draw its new lines. The initial plan proposed would uproot entrenched incumbents who were protected in the last redistricting effort in 2000, while making the map potentially more favorable to Democrats. What is more, the upheaval would likely cost California some prestige and strength as congressional leaders hailing from the state would not return to the legislature.[22] The impact on other states watching California for a sense of the potential advantages and shortcomings of using commissions is unclear as of this writing.

Drawing District Lines: Equal Population and Minority Representation

Two of the most important factors for mapmakers to consider are *equal population* and *minority representation*. Since 1962 and the "one person, one vote" cases, district populations must be all but equal—for congressional districts, "as nearly as is practicable," according to *Wesberry v. Sanders,* 376 U.S. 1 (1964). The advantage here is that if all votes are equal, it is easy for the court to see where a rule is violated. On the other hand, the requirements of equal population may lead to the division of a group with common interests, and it may be more difficult to draw a minority-dominated district where the group could choose its own candidate. *Minority representation* is a concept that has become more complex since the 2000 Census first accepted multiple responses for its category on race, a move that made possible

126 combinations of responses to racial and ethnic inquiries.[23] Basically, states comply by following the Voting Rights Act of 1965, especially Sections 2 and 5.

The Supreme Court has identified a number of "traditional" redistricting guiding principles that are often considered along with equal population and minority representation. One of these is *contiguity*, which refers to whether some- one could travel to any area within a district without crossing out of it. In other words, are the lines drawn around areas that touch one another as much as pos- sible? Another concept is *compactness*, which there are at least two ways to measure. First is by geography: Smooth borders are better than contorted ones; and the closer any single piece of the district is located to its center, the better. Second is by population: More compact districts have more people living near their geo- graphic midpoint. Compactness may in some cases make drawing districts with equal populations difficult or even impossible, as lines may need to be drawn in irregular ways to include the right number of people. Finally, attention may be paid to *political and geographic boundaries*, especially where political entities have been created by preexisting lines. As these lines were often created to separate a group with a common interest from others, these may be a starting point and a checkpoint for where future congressional district lines are drawn. Another issue that may enter into the calculus is the existence of *communities of interest*. A com- munity of interest is a group that lives close by others with similar characteristics and/or goals concerning politics, religious outlook, finances, racial/ethnic back- ground, culture, or interest in associating. What the common characteristic of the group members is may not always be apparent.[24]

Redistricting and the 2012 Elections

In 1900, the largest states (which also boasted the most representatives in Congress) were New York, Pennsylvania, Illinois, Ohio, Missouri, Texas, and Massachusetts. One hundred and ten years later, the most populous state, California, is followed by Texas, New York, Florida, Pennsylvania, Ohio, and Illinois. Americans have continued heading West (California) and South (Texas, Florida) at the expense of Midwestern "Rust Belt" states such as Indiana, Illinois, and Michigan, among others. "This is now the first time in history that the number of seats held by the Midwest and Northeast is less than 40 percent of the country," wrote Eric Oster- meier, editor of the Humphrey Institute's Smart Politics blog at the University of Minnesota. Arizona, Idaho, Nevada, Texas, and Utah are the states that have added residents fastest in the past ten years; eleven of the twelve congressional seats chang- ing hands come from the Midwest and Northeast, and eight new seats will emerge west of their prior homes. "The trend," said Census director Robert Groves, "is a growth in seats for Western and Southern states and a tendency to lose seats from the Midwest and Northeastern states."[25]

There are political dimensions to these migration patterns. According to scholar Nelson Polsby, an increase of Republican voters in the South following World War II may be attributed at least in part to "the growth in the South of residential air conditioning . . . [which] made the South habitable all year around to northerners, many of whom had adopted the custom of visiting the South during the winter months."[26] In addition, weakening unions and "right to work" laws in southern states that complicate union formation have helped draw workers away from the Rust Belt, thereby taking away representatives from formerly Democratic regions in the Midwest and Northeast while increasing the congressional voting strength of the South.[27]

In 2010, some observers predicted that projected Republican electoral gains at the state level could create an environment ripe for aggressive partisan gerrymandering of congressional district lines. According to Tim Storey of the National Conference of State Legislatures, in the 2010 elections, "Republicans won a commanding advantage in the redistricting process." Others were more skeptical, noting that a forty-seven-seat advantage in the U.S. House is the largest Republican majority in decades and would be difficult to expand. In larger states such as Texas, Pennsylvania, Ohio, and Florida, it is difficult to imagine how Republicans could add to their ranks in the House. Added to the mix are potential Democratic advantages: a Democrat in the White House and in charge of the Department of Justice for the first time in decades, an indecisive electorate that has changed its mind several times in the last few election cycles, and, finally, the fact that a lot of states are gaining more people in Democratic rather than Republican areas. Under the circumstances, it might be wise for Republicans to secure their gains rather than "get greedy" and try to add to their numbers.[28]

Populous States With Republican State Legislators in Control of Redistricting

Would Republican state legislators in charge of redrawing congressional district lines "get greedy" or instead opt to draw their maps conservatively? Early indications are that the GOP will aggressively approach its line-drawing opportunities and try to maximize gains rather than merely protect current seats. In Texas, the GOP appears to be trying to expand its influence as much as possible. Republicans held a twenty-three–nine congressional advantage over Democrats, and with four new seats coming thanks to the census, experts initially believed that Republicans might have to cede half of them to Democrats. After all, much of the state's population growth came from Hispanics, who often support Democrats, and given the GOP's already overwhelming majority, it would not have been a surprise for Republicans to draw two majority-Hispanic districts without much fanfare. Instead, their proposed map draws three new, barely Republican districts, draws one strongly Democratic district, and also redistricts Rep. Lloyd Doggett (D-Texas) into a new district dominated by the opposition. The result: ten deeply (Democratic) blue seats and twenty-six red ones in which the 2008 Republican presidential nominee, Sen. John McCain, won 52 percent or greater of the popular vote.[29]

Florida, which gained two seats in the recent reapportionment, amended its state constitution twice last November, and in doing so tied the hands of Republican map drawers hoping to improve an already favorable map. The changes force redistricters to propose districts that are essentially neutral for incumbents and parties, are "compact," and incorporate existing "geographical boundaries." The amendments were approved by the Department of Justice, but could be reevaluated in court. Much hinges on the result: Republicans could conceivably gain both of the new seats if the amendments are found lacking. Alternatively, an unsympathetic court could begin to undo the current map and take away the GOP's advantage.[30]

Conditions are not terribly encouraging in the Midwest for further Republican expansion. Pennsylvania has more Republican than Democratic members of Congress (twelve-seven), but the state is losing a seat after the new census. Several of the districts that Republican mapmakers drew in 2001 turned out to be too marginal to keep, and the GOP had only seven districts by 2008. The state tends to go for Democrats in presidential elections and is volatile on the congressional level, prompting speculation that rather than try to get thirteen or fourteen districts, as they did ten years ago, Republicans may settle for shoring up what they have. Similar to Texas, Florida, and Ohio, the Republican-dominated state legislature in Pennsylvania is in charge of redistricting, but is not likely to be able to improve the GOP's number of U.S. House members. There are thirteen Republican House members in the Buckeye State to just five Democrats. However, the state is losing two seats—one likely Democratic and the other Republican. In Michigan, Republicans are trying to hold ground as the Wolverine State loses one seat following the census. Attempting to keep their nine incumbents in office (compared to six Democrats), the proposed GOP map released on June 17 places Democrats Sander Levin and Gary Peters in the same district while aiding Republican incumbents Thaddeus McCotter and, to a lesser extent, Dan Benishek and Tim Walberg.[31]

Heading south, the news is more encouraging for the GOP. In North Carolina, Republicans can reasonably expect to gain seats. The state legislature (and the congressional redistricting process) is controlled by Republicans, and the Democratic governor cannot veto the result. Currently, Democrats have a majority of the congressional delegation (seven of thirteen total), but Republicans could pick up three or four seats as they dismantle the present configuration that was put into place by the Democrats a decade ago. The Tar Heel State may be following in the footsteps of California the next time around, however: The state House recently passed a bill where staff members would draw districts and then elected lawmakers would be able to pass or derail them, similar to the model provided by Iowa. In Georgia, state Republicans control the redistricting process, and the GOP has an eight-to-five advantage in the U.S. House. The news that Georgia is set to add one seat, thanks to the 2010 Census, might seem very welcome to Republicans. However, there is not much the GOP can do to improve its strong position within the Peach State unless it wishes to risk its thinning majority.[32]

Populous States With Democratic State Legislators in Control of Redistricting

Democrats have few opportunities to redistrict to their advantage because there are so few states where they control the process (just seven compared with eighteen for the GOP). In their most important state, Illinois, Democrats in the state legislature have a lot of potential ground to gain when they draw a new map that attacks the current GOP advantage of eleven to eight members of Congress.[33] Indeed, a proposed map expected to receive the governor's approval would redistrict ten of the eleven GOP representatives into districts with other members of their own party, potentially leading to the defeat of six incumbent Republicans.[34]

Populous States With Split Control of Redistricting

In the dozen states where Democrats and Republicans share control of state government, compromise on redistricting is more likely. The biggest state under split party control, New York, is losing two congressional seats because of the census, but the unlucky members of Congress being redistricted out may not be known for a while. In May 2011, Democratic candidate Kathy Hochul won a special election in the twenty-sixth congressional district, a consistently Republican district that lies between Rochester and Buffalo. The incumbent, Rep. Chris Lee, resigned after the media reported that Lee, who is married, had sent suggestive photos of himself to another woman. A month later, Rep. Anthony Weiner resigned from office after the media caught wind of several explicit photos the married Weiner apparently sent to several women, including a former porn star. The jury is still out on how these scandals will affect the new district lines. Weiner's former district (NY-9) ranges from southern Queens to southern Brooklyn, which is a heavily Democratic area.[35]

Current and Future Trends

The 2010 Census is history, but states are still working on a variety of different timelines to figure out their new district lines. A few states (notably Texas, Illinois, and Michigan) have plans, while the future of other states (see: New York) remains murky. Even at this early date, though, a few trends are becoming apparent. *These trends could have implications for an entire decade (as discussed later).*

More Active Redistricting Tactics by Republicans

An increasingly apparent tendency this time around is a willingness by Republicans to aggressively push their advantage to expand their influence, even at the risk of losing ground. A curious wrinkle highlighted by the census is that a significant amount of the population growth in Republican-dominated states such as Texas comes from minority (often Democratic-leaning) populations. Will Republican mapmakers be able to draw districts that account for the various required factors (equal populations, minority representation, etc.) and also increase Republican representation? The few early maps drawn so far seem to indicate that the GOP will (at least in some places) aggressively try to increase its margins, even if the likely result is a court date. *That means a long, drawn-out process that could extend into 2012 and beyond.*

Does Technology Help to Democratize the Redistricting Process?

One of the recurring features of redistricting where state legislators are responsible for drawing federal congressional districts has been that often "politicians pick voters instead of the other way around."[36] In theory, voters select politicians through elections, but technological advances have made it easier for politicians responsible for drawing districts to manipulate boundary lines for political purposes. Over the long term, this dynamic may change as voters become fed up with politically motivated districting decisions and use emerging technology to push for a greater democratization of the redistricting process. One possible emerging trend—as evidenced by California's movement to a bipartisan commission and other states such as North Carolina considering the same—suggests that the public may be moving away from a preference for politician-designed districts. California may lose some incumbents and, consequently, seniority in Congress once all of the dust settles, but its experience with a commission may cast a long shadow on redistricting plans for 2020.

Equally important is how faster, more powerful computers and more easily accessible data are allowing average voters to have a greater voice in the redistricting process, albeit in some cases at the expense of mapmakers' intellectual property. Florida invites computer users to visit a special redistricting website to create and turn in a proposed map to the state. Scholars Micah Altman and Michael McDonald created a website through which members of the general public may create maps at http://www.publicmapping.org. Students at Columbia Law School are also participating in redistricting exercises (http://www.law.columbia.edu/redistricting), as are students in Virginia colleges and Michigan state citizens.[37] In the long run, the increasing involvement of average citizens may be the legacy of these early twenty-first-century redistricting processes.

The Growing Population of Latinos — The Next Set of Majority-Minority Districts?

As the Latino population continues to grow in the United States, it becomes likely that more Latino majority districts will be drawn in southwestern and western states such as Texas, Arizona, New Mexico, and Colorado. If states can show they have drawn these districts for political and not principally racial reasons, consistent with the Supreme Court decision in *Shaw v. Reno* (as discussed earlier), then such plans are likely to withstand legal scrutiny. Whether the Supreme Court decides to revisit the *Shaw v. Reno* decision remains to be seen. What is known is that Latinos are the fastest-growing minority group in America. Today, they represent more than 14 percent of the nation's population, and that is expected to double over the next forty years according to the Pew Hispanic Center (to 29 percent in 2050).[38] Not only will redistricting issues affect more Latinos, but it will surely mean that more Latinos will participate in the redistricting process itself.

Conclusion

The redistricting process set forth in Article 1, Section 2, of the U.S. Constitution would scarcely be recognized by the founders today, as this complex, modern, technologically savvy practice currently employs hundreds of attorneys, redistricting experts, and politicians. Few could have imagined that the tools of redistricting could be stored in a personal computer, accessible to college students, redistricting experts, and everyone in between. Meanwhile, the shift of the population to the South and West continues, as it has over the last half-century. What remains to be seen is what impact that has on shaping districts in future elections, whether the states will move to a more merit-based or citizen-based system, or whether the status quo of state legislatures doing redistricting remains the norm.

Notes

1. Richard Stengel, "Tracking America's Journey" (*Time*, October 23, 2006).
2. Charles S. Bullock III, *Redistricting: The Most Political Activity in America* (Lanham, MD: Rowman and Littlefield, 2010), 4.
3. For political scientists' accounts of redistricting, see Mark E. Rush and Richard L. Engstrom, *Fair and Effective Representation? Debating Electoral Reform and Minority Rights* (Lanham, MD: Rowman and Littlefield, 2001); Gary W. Cox and Jonathan

N. Katz, *Elbridge Gerry's Salamander: The Electoral Consequences of the Reapportionment Revolution* (New York: Cambridge University Press, 2002); Jonathan Winburn, *The Realities of Redistricting: Following the Rules and Limiting Gerrymandering in State Legislative Redistricting* (Lanham, MD: Lexington Books, 2008); and Bullock, *Redistricting: The Most Political Activity in America.* Legal works include J. Gerald Hebert et al., *The Realist's Guide to Redistricting: Avoiding the Legal Pitfalls,* 2nd ed. (Chicago: ABA, 2010); Justin Levitt, *A Citizen's Guide to Redistricting, 2010 Edition* (Brennan Center for Justice at New York University School of Law, 2010). Accessed August 5, 2011, from http://www.brennancenter.org/content/resource/a_citizens_guide_to_redistricting_2010_edition/; Justin Levitt, *A 50 State Guide to Redistricting* (Brennan Center for Justice at New York University School of Law, 2011). Accessed August 5, 2011, from http://www.brennancenter.org/content/resource/a_50_state_guide_to_redistricting/. Works on the history of redistricting include Charles W. Eagles, *Democracy Delayed: Congressional Reapportionment and Urban-Rural Conflict in the 1920s* (Athens, GA: University of Georgia Press, 1990); David Butler and Bruce Cain, *Congressional Redistricting: Comparative and Theoretical Perspectives* (New York: Macmillan, 1992); and Thomas E. Mann and Bruce E. Cain, Eds., *Party Lines: Competition, Partisanship, and Congressional Redistricting* (Washington, DC: Brookings Institution Press, 2005). For a geography scholar's view, see Mark Monmonier, *Bushmanders & Bullwinkles: How Politicians Manipulate Electronic Maps and Census Data to Win Elections* (Chicago: University of Chicago Press, 2001). For an argument on adding members to the House, see Brian Frederick, *Congressional Representation & Constituents: The Case for Increasing the U.S. House of Representatives* (New York: Routledge, 2010). Redistricting works that focus on race include David Lublin, *The Paradox of Representation: Racial Gerrymandering and Minority Interests in Congress* (Princeton, NJ: Princeton University Press, 1997); David T. Canon, *Race, Redistricting, and Representation: The Unintended Consequences of Black Majority Districts* (Chicago: University of Chicago Press, 1999); and Dewey M. Clayton, *African Americans and the Politics of Congressional Redistricting* (New York: Garland, 2000).

4. Levitt, *A Citizen's Guide to Redistricting,* 6. Usually lines are redrawn only after the census, but not always: In 2003, the Republican-led Texas state legislature decided to voluntarily redraw the boundary lines to help GOP electoral prospects.

5. Levitt, *A Citizen's Guide to Redistricting,* 8. See also Cox and Katz, *Elbridge Gerry's Salamander.*

6. Levitt, *A Citizen's Guide to Redistricting,* 6.

7. Ibid.

8. Aaron Blake, "Census 2010 Shows Red States Gaining Congressional Seats" (*The Washington Post,* December 21, 2010). Accessed on November 18, 2011, from http://voices.washingtonpost.com/thefix/redistricting/red-states-gain-as-new-congres.html

9. Aaron Blake, "Republicans Ramp Up Redistricting Efforts" (*The Washington Post,* May 31, 2011). Accessed on November 18, 2011, from http://www.washingtonpost.com/blogs/the-fix/post/republicans-ramp-up-redistricting-efforts/2011/05/31/AGzpNSFH_blog.html

10. Bullock, *Redistricting*, 49. For an analysis of urban-rural rhetoric and reapportionment, see Eagles, *Democracy Delayed*.

11. Levitt, *A Citizen's Guide to Redistricting*, 10, 57, 58; Bullock, *Redistricting*, 14, 16, 17, 19, 51.

12. See Cox and Katz, *Elbridge Gerry's Salamander*, 12; Bullock, *Redistricting*, 28–29; *Colegrove v. Green*, 328 U.S. 549, 556 (1946): "Courts ought not to enter this political thicket. The remedy for unfairness in districting is to secure State legislatures that will apportion properly, or to invoke the ample powers of Congress."

13. Cox and Katz, *Elbridge Gerry's Salamander*, 210.

14. Bullock, *Redistricting*, 53.

15. Levitt, *A Citizen's Guide to Redistricting*, 48.

16. Levitt, *A Citizen's Guide to Redistricting*, 46, 47. See *Thornburg v. Gingles*, 478 U.S. 30 (1986).

17. Bullock, *Redistricting*, 55.

18. Bullock, *Redistricting*, 55, 60 (citing Lublin, *The Paradox of Representation*, 41), 64, 65, 66, 67, 72, 73, 77.

19. Bullock, *Redistricting*, 50, 79, 80, 159.

20. Micah Altman and Michael McDonald, "The Promise and Perils of Computers in Redistricting" (*Duke Journal of Constitutional Law & Public Policy*, Vol. 5, No. 69, 2010), 71, 75; Micah Altman, Karin Mac Donald, and Michael McDonald, "Pushbutton Gerrymanders? How Computing Has Changed Redistricting," in Mann ad Cain, *Party Lines: Competition, Partisanship, and Congressional Redistricting*, 52, 53, 54; Bullock, *Redistricting*, 39–40; Levitt, *A Citizen's Guide to Redistricting*, 42.

21. See *The Washington Post*'s Redistricting Scorecard, http://www.washingtonpost.com/wp-srv/special/politics/redistricting-scorecard/ (accessed August 5, 2011). See Levitt, *A Citizen's Guide to Redistricting*, 24, 34–36.

    Those states under Republican control are Alabama, Florida, Georgia, Indiana, Kansas, Louisiana, Michigan, North Carolina, Nebraska, New Hampshire, Ohio, Oklahoma, Pennsylvania, South Carolina, Tennessee, Texas, Utah, and Wisconsin. Democrats control redistricting in Arkansas, Connecticut, Illinois, Massachusetts, Maryland, Rhode Island, and West Virginia. Democrats and Republicans each have some control in Colorado, Iowa, Kentucky, Maine, Minnesota, Missouri, Mississippi, New Mexico, Nevada, New York, Oregon, and Virginia; Bullock, *Redistricting*, 100; Alex Isenstadt, "Census Results to Spark Map Fights" (*Politico*, December 22, 2010).

22. *The Washington Post*'s Redistricting Scorecard; Alex Isenstadt, "Political Earthquake Roils Calif. Delegation" (*Politico*, June 10, 2011); Aaron Blake, "Incumbents Lose, Democrats Win With California Redistricting Proposal" (*The Washington Post*, June 10, 2011); Ben Pershing, "New Redistricting Map Could Make California Less Golden on the Hill" (*The Washington Post*, June 20, 2011).

23. Levitt, *A Citizen's Guide to Redistricting*, 44, quoting *Wesberry v. Sanders*, 376 U.S. 1, 7,8 (1964); Levitt, *A Citizen's Guide to Redistricting*, 45, 46; Nathaniel Persily, "The Law of the Census: How to Count, Whom to Count, and Where to Count Them" (*Cardozo Law Review*, Vol. 32, 2010–2011), 755, 770.

24. See *Miller v. Johnson*, 515 U.S. 900, 916 (1995) and *Shaw v. Reno*, 509 U.S. 630, 647 (1993). Levitt, *A Citizen's Guide to Redistricting*, 50, 51, 52, 53, 54, 56.

25. Bullock, *Redistricting*, 4, 7; Alexander Burns, "2010 Census Results Show Power Shifting Westward" (*Politico*, December 21, 2010). Accessed on November 18, 2011, from http://www.politico.com/news/stories/1210/46683.html.

26. Bullock, *Redistricting*, 7; Nelson Polsby, *How Congress Evolves* (New York: Oxford University Press, 2004), 84.

27. Bullock, *Redistricting*, 7.

28. Huma Khan, "Redistricting Trends Favor GOP: Why You Should Care" (*ABC News*, November 2, 2010); Paul M. Barrett, Martin Z. Braun, and Tim Jones, "Republicans Win a Big Redistricting Edge," *Bloomberg Businessweek* (November 3, 2010); Aaron Blake, "Why the GOP's Redistricting Advantage Is Overstated" (*The Washington Post*, December 23, 2010); Richard E. Cohen, "GOP Plays It Safe on Redistricting" (*Politico*, March 16, 2011); Chris Cillizza, "Beware Incumbents! (Again)" (*The Washington Post*, May 19, 2011).

29. Aaron Blake, "Redistricting Battles Hit a Fever Pitch" (*The Washington Post*, June 3, 2011); Aaron Blake, "GOP Will Draw Map in Texas, But Gaining Seats Difficult" (*The Washington Post*, November 18, 2010); Aaron Blake, "The GOP's Big Texas Gerrymander" (*The Washington Post*, June 2, 2011).

30. Blake, "Redistricting Battles Hit a Fever Pitch"; Aaron Blake, "'Fairness' in Florida and How It Could Help Democrats" (*The Washington Post*, February 17, 2011); Wire Service, "U.S. Justice Department Clears Florida Redistricting Amendments" (*St. Petersburg Times*, May 31, 2011).

31. Aaron Blake, "Lots at Stake for GOP in Pennsylvania Redistricting" (*The Washington Post*, February 7, 2011); Aaron Blake, "Members Likely to Be Pitted Against Each Other With Ohio Losing Two Seats" (*The Washington Post*, January 5, 2011); Aaron Blake, "Michigan Map Highlights GOP Redistricting Challenges" (*The Washington Post*, June 20, 2011).

32. Aaron Blake, "North Carolina: The GOP's Golden Goose of Redistricting" (*The Washington Post*, March 3, 2011); "Non-Partisan Redistricting Bill Passes House" (*Charlotte Observer*, June 9, 2011); Aaron Blake, "Georgia Democrats Barrow and Bishop Confront an Uncertain Redistricting Fate" (*The Washington Post*, December 7, 2010).

33. Aaron Blake, "Illinois: Democrats' Lone Redistricting Prize Is a Big One" (*The Washington Post*, December 17, 2010).

34. Aaron Blake, "Illinois Redistricting Plan: DeLay Lite?" (*The Washington Post*, May 31, 2011).

35. Nate Silver, "Weiner's Seat Could be Scrambled in Redistricting" (*The New York Times*, June 8, 2011); Aaron Blake, "Hochul's Win Throws a Major Wrench Into New York Redistricting" (*The Washington Post*, May 25, 2011); David B. Caruso, "Anthony Weiner Resigns: Special Election, Redistricting Will Decide New York House Seat" (*The Huffington Post*, June 17, 2011).

36. Altman and McDonald, "The Promise and Perils of Computers in Redistricting," 70.

37. See Kimball Brace, Doug Chapin, and Wayne Arden, "Whose Data Is It Anyway? Conflicts Between Freedom of Information and Trade Secret Protection in Legislative Redistricting" (*Stetson Law Review,* Vol. 21, 1991–1992), 723, 727; Micah Altman and Michael P. McDonald, "The Dawn of Do-It-Yourself Redistricting?" (*Campaigns & Elections,* Vol. 32, 2011), 38, 42; Michael P. McDonald, "The 2010 Midterm Elections: Signs and Portents for the Decennial Redistricting" (*PS,* 2011), 314–315; Gregory Korte, "Software Opens Up Redistricting" (*USA Today,* March 21, 2011).

38. "U.S. Population Projections 2000–2050" (*Pew Hispanic Center,* Summary, February 11, 2008).

CHAPTER 12

Women and Campaigns—Growing Female Activism From the Grass Roots to the Top

Susan A. MacManus with the assistance of Renee Dabbs and Mary L. Moss

WHAT DO DEMOCRATS HILLARY CLINTON and Nancy Pelosi have in common with Republicans Sarah Palin and Michele Bachmann? They have all ascended to very powerful positions in the world of national politics, making them role models for aspiring female candidates running for national, state, and local offices. Each of these pathbreaking women has benefitted from the growing political activism of like-minded females—voters, grassroots-level party activists, campaign strategists and managers, and media consultants and media professionals. But because of their gender, each has been subjected to what, at times, appears to be an overemphasis on style rather than substance, much to their chagrin.

The imbalance is escalating, driven in large part by the increasingly visual nature of campaign coverage.[1] While campaign techniques have evolved and more women have ascended to key positions in campaigns, the disproportionate emphasis on "style" persists. A well-known former congressman from Texas, Democrat Martin Frost, recently acknowledged this in a column posted on a highly trafficked political website: "You can tell how a female politician is faring by looking at the photographs of her in print media like *The New York Times*, *POLITICO*, *The Hill*, *Roll Call*, and *The Washington Post*. When things are going well, the photos accompanying stories are flattering. When things start to go south for a politician, so do the photos."[2] (He admitted this was not always true for male candidates.) The sometimes visceral visual portrayal of women candidates is not limited to newspapers or television. It reaches deeply into the rapidly expanding world of social media retrievable online and via mobile devices such as smartphones and tablets.

Discussions of the substance-versus-style battle and its impact on campaigns are a major theme of this chapter. Here, we also discuss the growing presence of female professionals in campaigns—as managers, strategists, pollsters, and consultants—and in the media covering campaigns. We detail the increased diversity of female voters, the more sophisticated microtargeting of them via multiple media, and new get-out-the-female-vote (GOTFV) techniques. The chapter concludes with a look ahead to the role that gender is likely to play in future election campaigns.

Perennial Questions Concerning Female Candidates

Every election cycle, the same overriding question emerges: "Will *this* be the 'Year of the Woman, Again?'" In 1992, a record number of women were elected to the U.S. Congress, prompting that election cycle to be labeled "The Year of the Woman." This explains why every election year since, the question as to whether it will be another record year for women has been raised. Considerable media attention then gravitates to perennial questions:

- Will we ever have a female president?
- Will women continue to turn out to vote in higher proportions than men?
- How cohesive is "the women's vote"?
- How big will the gender gap be this year?
- Can female candidates raise as much money and get as many major media and celebrity endorsements as men?
- Do negative ads work as well for female candidates as for their male counterparts?
- Is there bias in the way the media describe female candidates?

The answers to these questions may vary depending on the specific electoral contest, but no campaign can ignore the role of gender. Nor can political parties, interest groups, or the news media. Knowing how to reach and mobilize women voters with an effective message is critical to a candidate's success.

The heightened role of visuals has increased attention on the physical appearance as well as the nonverbal behavior of women on the campaign trail—whether as candidates, surrogates and spouses, party or interest group spokespersons, or media (anchors, reporters, columnists, program hosts). The fact that style often trumps substance is well known. In the words of one analyst, "Women in politics have it rough. Not only is it a merciless, dog-eat-dog, male-dominated field, but they also have to be incredibly meticulous with their appearance, much more so than their male counterparts, lest they look weak, inexperienced, or unprofessional."[3]

For many women, this overemphasis on appearance is a step backward—one that tends to reinforce gender stereotypes. But for those heavily involved in campaigns, the "emphasis on the visual" is simply a reality of the technological times that we live in. Campaigns must have proactive and reactive strategies in place when it comes to women now that videos and visuals have become a more prominent feature (and concern) of campaigns. For example, in 2008, Tina Fey's wildly popular weekly *Saturday Night Live* portrayal of Sarah Palin as "ditzy" ultimately forced Palin to agree to appear side-by-side with Fey in an attempt to minimize the damage. Similarly, a YouTube video that made fun of Hillary Clinton's tears as she responded to a question of how she kept going on the campaign trail in light of all the criticisms against her prompted Clinton's campaign to quickly get Clinton on the national airwaves and YouTube explaining her emotional response to the question. Female support for her actually increased as more women saw Clinton's tears as a sign of her compassion rather than as a weakness. Knowing how to reach women voters allowed the campaign to turn bad coverage into good.

The Growing Presence of Women in Campaigns

More women are taking the controls of national campaigns and playing prominent roles as consultants. Several Democratic presidential candidates have had female campaign managers (Michael Dukakis—Susan Estrich, 1988; Al Gore—Donna Brazile, 2000; John Kerry—Mary Beth Cahill, 2004; Hillary Clinton—Patti Solis Doyle, then Maggie Williams, 2008). On the Republican side, Jen O'Malley Dillon served as George W. Bush's communications director in his 2004 reelection bid, while Carly Fiorina served as John McCain's campaign economic adviser in 2008. The need to have "female faces in high places" in a campaign became abundantly clear to Democrat Barack Obama who took a lot of heat for the absence of women at the top levels of his 2008 campaign. He selected two women as deputy campaign managers for his 2012 reelection campaign.

Women as Campaign Consultants

Virtually every major campaign now has managers, strategists, pollsters, and consultants on board to ensure that female voters are targeted and mobilized. Many of these campaign professionals are women talented at reaching other women. For example, each major political party uses female pollsters skilled at capturing the opinions of likely women voters (Kellyanne Conway for the Republicans; Celinda Lake for the Democrats).

The larger the campaign, the more diverse the female staff is likely to be, particularly in its age, racial/ethnic, and religious composition. Why? Because age, race, and religion often affect what issues are deemed by a voter to be of the highest priority. Age is also an important predictor of what type of media a female voter is most likely to access to get information about a particular candidate or issue.[4] Obviously, younger staffers are more alert to the use (and abuse) of social media than some older staffers, although that gap has narrowed considerably.

Female Candidacies on the Rise

Female candidacies at all levels—federal, state, and local—are on the rise, even though female candidacy rates still lag behind male candidacy rates.[5] There are increasingly more contests with women running against women. The number of women in elected office at all levels has increased over the past decade.[6] Savvy political party leaders and politically oriented special interest groups now actively recruit women to run, especially in open districts with no incumbent in the race. They often conduct campaign schools designed just for female candidates. There are even political interest groups that specialize in fundraising for female candidates (EMILY's List for Democrats; the WISH List for Republicans).

At the same time, more women are deciding to run on their own. A bad economy, a strong anti-incumbent mood, and citizen perceptions of widespread corruption/collusion in both the public and private sectors have prompted more women to jump into the political ring. There is some research suggesting that such circumstances allow women to run as outsiders or reformers and to capitalize on their positive gender stereotypes—of being "more honest, more compassionate and better on issues involving families and children."[7] There has also been an upswing in the number of female corporate chief executive officers (CEOs) who have run for office based on the belief that women have more credibility on fiscal issues since women control the purse strings in many households. Prominent examples in 2010 were California Republicans Meg Whitman, former CEO of eBay, and Carly Fiorina, former CEO of Hewlett-Packard, who ran for governor and U.S. Senate, respectively. The same year, Democrat Alex Sink, former president of Bank of America in Florida, ran for governor in Florida.

Women and Media Presence

Women are omnipresent in the media that cover campaigns as well—as anchors, reporters, political pundits, commentators, columnists, and bloggers. Virtually every broadcast and cable television network has female political analysts, as do radio talk shows (liberal and conservative), newspapers, newsmagazines, and online political sites. Women with high profiles are often given important political party or interest group leadership posts specifically to ensure they appear as guests on all types of news-oriented programming, including half-hour newsmagazine shows on broadcast and cable television and radio. In 2011, Democrats chose media-savvy

Congresswoman Debbie Wasserman Schultz of Florida as chair of the Democratic National Committee. A frequent guest on national news programs, Wasserman Schultz will get plenty of airtime in 2012 as she presides over the Democratic National Convention in Charlotte, North Carolina. Miami's Cuba–born Republican congresswoman Ileana Ros-Lehtinen, tapped by Republican leadership in the House as chair of the House Committee on Foreign Affairs, will have a major presence in media coverage of the 2012 Republican National Convention in Tampa, Florida.

As part of their media strategy, campaigns also promote appearances of female candidates, party leaders, surrogates with celebrity status (whether spouses,[8] family, friends, or Hollywood) on *non-news* programs. Popular daytime female-oriented shows (*The View, The Ellen DeGeneres Show,* Katie Couric) attract large female audiences. So do late-night entertainment/comedy shows (Leno, Letterman, Colbert, Stewart), albeit a younger female audience. Woman-to-woman campaigning— whether on television or in person—is generally seen as more effective in turning out female voters *if* the two are somewhat like-minded on issues.[9] It is important to remember that women are *not* monolithic politically or socioeconomically. Also, some women are much more critical of other women than are men, especially with regard to physical appearance. (Some refer to this as the "mean girl" phenomenon.) And some women do not like to be supervised by other women, especially if the female supervisor is perceived to be a "queen bee."[10] The latter situations can be challenging in putting together a smoothly operating campaign team.

Female Voters: Not a Solid Bloc of Like-Minded Voters

The truth is that women have never been a solid bloc of like-minded voters. When a female candidate enters a race naively believing she can win "the women's vote," her political consultants must remind her "that women can be deeply suspicious and critical of one another,"[11] often stemming from ideological/partisan divides. Nothing better reflects this than the debate between conservative and liberal women over the meaning of the term *feminist* as it applied to Sarah Palin in 2008.

Regardless of party affiliation, regional location, or incumbent status, the question remains: "In a media-dominated world, is it really harder for female than male candidates?" Some say no and argue that both genders are under the same bright lights and are equally subject to attack based on their issue stances or personal behavior. Others say yes, female candidates do have a tougher time. They point to differences in labels used to describe similar positions or behavior by male and female candidates. The labels are generally far more pejorative and damaging to women. An example of such a difference in word choice is seen in the description of past extramarital relationships: *slut* (female) versus *stud* (male).[12] It is hard to combat language that reinforces sexist stereotypes.

The "Brains Versus Beauty" Battle: Substance Versus Style

Female candidates desperately want media and voter attention to be focused on their issue stances and qualifications rather than their looks. Yet new technologies like high-quality cell phone and handheld video cameras have made it more difficult for women. Why? Because it is easier to catch a shot of a female candidate (or surrogate) looking "less than her best"—and to quickly project that unflattering image to a large audience of attentive voters. For some female candidates, particularly those with more traditional lifestyles and thicker accents, the potential for these instantaneously projected image-damaging pictures can be rather worrisome and intimidating—and rightfully so. There is widespread agreement that "cultural stereotypes, media framing, and public perceptions are among the factors female candidates must confront when running for public office."[13] The media's past fixation on physical appearances and marital status is described by Georgia Duerst-Lahti as women candidates' "hair, husband, and hemline" problems.[14] Television and online videos make it easy to prompt the voter to focus on all three.

Women Judged Differently Than Men

Television remains a major source of political information for a majority of Americans. It is a powerful medium because it projects visual images of a woman's physical attributes and mannerisms and meshes them with audio. So do online videos. Both types of media are particularly challenging for women: "It's tough for women to come across as strong as men. Their voices are higher pitched, their features are softer, their mannerisms are not firm; and if they are, people are turned off because it's not feminine."[15] Yet, voters pay closer attention to the physical attributes and mannerisms of female candidates than to those of their male counterparts, particularly when viewing television/video campaign ads.

Having a female candidate as a client makes the job of the political consultant considerably more challenging—and risky. It is not easy to tell a woman candidate that she needs a major makeover. But it is especially difficult when the political consultant is a man—and most consultants are men, although the number of female-headed image consulting firms is on the rise. The bottom line is that it is more difficult and time-consuming to develop effective video-based campaign ads for female candidates, primarily because physical images matter so much more than for male candidates. While the double standard is hard to swallow, its presence is all too real, as evidenced by the comments of the former congressman cited earlier in the chapter.

Physical Appearance

Some attribute the media's and the public's overemphasis on female candidates' appearance to sexism, while others attribute it to the fact that women are simply more fashionable than men—and have more choices affecting how they look. As one analyst puts it, "A man decides to run for office: He plans the substance of his campaign and then buys a few black or navy suits and some red and blue ties. A woman decides to run for office: She does the same, and then has to consider hair, makeup, jewelry and shoes, in addition to her wardrobe."[16]

Minimizing distractions and excessiveness is a challenging task, but one that is necessary to prompt voters to focus more on the message. "[Selecting] anything out of the ordinary will get commentary. That is, anything excessive: Anything excessively casual, excessively feminine, too much makeup, a hairstyle that seems excessive and out of the ordinary."[17]

Hairstyle and Color. "If you're running for something, you'd better have good hair,"[18] especially if you are a woman. Whether and how often to change one's hairstyle are both important decisions female candidates must make. The more you change your hairstyle, the more you make that part of a news story. The trick is to keep a consistent hairstyle that doesn't look out of date and is easy for the candidate to maintain without needing to have a personal hairstylist on the campaign trail with her. There is, however, no "one style fits all" hairstyle.

Older female candidates must make a decision about whether to color their hair. If they decide to do so, it must be maintained, which is expensive. Length of hair and use of bangs seem to be inversely related to age. Younger women can have longer hair; older women cannot. Hair that constantly must be pushed out of the face creates an extremely distracting mannerism.

Black female candidates have some other challenges with regard to hair. As noted by Regina Jere-Malanda, editor of *New African Woman* magazine, "Next to skin colour, hair is truly the other most visible stereotype of being a black woman. There is no other group of people in the world today who experience so much ado about their ever-evolving hairdos as we black women." In the late 1960s, the Afro or natural look ruled the day. But today, "the hairstyle that said 'I'm black and proud,' has almost disappeared, replaced by sleek fake-hair weaves and hair extensions or, worse still, hair straightened into submission through chemical cream."[19]

Fortunately, the cost of a hairstyling is not as much of an item for ridicule for female candidates as it is for males. (Witness John Edwards, who spent $400 on a hairstyling session.) But hairstyling is a recurring expense for women that must be built into campaign budgets in terms of both time and money.

Makeup. Understatement is the goal here. According to one image consultant: "Less is more. A woman should never look like she's wearing makeup, and anything that is outside the norm will welcome controversy that she must be prepared for."[20] The effect of too much makeup is to raise questions about the professionalism of the candidate among male and female voters alike. Such was the case with former Florida secretary of state Katherine Harris who was at the center of the 2000 presidential election recount between George W. Bush and Al Gore. She was once described as "the rigid, heavily made up woman reading statements on CNN [and as] a crazed floozy played by a Saturday Night Live actor."[21] She subsequently and successfully ran for Congress two years later, but had markedly tamped down her makeup.

Botox, Anyone? Long days on the campaign trail have a tendency to create weary eyes and tired faces. Botox can quickly rejuvenate areas around the eyes, cheeks, and jawline. As one plastic surgeon has put it, "In a day and age when lunch hour liposuction is a reality, politicians are turning to the knife or the need for the quick fix to the age old problem of well, age."[22] But it can also generate *more* attention on appearance and age as the "does she or doesn't she?" question gets raised by the media.

Clothes. The importance of clothes cannot be underestimated. For women in power, finding balance in the wardrobe is difficult but imperative. A *Wall Street Journal* article points out the dilemma: "The attention brought to clothing is a two-edged sword for authoritative women everywhere. A style misstep can be career-limiting. Yet paying too much attention to one's appearance risks accusations of frivolity—which is equally career-limiting."[23]

For years, a debate as to whether female candidates should look feminine or masculine has raged in the academic literature on women in politics.[24] The debate has calmed down a bit now that more women are in elected office. Whether one chooses a conservative-looking dress, suit, or pantsuit, one can still look feminine with the choice of color and accessories. When choosing color, it is critical to consider hair color and skin tone. The rule seems to be that the older the woman, the more conservative the cut/lines of the clothing should be, but not necessarily the color. Hillary Clinton's choice of a bright orange pantsuit in her speech to the Democratic National Convention in 2008 endeared her to many older women, because of its boldness and its femininity.

Clothing that fits well, holds up well, and looks nice is expensive. In the past, it was women's clothing costs that seemed to garner the most negative media attention (for example, Pelosi and Palin). The old saying was that "the media won't notice a man's $5,000 suit,"[25] but will criticize the price tag for a woman's suit or dress if it seems excessive. That has changed somewhat as more extremely wealthy men have thrown their hats into the political ring, giving rise to more stories about male clothing and grooming costs, although still not many.

Necklines and Hemlines. How low is too low? How short is too short? The media had a heyday with their coverage of Hillary Clinton and Sarah Palin. With Clinton, it was her wearing of a shell that showed a little cleavage. With Palin, it was her dress length and high heel shoes that prompted crude photos featuring her legs. In each instance, the coverage distracted from the campaign messages.

The 2008 campaign left many Clinton and Palin supporters feeling disappointed with the outcome, but even angrier with the media coverage of female candidates, which they perceived to be biased and sexist—retrogressive, not progressive. The "tabloid-like" treatment of these accomplished candidates infuriated women. In many instances, it made women more determined to go vote; for others, it prompted them to stay home. In a postelection poll of women (voters and nonvoters), 65 percent of the women surveyed—majorities in *every* demographic and political group—said that women candidates are held to different standards on the campaign trail.[26]

Accessories: Jewelry (Earrings, Necklaces, Pins, Bracelets, Rings, Watches), Hats, Belts, Purses, Shoes. Campaign image consultants consider accessory selection as part of a candidate's overall image. Some women like to make political statements with their jewelry selection (former secretary of state Madeleine Albright, with her fashion pins, is an example); men do, too, with their lapel pins (for men, the absence of an American flag lapel pin can be an unwelcome newsmaker, as candidate Obama learned firsthand in the 2008 campaign). The key for candidates of both genders is to select jewelry that reflects who they are. Clearly, women wear more accessories than men. *Complementary,* not *dominant,* should be the operative word here. *Dangling, jingling, glittering, dazzling, dizzying,* and *oversized* are not optimal adjectives for accessories of any type.

Accessory fashions differ by age, region, and race/ethnicity. For example, older women tend to feel more at ease wearing a strand of pearls or a gold necklace; younger women prefer pendants. Belt buckles the size of Texas may work well in the Lone Star State but not elsewhere. Expensive designer handbags are likely to catch less attention in metropolitan settings than in poorer, more rural areas. Minority women (African Americans in particular) often prefer more culturally linked necklaces or stylish hats that become their trademarks. Former Florida Democratic state senator. Frederica Wilson, now Congresswoman Wilson, is known for her "flamboyant, glittering hats and coordinating skirt suits."[27] Latina candidates, especially younger ones, tend to wear brighter lipstick.

Eyewear: Contacts or Glasses? If voters are used to seeing a candidate wear glasses, switching to contacts when filming an ad can be similar to changing a hairstyle. People notice. Voters are more inclined to anticipate that older women will wear glasses, but they do not expect it from younger candidates. When Palin debuted on the political stage at the Republican National Convention wearing a pair of $375 rimless titanium glasses created by a Japanese designer, Kazuo Kawasaki, she created a rush on those glasses, although, as one optician noted, they generally don't look as good on others as on Palin. Palin's decision to wear glasses instead of contacts resonated well with younger and middle-aged women who either choose to or must wear glasses.

Nonverbal Behavior: Personal Attributes and Mannerisms

Nonverbal behavior matters. Research has shown that it is often a more powerful voting cue than experience or issue stances. Several researchers have even linked facial expressions and party identification.[28] Snap judgments are often made not just on a candidate's physical appearance, but on height, voice (tone, speaking rate, pitch), name recognition, facial features, eye contact, gestures, and stance (posture). More and more campaigns are adding body language experts to their staffs, recognizing that nonverbal behavior plays an integral part in portraying important emotions (anger, compassion, passion, and optimism, to name a few) and leadership qualities (sincerity, confidence, inspiration, honesty). Many believe that "when reason and emotion collide, emotion invariably wins."[29]

Political consultants advising female (and male) candidates tend to pay closest attention to the nonverbal behaviors/attributes that seem idiosyncratic or excessive. However, opinions as to whether those thresholds have been reached often vary among campaign staff and political consultants. Among the behaviors most closely monitored are:

1. *Hand gestures.* Women tend to use their hands to "talk" more than men. Some gesturing is good, but excessive flailing of hands in videos is not optimal. Gestures need to underscore a message.
2. *Eye contact.* Direct contact with the camera and one's opponent or the moderator (in debates) is best.
3. *Facial expressions.* Women generally smile more than men. In certain circumstances that is good, but in others it is less so (for example, when a situation calls for anger or disgust).
4. *Tears.* While appropriate and expected more from women, tears always end up being the subject of negative news stories, particularly those written by male reporters. However, in certain circumstances, tears (if genuine) may be quite powerful—and positive.
5. *Laughs.* Women are advised to "make sure your laugh is a laugh" rather than a giggle or a "cackle." The latter can make a candidate fodder for disparaging "YouTube" videos and late-night comedy shows, as Hillary Clinton found out firsthand.
6. *Voice volume and pitch.* Women have a tendency to be more soft-spoken and less emphatic than men, although that seems to be less of a problem today than in the past.
7. *High-pitched voices,* more common among women, are not as desirable as deeper voices when it comes to audio sound. But little can be done to change that. One way around it is to "use anonymous announcers as the dominant speaker in their television spots."[30]

8. *Tone of voice/message.* Anything that can be perceived as "whining" is not good because it feeds into negative stereotypes about women. It also underscores the difficulty women face in finding the right balance between toughness and femininity. There has been considerable debate about whether it is easier for a woman than a man to run a negative ad. The general consensus is that it is, precisely because the "softness" of her voice tamps down the negativity somewhat.

The Most Personal Attributes? How Kisses, Hugs, and Handshakes Are Viewed

Kisses, hugs, and handshakes have great importance as well. At one time, the dominant question was whether women should extend their hand for a handshake first. Now, it is not simply whether to engage in a handshake but whether to hug and/or kiss running mates or opponents on the cheek. Geraldine Ferraro, vice presidential running mate of Democratic presidential candidate Walter Mondale, said that in 1984, anything beyond a handshake gave the appearance of intimacy that was damaging to both male and female candidates. As Ferraro noted, anything more, and "people were afraid that it would look like, 'oh my God, they're dating,'"[31] "Back then, Mr. Mondale had a strict 'hands off' policy and did not even put his palm on Ms. Ferraro's back when the two stood side-by-side and waved with uplifted arms."[32]

Today's debate has changed a bit, especially when it comes to interactions with persons of the opposite sex. At issue is "the hug." It was thrust to the forefront in 2008 when Republican presidential candidate John McCain publicly hugged vice presidential running mate Sarah Palin after her speech at the Republican National Convention. It raised the age-old question of the appropriateness of a male candidate hugging a female who is not his wife. But it is now an equally challenging decision for women candidates. When asked about handshakes and hugging, Jefferson County (Alabama) commissioner Shelia Smoot said: "It's funny, because I've been struggling with that issue myself—whether to do the traditional handshake, or when appropriate, a hug." But she had no idea of whether a female would be seen as less credible if she were a "hugger." [33]

Males hugging males seem to get little attention on the campaign trail, reflective of the double standard that infuriates women candidates. But there is another side to "man hugs" that is equally disconcerting. Their use of the *Sopranos*-style hug as a greeting is seen by some female candidates as exclusionary because it projects the image that the two males are in "the family" or "the club" and women are not.

Kissing opens up even more controversy. Across the board, the consensus is to leave the kissing for loved ones. The kiss is awkward and leaves much room for interpretation. No serious women candidate wants to be part of a dialogue about how her male counterpart's spouse would feel about the kiss. This was a huge story around the McCain–Palin relationship and continued to take away from the seriousness of the Palin candidacy.

Family as Props in Ads?

There is considerable debate as to whether women should feature their spouse and children in ads. Studies show they are more reticent to do so than men, primarily because they believe it makes them seem less able to focus on the office they are seeking. When a mother runs, voters of both genders often wonder, "'Who will care for the children while she campaigns?'—a question for Pauline but not Paul."[34] Some refer to this phenomenon as the "mommy penalty." Not surprisingly, social scientists have found that women candidates tend to distance themselves from their roles as wives and/or mothers by picturing their families in only 8 percent of their ads.[35] Men are twice as likely to do so. Women candidates are also quite aware that the media are more likely to hold them accountable for the actions of their husbands and children.

The growing number of single women (never married) and single-parent moms running for office has prompted debates over how to handle the issue of marital status in ads, especially in the more traditional conservative areas of the South. Stereotypes regarding sexual preference and behavior must be anticipated. Some political consultants have advised single women to smile, use gestures, and picture young children as a way to deflect these biases. The situation clearly reflects how women are cross-pressured by the need to "show personal warmth, preferably in a role of mother, daughter, sister, or wife" and the need to project toughness and competence.[36]

The irony here is that as campaigning and media have become more visual, it appears that more attention is being paid to a female candidate's "style" than to her issue positions. In fact, one could argue that the overemphasis on visuals has reached a point where it has become a deterrent to women running for office, just as have "the toxicity of the political environment today, the gridlock in Congress and state legislatures, and the invasion of privacy that inevitably accompanies a campaign."[37] The danger to both female and male candidates is if such nonparticipatory attitudes spill over into the female electorate.

Strategies to Get Out the Female Vote

For years, women have made up a larger share of the electorate and turned out at higher rates, especially in presidential elections (see Figure 12.1). Registering women and then getting them to vote are key goals of every campaign—from start

FIGURE 12.1 Voter Turnout in Presidential Election Years: A Gender Comparison

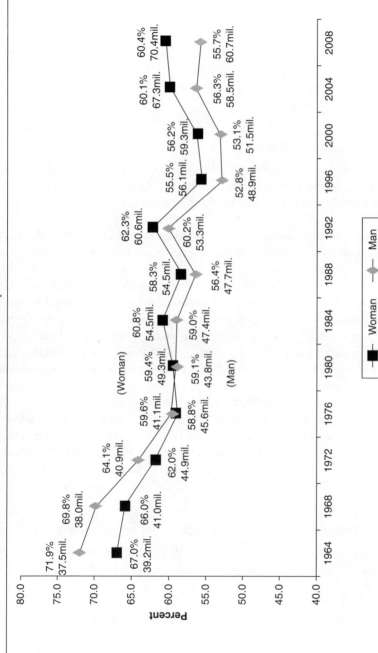

Source: Center for American Women and Politics (CAWP), Eagleton Institute of Politics, Rutgers University, "Fact Sheet: Gender Differences in Voter Turnout," November, 2009.

to finish. Some groups are harder to mobilize than others. For example, older women turn out at higher rates than younger women. Poorer and lesser-educated women turn out at lower rates than their more affluent, better-educated counterparts. And turnout rates among black women are higher than those of white, Hispanic, or Asian/Pacific Islander women. This means that a campaign's outreach strategies must be narrowly tailored (micro-targeted) to different groups of female voters, in recognition that women differ generationally, socioeconomically, culturally, and racially/ethnically.

Microtargeting on the Upswing

Microtargeting as a mobilization (GOTV) strategy began in the 2004 presidential campaign and has escalated with every subsequent election. It recognizes that using "one size fits all" tactics to energize women voters can result in a candidate's defeat. As Donna Brazile advises, "To pull more women into the voting process—and to win votes—the two major parties should drop any idea of a 'one size fits all' approach to women. Instead, they should target their messages to diverse groups of women."[38]

In today's campaigns, political parties and advocacy groups alike use a wide variety of GOTFV tools—everything from text messages, online social networks, recorded ("robo") phone calls from candidates and celebrities, and appearances by the candidates and high-profile surrogates to precisely targeted mail, radio spots, television (broadcast and cable), and online ads and videos on their websites and on sites like YouTube. Feedback and insights from focus groups and public opinion surveys (telephone and online) are used to craft the content, format, and placement of political ads to narrowly defined groups of potential female voters.

Targeted ads also play a key role in informing women about how to vote early in person or how to cast an absentee ballot. These forms of voting are often more convenient to single parents, the disabled, and women who work evenings or shifts. They can cast their ballot at a time and place that is more in sync with their schedules and needs.

Timing of Mobilization Efforts and Message Delivery Mode Are Tricky

The timing of mobilizing women voters is often tricky. Historically, women have been "late deciders"—in terms of both whom to vote for and the decision to actually go vote. For some women, especially older women, direct mail is still the best way to reach them. However, according to direct mail specialists, it has to happen between the time a person picks up a mailer and the time she reaches the first trashcan. It's more likely to happen if the recipient can immediately see something of herself and her sentiments in the piece. That means compelling pictures and a simple, straightforward message. The timing of when to send mail ads is getting trickier, with more states adopting early voting. Repetition is critical—but expensive.

For many women, especially younger and working women, mobilization via television and the Internet (especially social networking sites) is now considerably more effective than direct mail. Television and the Internet are increasingly converging, prompting some analysts to now characterize voter mobilization efforts as "YouTube/social network" campaigns. Women make up the majority of online users, and evidence is mounting that the woman-to-woman approach via social networking sites and blogs is quite effective. One recent Harvard University study concluded that "some of the most visible and creative users of social media in the political realm have been women."[39] For example, the author of *Mothers of Intention: How Women and Social Media Are Revolutionizing Politics in America* began her activism by creating a popular blog (PunditMom) aimed at progressive (liberal) mothers.[40] Social networking has been equally effective in mobilizing conservative women. Many stay-at-home mothers with young children used Twitter and other social networking platforms to connect conservative activists with the Tea Party movement and to spike turnout in the 2010 midterm elections.[41]

At the same time, the Harvard study found that social media can be a mixed blessing for female politicians and activists—again because the visuals elevate the importance and impact of females' physical appearance and nonverbal behavior. Political scientist Susan Carroll sees social media as "a mixed blessing for women" because "it lets people be more hostile, negative and vile. The normal social sanctions don't exist." She cautions that the vile factor "is worse on the blogosphere, more intense."[42] It is here that crude Photoshopped images of women activists and candidates often appear and take on a life of their own as they are shared with politically like-minded "friends." Combating such practices has been difficult with the proliferation of social networking sites.

Looking Ahead

Gender will continue to play a critical role in election campaigns in the future. However, there is not likely to ever be a cohesive "women's vote." Women will continue to differ by their age, racial/ethnic, socioeconomic, cultural, and political attributes. What may change is the degree to which beauty trumps brains. Today's YouTube-dominated elections, which tend to overemphasize the importance of females' looks, may not have the same powerful impact in future election cycles.

It will become increasingly more difficult to create a "viral video sensation." The impact of visuals on women may also be lessened as more women play active roles on the campaign trail and the novelty of a female candidate, consultant, or media star wears off. The proliferation of more politically homogeneous online communities may also help minimize the "style" factor and increase the focus on substance. Until then, appearance and nonverbal behavior will continue to matter more to the successes of female candidates than to male contenders. It makes the job of political consultants considerably more difficult, the need for more female voices among their ranks even more critical, and the effectiveness of microtargeting the female electorate markedly more essential.

Notes

1. We conducted in-depth telephone interviews of eleven political operatives and consultants (seven males; four females) in February and March 2010. These campaign professionals (general consultants, pollsters, media specialists, new media specialists, and direct mail experts) included both Republicans and Democrats. Some work on the national stage, others primarily in the South. Several specialize in working with minority and ethnic candidates.
2. Martin Frost, "The Politics of Photos" (*Politico,* July 17, 2011).
3. Anonymous, "Power Hair" (Television Tropes & Idioms). Accessed on February 27, 2010, from http://tvtropes.org/pmwiki/pmwiki.php/Main/PowerHair.
4. Aaron Smith, *The Internet and Campaign 2010* (March 17, 2011). Accessed on November 18, 2011, from http://www.pewinternet.org/Reports/2011/The-Internet-and-Campaign-2010.aspx.
5. Reasons for the lower candidacy rates are wide-ranging, and include a lack of confidence in their ability to be competitive with males in raising money, securing party help or endorsements, and winning; family responsibilities, especially young children at home; and fear of the media—intense scrutiny and negative stereotyping of female candidates. See Julie Anne Dolan, Melissa M. Deckman, and Michele L. Swers, *Women and Politics: Paths to Power and Political Influence,* 2nd ed. (New York: Longman, 2010); Jennifer L. Lawless and Richard L. Fox, *It Takes a Candidate: Why Women Don't Run for Office,* revised ed. (New York: Cambridge University Press, 2010).
6. Detailed historical statistics are available from the Center for American Women and Politics Fact Sheets posted at www.cawp.rutgers.edu?fast_Facts.
7. Nicholas J. G. Winter, "Race, Gender, and Politics: Dangerous Frames" (The [University of] Chicago Blog, March 17, 2008). Accessed February 27, 2010, from http://pressblog.uchicago.edu/2008/03/17/race_gender_politics_danger.html.
8. For an overview of the historical role of presidential wives on the campaign trail, see Susan A. MacManus and Andrew F. Quecan, "Spouses as Campaign Surrogates: Strategic Appearances by Presidential and Vice Presidential Candidates' Wives in the 2004 Election" (*PS: Political Science and Politics,* April 2008), 337–348.
9. Susan A. MacManus, "Voter Participation and Turnout: Female 'Star' Power Attracts Women Voters," in *Gender and Elections: Shaping the Future of American Politics,* edited by Susan J. Carroll and Richard L. Fox (Cambridge: Cambridge University Press, 2006), 43–73.

10. A Queen Bee is a woman in power who tries to preserve her power at all costs. Rather than helping other women advance, she feels threatened by them and ends up blocking their promotions.

11. Anne E. Kornblut, *Notes From the Cracked Ceiling: Hillary Clinton, Sarah Palin and What It Will Take for a Woman To Win* (New York: Crown Publishing Group/Random House, 2010).

12. In a quote from the movie *Definitely Maybe,* a young girl asks her father what the boy word is for *slut.* After giving it a brief moment of thought, he comments, "They still haven't come up with one yet."

13. Kristina K. Horn Sheeler, *Gender and Candidate Communication: VideoStyle, WebStyle, NewsStyle* (Review) (*Rhetoric & Public Affairs,* Vol. 8, No. 4, 2005), 701–704.

14. Georgia Duerst-Lahti, "Presidential Elections: Gendered Space and the case of 2004," in *Gender and Elections: Shaping the Future of American Politics,* Carroll and Fox 37.

15. Milena Thomas quoted by Monica O'Brien, "How to Become a Leader When You're a Woman" (December 5, 2009). Accessed on February 27, 2010, from http://blog .monicaobrien.com/category/lifestyle/women-lifestyle.

16. Theodora Blanchfield, "Superficial Significance: Tailoring the Perfect Female Candidate" (*Campaigns & Elections,* January 2007), 35.

17. Susan J. Carroll quoted in Blanchfield, "Superficial Significance," 35.

18. Giacomo Forbes, Austin, Texas, celebrity hairdresser, quoted by Helen Anders, "Governor Candidates Go Head to Head: What Will the Outcome Be?" (*Austin American-Statesman,* February 19, 2010).

19. All quotes are from Regina Jere-Malanda, "Black Women's Politically Correct Hair" (*New African Woman,* Summer 2009), 44. Accessed on November 19, 2011, from http:// www.exacteditions.com/exact/browse/432/961/6149/2/44.

20. Ginger Burr quoted in Blanchfield, "Superficial Significance," 35.

21. Adam C. Smith, "Harris Could Have Last Laugh" (*St. Petersburg Times,* June 2, 2002). Accessed on February 27, 2010, from http://www.sptimes.com/2002/06/02/State/ Harris_could_have_the.shtml.

22. Finesse Aesthetic & Plastic Surgery, "Plastic Politics: How Plastic Surgery Gives Politicians a Life." Accessed on May 26, 2011, from www.finesse-aesthetics.com/plastic-politics.html.

23. Christina Binkley, "Women in Power: Finding Balance in the Wardrobe" (*The Wall Street Journal,* January 24, 2008), D1.

24. Dianne G. Bystrom and Narren J. Brown, "Videostyle 2008: An Examination of 'Feminine' v. 'Masculine': Television Advertising Strategies," paper presented at the annual meeting of the National Communication Association, November 2009.

25. Political image consultant Maurice Bonamigo quoted in Blanchfield, "Superficial Significance," 35.

26. Telephone poll of 600 women conducted November 21–24, 2008, for Lifetime Network by Republican pollster Kellyanne Conway and Democratic pollster Celinda Lake; margin of error +/-4.4 percent.

27. Shannon Colavecchio, "Sen. Frederica Wilson: A Woman of Many Hats" (*St. Petersburg Times,* May 11, 2009).

28. Nicholas O. Rule and Nalini Ambady, "Democrats and Republicans Can Be Differentiated From Their Faces," PLoS ONE 5(1): e8733.doi:10.1371/journal.pone.0008733, 2010.

29. Westen in Enika Packard, "The Brain in the Voting Booth" (*American Psychological Association Monitor,* Vol. 39, No. 2, 2008). Accessed on March 1, 2010, from www.apa.org/monitor/feb08/brain.aspx.

30. Ibid.

31. Elisabeth Bumiller, "To Have (as a Running Mate) and to Hold (Politely)" (*The New York Times,* September 8, 2008).

32. Ibid.

33. Bill Meyer, "McCain's Hug of Palin Raises Eyebrows" (*Cleveland Plain Dealer,* September 28, 2008).

34. Swanee Hunt, "Women, Start Your Campaigns" (*The Boston Globe,* January 28, 2010). Accessed on February 27, 2010, from www.boston.com/bostonglobe/editorial_opinion/oped/articles/2010/01/28/women.

35. Bystrom and Brown, "Videostyle 2008," 2009. The study was based on an examination of television commercials run between 1990 and 2006.

36. Angie Drobnic Holan, "Review: Want to see a female president? Read Anne E. Kornblut's 'Notes From the Cracked Ceiling.'" *Tampa Bay Times,* February 21, 2010. Accessed on August 8, 2011 from www.tampabay.com/features/books/review-want-to-see-a-female-president-read-anne-e-kornbluts-notes-from-the/1074001.

37. Naureen Khan, "Galvanizing Women Candidates" (*National Journal,* March 31, 2011).

38. "Energize the Women's Vote in 2004" (Women's eNews, July 3, 2004).

39. Alexis Gelber, "Digital Divas: Women, Politics, and the Social Network". Harvard University John F. Kennedy School of Government, Joan Shorenstein Center on the Press, Politics, and Public Policy Discussion Paper Series, #D-63, June 2011.

40. Joanne Bamberger, ed. *Mothers of Intention: How Women and Social Media are Revolutionizing Politics in America* (Houston, TX: Bright Sky Press, 2011).

41. Gelber, "Digital Divas," 2.

42. Susan Carroll, quoted in Gelber, "Digital Divas," 27.

CHAPTER 13

Minority Candidates and the Changing Landscape of Campaigns in the Twenty-First Century

Atiya Kai Stokes-Brown

THE INCREASING POPULATION of racial and ethnic minorities, particularly Latinos and Asian Americans, is transforming America's political landscape. Furthermore, the election of Barack Obama to the presidency highlights how candidates of color are gaining increased access to positions of political power, ascending to the highest levels of political leadership. The success of these candidates today has been attributed to the manner in which these candidates run their campaigns, adopting successful employing electoral strategies designed to encourage greater support among white voters while maintaining electoral backing in minority communities—especially in the second decade of the twenty-first century. In addition to using traditional communication methods such as television and radio advertisements and more traditional elements of outreach and fieldwork (e.g., targeted mobilization, direct mailing, door knocking, phone banking, get-out-the-vote activities), these candidates have also adopted a new style of political campaigning that takes advantage of the latest technologies. In this chapter, we will explore the various ways in which minority candidates are using these technologies to influence elections. Following a brief discussion of the role of race and ethnicity in elections, we focus on the transformative character of campaign experiences for minorities and what implications they have for the future.

Minority Campaigns and Candidate Behavior

While candidates of color in general are severely underrepresented in U.S. politics, their numbers have been increasing in recent years. The most recent data available show that African Americans hold more than 9,000 elected offices.[1] Latinos hold

5,739 elected offices nationwide, a 53 percent increase in the total number of Latinos serving in elected office since 1996.[2] Asian Americans hold over 2,000 elected offices in national, state, and local governments, in addition to a number of appointed officials and judges.[3] The rising number of racial and ethnic minorities serving in elected office is largely a result of the creation of majority-minority districts where these groups (together or singularly) make up a majority of the population in the district. These districts have played a central role in creating opportunities for African American candidates and, to a lesser extent, Latino candidates.[4]

Many African Americans and Latinos serving in Congress today represent these types of districts. For example, Democrat Terri Sewell, the first African American woman to represent Alabama in Congress, ran for and won the state's seventh congressional district—a majority African American (62 percent) district in 2010. The seat had been held previously by Representatives Artur Davis (2003–2011) and Earl Hilliard (1993–2003). Elected to a newly created district as a result of the 2000 Census, Democrat Raúl Grijalva won the 2002 election in Arizona's seventh congressional district. Situated in the southwestern part of the state, Latinos make up 51 percent of the district's population. This is in stark contrast to the electoral realities of Asian American elected officials who have mostly emerged from districts where Asians do not constitute a majority of the population and are therefore "most likely among all minority groups to be elected by another racial group."[5] This was the case for Democrat Judy May Chu, who won a special election held in 2009 in California's thirty-second congressional district to replace Hilda Solis. Solis vacated the seat to become U.S. secretary of labor. Chu won the election in the majority Latino (62 percent) district, becoming the first Chinese American woman to be elected to Congress.

With the future of majority-minority districts in question, a growing number of African American and Latino candidates have in recent years run for office and won outside of these districts. Elected in 2010 to Washington State's third congressional district seat, Republican Jaime Herrera Beutler won in a majority white district (88 percent) where Latinos make up approximately 5 percent of the population. Democrat Emanuel Cleaver, elected in 2004 with 55 percent of the vote, won in Missouri's majority white (69 percent) fifth congressional district where African Americans make up 24 percent of the district's population.

The success of these candidates and others like them has been attributed to candidates' use of electoral strategies designed to build a successful electoral coalition. As part of a strategy designed to attract white moderate voters, deracializing candidates project a nonthreatening image, avoid employing direct racial appeals, and avoid emphasizing a racially specific issue agenda.[6] An alternative perspective to deracialization suggests that multiple strategies can be coupled in an election to build a successful electoral coalition. Noting the fluidity of a campaign and the elasticity of campaign strategies, this alternative perspective suggests that minority candidates can adopt a "mainstream" strategy to appeal to white voters, showing that they are not "merely" representatives of their group and that they can speak for a broad coalition of interests, but simultaneously make appeals to minority constituencies through political surrogates and tailored messages in racial and ethnic media.[7]

Campaign Activities of Minority Candidates

Minority campaigns adopt tactics to mitigate the electoral disadvantage often attributed to the racial conservatism of some white voters and to mobilize enthusiasm and support in minority communities. In an effort to secure political office, minority campaigns rely on a wide range of tactics. Most rely primarily on traditional campaign methods and communication strategies that include television, radio, and print and mobilization tools including get-out-the-vote drives and phone banking. But like their white counterparts, minority candidates are also using such new technologies such as Facebook, Myspace, and Twitter to make targeted contacts with individual voters and rally supporters, and cutting-edge fundraising techniques to pursue their electoral goals.

Traditional Media

Communication is a key component of any political campaign. Candidates rely heavily on paid mass media advertising to communicate their message to voters for several reasons. Television is quite popular, and television viewing remains high, as the average American watches approximately 153 hours of television every month.[8] Candidates are also likely to use this medium (in addition to radio) because it attracts a good deal of media attention and can help drive the media narrative.[9] Finally, it is worth noting that despite the rise of the digital era, not everyone is on the Internet. Older voters in particular, who are more likely to vote than younger voters, may be less familiar with technology and rely on television for political information.[10] Like their white counterparts, minority candidates take a more conventional approach to mass media, spending a significant portion of their funds on television and (to a lesser extent) radio advertising. According to the Campaign Media Analysis Group, spending for federal candidates in 2010 surpassed $200 million while state candidates purchased more than $380 million in ads.[11] In Florida's competitive twenty-second congressional district race between incumbent Democrat Ron Klein and his Republican challenger, Allen West, West allocated $3,066,000 (approximately 50 percent of his budget) for television ads.[12] West went on to win the election, becoming the first African American Republican congressman from Florida since Reconstruction. Oregon Republican Jaime Herrera Beutler invested $869,480 (approximately 59 percent of her budget) in broadcast television.[13] Upon defeating Democrat Denny Heck for the seat vacated by retiring Democratic representative. Brian Baird, Herrera Beutler became the first Latino to represent the state in Congress.

The Internet

In recent years, the Internet has become a more central part of the campaign environment. Voters are embracing the Internet to engage in political decision making, and candidates are using the Internet as a more efficient means of communicating. The Internet also helps candidates establish online communities of supporters, which ultimately enhances their grassroots campaign. The most prominent example of the role that new media can play in elections is that of then-candidate Barack Obama, who in 2008 became the first African American president of the United States. Obama's success in the 2008 presidential election has been linked to his use of information technology, including personal websites, Facebook, Myspace, Twitter, and YouTube, to connect with followers and organize the campaign.

Campaign Websites

Campaign websites have become more common each election cycle as candidates realize their potential for giving them an almost unlimited ability to introduce themselves and their issue positions to voters. Controlling both the content of the site and how users interact with it, candidates use websites to provide information on as many issues and in as much detail as they choose. As a result, almost all candidates, regardless of level of office, have personal websites where voters can find information about the candidate. Obama had approximately sixteen different websites where voters could access information. The main website, my.barack-obama.com, contained videos, speeches, photos, and how-to guides that gave people the materials they needed to create their sites in support of Obama. It proved to be extremely successful, helping the candidate "attract 3,306 grassroots volunteer groups, 4,416 personal fundraising pages, 6,706 personal blogs, and 38,799 people with individual profiles building networks to support Obama."[14]

Social Networks

Unlike websites, social networks connect people in online communities, and the sites allow users to contribute to content and to initiate contact with other users. Facebook is the largest online social network with over 200 million active users, surpassing other online social networks such as Myspace and Friendster. The site is especially popular among younger generations, college students, and racial and ethnic minorities, who are spending more time on social media sites. Facebook allows candidates to set up pages where they can post information about themselves, photos, and information about upcoming and past events, and has a section for people to donate to the campaign and/or volunteer. It also allows others to form groups in support of candidates. The Obama campaign encouraged supporters to build their own sites, and more than 900,000 people joined the "One Million Strong for Obama" group on Facebook. Supporters on numerous college campuses also created Facebook groups for the candidate. Even before he announced his candidacy for president, the group "Barack Obama for President in 2008" had accumulated over 50,000 members, and the group "One Million Strong for Barack" gathered 200,000 members in less than three weeks.[15]

In 2010, Hansen Clarke used his Facebook page to connect with voters in Michigan's thirteenth congressional district to defeat seven-term incumbent Carolyn Cheeks Kilpatrick in the Democratic primary. Clarke went on to defeat Republican John Hauler, becoming the first Bangladeshi American elected to Congress. The rise of Twitter has also altered the media landscape. Twitter is a microblogging website where users can send and receive short messages called tweets on a variety of topics from the people they follow. On the web, Obama's Twitter site had more than 100,000 followers, who received updates from Obama's town hall meetings and links to his website. Obama's number of followers has since increased to more than 10 million. In the 2010 Florida Senate race, Republican Marco Rubio encouraged supporters to follow him on Twitter to join in on conversations about "Florida's future and to stand with him for less government and lower taxes."[16] Rubio went on to win the election with 49 percent of the vote against Democrat Kendrick Meek and Independent Charlie Crist.

Minority candidates' campaigns also benefit from the popularity of social media sites like YouTube, a site where users are able to share, upload, and watch videos on the Internet by uploading or downloading video clips to and from websites, mobile devices, blogs, and e-mail. As one of the fastest-growing websites on the Internet, candidates use this tool to communicate with young people in particular, who make up the vast majority of users.[17] YouTube enables candidates to reach segments of the population with minimal costs and attract mainstream media attention. During the 2008 campaign, 14.5 million hours of campaign-related videos were watched on YouTube, and by all accounts, the Obama campaign took advantage of YouTube for free advertising.[18] YouTube was particularly useful for Allen West, whom we discussed earlier. West ran for Florida's twenty-second congressional district seat in 2008 and lost against Democrat Ron Klein by ten percentage points. His success against Klein in 2010 has been attributed in some part to a YouTube video of him delivering what amounted to a conservative call to arms before a Florida Tea Party audience. Viewed more than 2 million times, the video became an Internet sensation helping him secure the backing of high-profile anti-establishment conservatives including former Alaska governor. Sarah Palin.[19]

Online videos from former soldiers praising West's leadership were also attributed to helping him circumvent allegations of misconduct during his time of service in the military when he was stationed in Iraq.[20]

Political Blogs

Minority candidates also use political blogs to inspire supporters through open discussion and inspire them to get engaged in the campaign. Some blogs tend to be somewhat controlled by the campaign whereas others give visitors to the blog unrestricted access to post comments. In addition to creating and maintaining blogs, campaigns also coordinate with grassroots supporters who have created their own blogs. For example, in 2008 Democratic candidate Kesha Ram reached out to graphic designer Pat Floyd to post on his blog information about her campaign, including posters, logo designs, stickers, and other deliverables.[21] Ram went on to win the Vermont state legislative election, becoming the youngest member of the Vermont House of Representatives, and its only person of color. Official candidate blogs, in addition to other forms of media, also help candidates keep supporters updated about the campaign in real time. In the 2010 Nevada gubernatorial race between Democrat Rory Reid and Republican Brian Sandoval, Sandoval, who won the election, featured a blog on his campaign website that offered a campaign diary and information about events—but did not offer supporters the opportunity to share their views.

Finally, in an effort to mobilize communities of color, social media can also be used by minority candidates for targeted mobilization. Despite the breakdown of formal barriers to participation, racial/ethnic gaps in voting still persist with whites voting at a higher rate than racial and ethnic minorities. High minority voting has been shown to be crucial for candidates of color. Alienating African American voters is often cited as one of the reasons why Democrat Tom Bradley lost the 1982 California gubernatorial election. Some argue that his "color-blind" campaign style, designed to "lower the ethnic relevance of his candidacy for governor," led to relatively lower levels of racial bloc voting and failed to stimulate African American turnout.[22] Andrew Young and Carl McCall, gubernatorial candidates in Georgia and New York, respectively, also lost in part because they alienated and ignored African American voters.[23]

Mindful of this, the Obama campaign chose to create profiles on influential social networks for racial and ethnic communities like AsianAve.com, MiGente.com, and BlackPlanet.com. By participating on these networks, the campaign was able to blog about important issues of concern to those communities and could send carefully honed messages to a specific community.[24] Similarly, in his campaign to become the first Vietnamese American member of the California State Assembly in 2004, Van Tran distributed press releases to Vietnamese radio, print, and online media focused on mobilizing by discussion of issues relevant to Vietnam and the power of ethnic unity.[25] Information released to white, mainstream media made no mention of these issues.

E-mail and Texting

E-mailing and texting have also become part of most political campaigns. E-mails are relatively cheaper to circulate, are easier to initiate, and can reach people faster than traditional mail. Candidates often use e-mail to inform supporters about upcoming events, solicit donations, organize volunteers, publicize press releases, and mobilize their get-out-the-vote efforts. In addition to email, minority candidates rely on additional new approaches such as robocalls and text messaging.

In 2008, Anh "Joseph" Quang Cao, running against incumbent William Jefferson in Louisiana's second congressional district, authorized his campaign to launch a surprise, last-minute offensive with automated phone calls urging voters to pull the lever for Cao.[26] He went on to defeat Jefferson, becoming the first Vietnamese American elected to Congress.[27] Former Alaska governor Sarah Palin recorded robocalls urging Republicans in South Carolina to vote for Nikki Haley in the state's GOP gubernatorial primary.[28] Haley eventually won the election, becoming the first woman to serve as governor in the state and the second Indian American to serve as governor in the country. Minority candidates have also become savvy about using mobile devices to communicate with potential supporters. Text messaging is a relatively cheap and effective tool that offers an opportunity to reach supporters directly at any place and time. Over the course of the presidential campaign, the Obama campaign collected hundreds of thousands, if not millions, of cell phone numbers from people and used those numbers to send out text messages reminding people to register to vote, to go to the polls, and to organize others on behalf of the campaign. Obama also used text messaging to make major campaign announcements, such as his choice of Senator Joe Biden as his running mate.

Fundraising

In addition to communications, the Internet has been used most powerfully by candidates to facilitate fundraising. The Internet has, in many ways, reinvented campaign fundraising, shifting it from a few big donors to countless small donors. Obama's website, my.barackobama.com, helped him set records in terms of donations. In the first month of the nomination contest, Obama raised $32 million, $27 million of which came from online supporters who gave less than $50.[29] Deval Patrick also successfully leveraged online marketing tools to bring in more donations to his campaign. His Internet donations made up about 15 percent of the

$1.6 million Patrick raised from donors.[30] During the 2010 U.S. Senate race in Arizona, Democratic primary candidate Randy Parraz raised most of his campaign funds from online donations.[31]

Despite the rise of the Internet as a fundraising tool, minority candidates, like their white counterparts, still rely on interest groups for funds. Interest group support proved vital for candidates like Gwendolynne Moore, who in 2004 became the first African American elected to Congress from Wisconsin. Running in a majority white district, Moore received monetary support from a wide range of groups including African American and women's groups.[32] Women's political action committees also played a significant role in Moore's and Terri Sewell's campaigns—Moore received $259,000 from EMILY's List contributors, and Sewell received $47,000.[33] Tim Scott also benefited from campaign contributions from prominent elected officials in his 2010 election to represent South Carolina's first congressional district. Scott, the first black Republican elected to the House from the state since Reconstruction, received campaign contributions from Karl Rove, a top adviser to former president George W. Bush, and Representatives Eric Cantor of Virginia and Kevin McCarthy of California, two House Republican leaders. He also received more than $100,000 from the antitax Club for Growth.[34] During her primary campaign to become the first Latina governor of New Mexico, Susana Martinez relied heavily on the oil industry for campaign contributions.[35]

Voter Mobilization of Minorities, Part I—Microtargeting

Campaigns have the task of determining which voters to communicate with and what messages to send. Targeting helps campaigns preserve scarce resources while maximizing their impact. Microtargeting is a technique that makes use of commercial data mining and large-scale polls to do this more precisely. Microtargeting involves using voter files that overlay previous election results with individuals' voter turnout histories, contact information, and detailed demographic and consumer information that is correlated with political preferences.[36] Campaigns often use new technology (i.e., websites, text messaging, e-mails) to collect some demographic and consumer information. Enabling candidates to concentrate their efforts on supporters or persuadable voters, these sophisticated databases of voter information can then be used for multiple purposes, including guiding direct mail programs, media purchases, and voter drives designed to register and mobilize segments of the electorate.

Recognizing the successful use of microtargeting to help Republican president Bush win the White House in 2000 and 2004, the Obama campaign also used this technique to understand more advanced voter behavior so that the campaign could send highly specialized messages to voters. Identifying crucial constituencies of voters, the campaign was better able to track down likely supporters, which helped put states once considered unwinnable by a Democratic candidate into play. [37]

Voter Mobilization of Minorities, Part II—Get-Out-the-Vote

As discussed earlier, campaigns are giving renewed attention to "the ground game" and are increasingly using the Internet as a cost-effective tool to target and mobilize supporters. Much like Obama, Deval Patrick received national attention for employing a grassroots election strategy that made use of new media technologies in his 2006 (and 2010) gubernatorial campaigns. Using social media primarily for organizing and messaging in 2006, the campaign's e-mail list numbered over 40,000, each of whom sent messages to at least ten others, thereby reaching an estimated 400,000 field volunteers, supporters, and potential supporters who turned out in high numbers for "Meet Deval" events all over the state.[38] Using cell phones and e-mail to get out the vote among young people, the Obama campaign turned over its voter lists to volunteers who then used their personal laptops and cell phones to contact people from the lists.[39]

More than ever, campaigns are expected to use modern technology given that racial and ethnic minorities (particularly African Americans and Latinos) are more likely than the general population to access the Internet by cellular phones, and they use their phones more often to do more things.[40] However, remaining racial and ethnic differences in rates of computer and Internet use make it likely that most candidates will also rely on traditional models of targeting voters. For instance, Obama aggressively courted Latino voters using radio, television, and mail.[41] Patrick also had a strong traditional GOTV effort, using door-to-door canvassing and town hall meetings.[42] Hansen Clarke's campaign, not having the resources for a television campaign, relied heavily on door-to-door canvassing and held numerous town hall meetings in soup kitchens, churches, and polling places.[43] Piyush "Bobby" Jindal's election to the Louisiana governor's mansion in 2007 has also been attributed to "old-fashioned" politicking, including traditional voter mobilization techniques in more rural and remote sections of the state.[44] Door-to-door canvassing also proved successful for Ohio representative Jay Goyal (D, seventy-third district), who noted that "the key to my [2006] campaign was to knock on doors. So I went around from door to door to door to door; I knocked on 15,000 doors, and by doing that, I was able to connect to people on a one-on-one basis."[45]

Challenges for Minority Candidates in Future Elections

While the changing demography of the United States is transforming the political landscape, it also poses unique challenges for minority candidates looking to run in districts where one racial or ethnic group is a dominant majority. For example, in some communities where African Americans were once a majority of the population, they now make up a plurality of the population as African American families leave and Latino families take their place. This increases the chances that minority candidates will run against each other as legislative seats become available. This was the case in 2007 in California's thirty-seventh congressional district's special election to replace the late representative Juanita Millender-McDonald. The Democratic primary contest pitted Laura Richardson, who is African American, against Jenny Oropeza, who is Latina, in a district where Latinos and African Americans make up 43 percent and 25 percent of the district, respectively. Richardson won the primary, garnering 38 percent of the vote compared to Oropeza's 31 percent of the vote.[46] She then went on to win the general election, defeating Republican John Kanaley with 66 percent of the vote. While the last three members of Congress representing the district have been African American, the growth and engagement of the Latino population could raise social and political tensions in the district should the political dynamics in the district change. This not only impacts the district but has implications for the racial and ethnic composition of Congress.

With the emergence of an increasing number of heterogeneous districts, it is vital for minority candidates to establish a broad coalition. However, the outcome of California's thirty-second congressional district's special election in 2009 shows that candidates who adopt modern communication technology to reach voters also have a greater chance of success in homogenous districts. Democrat Judy Chu won the primary election against her Latino opponent, Gil Cedillo, in a district that is 62 percent Latino and only 18 percent Asian. Using websites and social media sites like Facebook, Twitter, and YouTube, Chu earned the support of many Latino voters and won a seat that has exclusively sent Latino members to Congress for the past two decades.[47]

Yet while it is useful for minority candidates to adopt modern communication technology to maximize minority turnout and appeal to races and ethnicities beyond their own, they may be somewhat limited in their ability to run a dual campaign given the accessibility of that technology. Candidates' ability to convey different messages to distinct constituencies is strongly influenced by the degree to which race-conscious messages can be confined to the appropriate audience so there is minimal risk of alienating out-group voters. Advances in mobile technology make it possible for almost anyone to capture candidates on video and post the video on the Internet using websites, blogs, and e-mail. Furthermore, campaigns often employ workers to search for comments (and actions) that can be used to discredit their opponent. Knowing that opposition researchers routinely search for damaging evidence of improper behavior or character flaws, minority candidates may increasingly turn to surrogates to present explicitly racial messages that can mobilize minority voters. This was the case for Democrat Harold Ford Jr. who, in the 2006 Tennessee Senate election, used African American clergy, labor activists, students from black colleges and universities, and Democratic Party functionaries to discuss racial policies and issues.[48] Yet, the degree to which alternative ethnic and racial media are segregated from mainstream media will also influence the usefulness of this approach. For example, this approach may be less risky for Asian American and Latino candidates than for African American candidates because of the costs involved in translating messages into English.[49]

Using Social Media

While personal contacts are often viewed as the most influential form of voter mobilization, most political consultants perceive social media to be a necessary component of an effective minority outreach strategy. As such, minority candidates and their campaigns will have to invest time and energy into learning how to use these tools effectively and with caution. Whereas the earliest candidate websites were often word-for-word copies of traditional campaign literature, today's websites and social media sites are expected to be interactive and comprehensive. In 2011, Herman Cain, an affluent African American businessman running for the Republican presidential nomination, held a social media day on July 1. In fact, there was a Facebook list for the event from a group called "Sarah Palin supporters for Herman Cain 2012."[50] Given the level of sophistication expected by typical Internet users, minority candidates who use new communication technology will have to keep up with the latest advances to attract supporters and motivate activists. Similarly, campaigns that choose to take advantage of the web's ability to offer interactive content will have to monitor sites to prevent potential damaging information or inappropriate comments or videos from appearing on them.

Conclusion

While the election of President Barack Obama is often cited as a defining moment in which the nation transcended racial and ethnic politics, race and ethnicity undoubtedly remain central cleavages in American politics. How, then, can we come to understand the relevance of race and ethnicity as we look to historic "colorblind" or "postracial" victories of minority candidates? Focusing on the campaigns of minority candidates, this chapter suggests that these recent successes are due in some part to minority candidates' adoption of a new style of political campaigning. Thus, the development and adoption of new technologies can facilitate the mainstreaming of minority candidates, enabling them to transcend their minority status and reducing the likelihood that their candidacies will be marginalized.

Future minority campaigns will be characterized by diverse campaign strategies and communication methods to win elective office in districts and states across the country. This will be due, in large part, to a shift in perspective among individuals, who will care more about how a candidate is going to represent his or her issues and concerns than about who the candidate is. Thus, the future of minority campaigns is the enduring tradition of minority candidates working to solidify their base but also working toward building a multiracial electoral coalition.

Notes

1. David Bositis, *Black Elected Officials: A Statistical Summary 2001* (Joint Center for Political and Economic Studies, May 2002). Accessed on November 19, 2011, from http://www.jointcenter.org/research/black-elected-officials-a-statistical-summary-2001.
2. National Directory of Latino Elected Officials, http://www.naleo.org/directory.html
3. James S. Lai, Wendy K. Tam Cho, Thomas P. Kim, and Okiyoshi Takeda, "Asian Pacific-American Campaigns, Elections, and Elected Officials" (*PS: Political Science and Politics*, 2001), 611.
4. In 1982, Section 2 of the Voting Rights Act was amended by Congress and interpreted by the Justice Department to mean that majority-minority districts should be created when possible so that minority voters would have a reasonable chance to elect their preferred candidate (Keith Reeves, *Voting Hopes or Fears? White Voters, Black Candidates and Racial Politics in America* [New York: Oxford University Press, 1997]). These districts are created within a single-member winner-take-all system because multimember districts greatly diminish the voting strength of racial minorities.
5. Lai, Tam Cho, Kim, and Takeda, "Asian Pacific-American Campaigns, Elections, and Elected Officials", 611.
6. Joseph P. McCormick and Charles E. Jones, "The Conceptualization of Deracialization: Thinking Through the Dilemma," in *Dilemmas of Black Politics: Issues of Leadership and Strategy,* edited by Georgia A. Persons (New York: HarperCollins College, 1993).
7. Christian Collet, "Minority Candidates, Alternative Media and Multiethnic America: Deracialization or Toggling?" (*Perspectives on Politics,* Vol. 6, 2008).
8. Nielsen Wire, "Americans Watching More TV Than Ever; Web and Mobile Video Up Too" (May 20, 2009). Accessed November 19, 2011, from http://blog.nielsen.com/nielsenwire/online_mobile/americans-watching-more-tv-than-ever/.
9. Travis N. Ridout and Glen R. Smith, "Free Advertising: How the Media Amplify Campaign Messages" (*Political Research Quarterly,* Vol. 61, 2008), 598–608.
10. Travis Ridout, "Campaign Microtargeting and the Relevance of the Televised Political Ad" (*The Forum,* Vol. 7, 2009), 11.
11. Ashley Parker, "Spending on Campaign TV Ads Expected to Break Record" (*The New York Times,* October 6, 2010). Accessed on March 20, 2011, from http://thecaucus.blogs.nytimes.com/2010/10/06/television-ad-spending-expected-to-break-record/.
12. Compiled from data provided by Political Money Line (http://www.tray.com).
13. Ibid.
14. John K. Wilson, *Barack Obama: This Improbable Quest* (Boulder, CO: Paradigm Publishers, 2008).

15. Zachary A. Goldfarb, "Facebook Flexes Political Might" (*The Washington Post*, February 3, 2007).

16. See http://twitter.com/#!/marcorubio/ (accessed March 1, 2011).

17. Greg Sterling, "YouTube Video and Usage Facts" (*Sterling Marketing Intelligence*, August 31, 2006).

18. Claire Caine Miller, "How Obama's Internet Campaign Changed Politics" (*The New York Times*, November 7, 2008). Accessed February 15, 2011, from http://bits.blogs .nytimes.com/2008/11/07/how-obamas-internet-campaign-changed-politics/.

19. Alex Isenstadt, "West Rakes in Cash" (*Politico*, July 9, 2010), http://www.politico.com/ news/stories/0710/39541.html; Alex Isenstadt, "Florida Challenger Raising Cash Fast" (*Politico*, August 13, 2010), http://www.politico.com/news/stories/0810/41028.html. Both accessed on April 2, 2011.

20. Michael M. Philips, "A Colorful, Costly Dogfight Takes Shape in House Race" (*The Wall Street Journal*, October 12, 2010). Accessed on May 1, 2011, from http://online.wsj .com/article/SB10001424052748703927504575540330106432228.html.

21. See http://patfloyddesign.blogspot.com/2008/09/kesha-ram-campaign-for-state.html (accessed May 1, 2011).

22. Jack Citrin, Donald Philip Green, and David O. Sears, "White Reactions to Black Candidates: When Does Race Matter?" (*Public Opinion Quarterly*, Vol. 54, 1990), 74–96.

23. Carol A. Pierannunzi and John D. Hutcheson, "The Rise and Fall of Deracialization: Andrew Young as Mayor and Gubernatorial Candidate," in *Race, Politics, and Governance in the United States*, edited by Huey L. Perry (Gainesville: University Press of Florida, 1996). Some scholars also suggest that Pataki won the election because Latinos formed a coalition with white conservative and Republican interests to replace to defeat McCall.

24. Daniel M. Shea and Michael John Burton, *Campaign Craft: The Strategies, Tactics, and Art of Political Campaign Management*, 3rd ed. (Westport, CT: Praeger, 2006).

25. Christian Collet, "Minority Candidates, Alternative Media and Multiethnic America: Deracialization or Toggling?" (*Perspectives on Politics*, Vol. 6, 2008), 716–717.

26. Michelle Krupa, "Anh 'Joseph' Cao beats Rep. William Jefferson in 2nd Congressional District" (*The Times-Picayune*, December 6, 2008). Accessed on March 20, 2011, from http://www.nola.com/news/index.ssf/2008/12/jefferson_cao_in_dead_heat.html.

27. It is worth noting that the district Congressman Cao competed in has a population of about 650,000, of which only 2.7 percent are Asians, and that the district was specifically drawn to give African Americans an electoral advantage.

28. Peter Hamby, "Palin Records Robocall for Nikki Haley" (CNN, June 3, 2010). Accessed on May 1, 2011, from http://politicalticker.blogs.cnn.com/2010/06/03/palin-records-robocall-for-nikki-haley/.

29. Christine B. Williams and Girish J. "Jeff" Gulati, *What Is a Social Network Worth? Facebook and Vote Share in the 2008 Presidential Primaries*, presented at the 2009 annual meeting of the American Political Science Association; Dewey M. Clayton, *The Presidential Campaign of Barack Obama: A Critical Analysis of a Racially Transcendent Strategy* (New York: Routledge, 2009), 147.

30. Frank Philips, "Patrick Campaign Says Online Giving Generates $240,000 Aide Says System Boosts Number of New Supporters" (*Boston Globe*, December 21, 2005).

31. Teresa Puente, "If Randy Parraz Wins Arizona Democratic Primary for U.S. Senate, He Could Face John McCain" (*Chicanisima*, August 24, 2010). Accessed on March 25, 2011, from http://www.chicagonow.com/blogs/chicanisima/2010/08/if-randy-parraz-wins-arizona-democratic-primary-for-us-senate-he-could-face-john-mccain.html#ixzz1Nwz5u3TQ.

32. Wendy Smooth, "African American Women and Electoral Politics: Journeying from the Shadows to the Spotlight", in *Gender and Elections: Shaping the Future of American Politics,* edited by Susan J. Carroll and Richard L. Fox (Cambridge: Cambridge University Press, 2006), 136.

33. Holly Yeager, "Does EMILY's List Still Matter?" (*The American Prospect,* July 7, 2008). Accessed on April 23, 2011, from http://prospect.org/cs/articles?article=does_emilys_list_still_matter; Mary Orndorff, "Campaign 2010: Terri Sewell's 7th District Fundraising Hits $1 Million Mark" (*The Birmingham News,* July 3, 2010). Accessed April 22, 2011, from http://blog.al.com/sweethome/2010/07/campaign_2010_terri_sewells_7t.html on.

34. Patrick O'Connor, "Tim Scott, Black Republican, Nominated for House Seat" (*Businessweek,* June 22, 2010). Accessed on March 20, 2011, from http://www.businessweek.com/news/2010-06-22/tim-scott-black-republican-nominated-for-house-seat.html.

35. See National Institute on Money in State Politics, www.followthemoney.org (accessed May 1, 2011).

36. Paul S. Herrnson, *Congressional Elections: Campaigning at Home and in Washington* (Washington DC: CQ Press, 2008), 110.

37. Leslie Wayne, "Democrats Take Page From Their Rival's Playbook" (*The New York Times,* October 21, 2008). Accessed on June 10, 2011, from http://www.nytimes.com/2008/11/01/us/politics/01target.html.

38. Christine B. Williams, "Government, the Permanent Campaign, and e-Democracy: Massachusetts Governor Deval Patrick's Interactive Web site" (May 1, 2009). Accessed on May 2, 2011, from http://ssrn.com/abstract=1397686.

39. Dewey M. Clayton, *The Presidential Campaign of Barack Obama: A Critical Analysis of a Racially Transcendent Strategy* (New York: Routledge, 2009), 108.

40. Jesse Washington, "For Minorities, New 'Digital Divide' Seen" (MSNBC, January 11, 2011). Accessed on April 20, 2011, from http://www.msnbc.msn.com/id/41023900/ns/us_news-life/t/minorities-new-digital-divide-seen/.

41. Alicia Menendez, "Margin of Error: How McCain Lost Latinos—And What Obama Must Do To Keep Them" (*Campaigns and Elections*, January 1, 2009). Accessed on May 1, 2011, from http://www.campaignsandelections.com/publications/campaign-election/2009/january-2008/margin-of-error.

42. Angela K. Lewis, "Between Generations: Devel Patrick's Election as Massachusetts' First Black Governor," in *Whose Black Politics? Cases in Post-Racial Black Leadership,* edited by Andra Gillespie (New York: Routledge, 2010), 177.

43. See http://news.rediff.com/slide-show/2010/sep/08/slide-show-1-hansen-clarkes-amazing-story-continues.htm.

44. Jill Konieczko, "10 Things You Didn't Know About Bobby Jindal" (*US News and World Report*, May 22, 2008). Accessed on May 1, 2011, from http://www.usnews.com/news/campaign-2008/articles/2008/05/22/10-things-you-didnt-know-about-bobby-jindal).

45. Sabeen H. Ahmad, "Election Day 2010: More South Asian Candidates Than Ever!" (*Divanee—South Asian News and Entertainment*, November 2, 2010). Accessed on May 1, 2011, from http://divanee.com/2010/11/02/election-day-2010-more-south-asian-candidates-than-ever/.

46. Josh Kraushaar, "Black Candidate Wins Disputed District" (*Politico*, June 27, 2007). Accessed on May 30, 2011, from http://www.politico.com/news/stories/0607/4693 .html. It should be noted that Millender-McDonald's daughter, Valerie McDonald, also ran for the seat and won only 9 percent of the vote.

47. Josh Kraushaar, "Will Chu Change 32nd?" (*Politico*, May 14, 2009). Accessed on June 10, 2011, from http://www.politico.com/news/stories/0509/22492.html.

48. Sekou Franklin, "Situational Deracialization, Harold Ford, and the 2006 Senate Race in Tennessee," in Gillespie, *Whose Black Politics? Cases in Post-Racial Black Leadership*, 222.

49. See Collet, "Minority Candidates."

50. "Sarah Palin Supporters for Herman Cain 2012 [Group]" (July 2011). Accessed on July 21, 2011, from Facebook.com.

CHAPTER 14

New Political Campaigns and Democracy

Dick Simpson

WHEN HE WAS A STATE LEGISLATOR in Illinois, Abraham Lincoln said there are three basic tasks in a political campaign: Canvas the district, identify your voters, and get them to the polls. Nothing much has changed, except for the technology. To win elections you still have to talk to the voters, find out who supports your candidate, and get them to vote on Election Day. The fact that we use computers, e-mail, websites, paid media ads, public opinion polls, microtargeting, automatic phone calls with potential voters, and direct mail appeals does not change the fundamentals of campaigning. Yet, technology in new political campaigns does make a difference. It provides the opportunity to increase democratic participation in elections. It also provides Orwellian opportunities to manipulate voters and citizens.

The Cost of New Political Campaigns

Because of new technology and the cost of staff and campaign consultants, new political campaigns have gotten very expensive. In local campaigns for city council in large cities as well as for county board, state legislature, and citywide offices in smaller towns or suburbs, there are usually at least three paid staff members. There is also the need to buy paid campaign ads at least on cable TV, on the radio, and in local newspapers. Direct mail and phone campaigns and a candidate website in addition to the traditional precinct operations are also expensive. Often these local campaigns of even a city council seat in a larger city now cost from $100,000 to $250,000.

In 2008, all state candidates and political action committees spent $2.7 billion. In the most expensive states such as California the average cost of winning a state assembly seat was $769,000, and winning a state senate seat cost $1,098,000.[1]

A large congressional campaign will often require as many as five or six paid staff members and paid public relations, advertising, and campaign consultants. The need to have websites and to utilize sophisticated Internet technology adds to the costs. Successful congressional campaigns in competitive districts now cost an average of nearly $1.5 million to run.[2] Campaigns for statewide office, at least in the larger states, cost more than $10 million, with the average U.S. Senate seat costing $8.5 million.[3]

Presidential campaigns cost hundreds of millions of dollars, with more than $40 million raised before the first primary or caucus vote is cast. These expensive campaigns cannot be funded just by the candidate, a few modestly wealthy friends, and excited volunteers. Professional fundraising and larger campaign contributions by interest groups, political parties, and political action committees (PACs) are required along with the parallel expenditures of the newer 527 organizations. For instance, on the conservative side of the political spectrum, the wealthy Koch brothers have pledged to raise at least $88 million and Karl Rove's group American Crossroads another $130 million to defeat President Barack Obama in 2012.[4] These huge sums of money are bound to escalate the cost of campaigns and affect their outcome. As Boatright points out in his chapter on fundraising, new technology has expanded the tools of fundraising, which enables candidates, parties, and outside groups to raise more money. As a result, the cost of elections continually increases.

So, in addition to the general campaign electioneering plans, specific serious fundraising plans have to be developed from the beginning. In short, high-tech, candidate-centered, multimedia, new technology campaigns are too expensive for just a good candidate running on good issues to win regularly. The high cost of these campaigns undermines democracy because it is often the candidates with the most money, not the best character and the best ideas, who win. Candidates without personal wealth or the ability to raise large campaign donations are eliminated. Individuals and highly partisan interest groups can intervene in campaigns with few restraints. James Madison, one of the authors and advocates of the U.S. Constitution, famously warned about the need to provide "checks and balances" to prevent "factions" or interest groups motivated by ideology or self-interest. He argued that if they were unchecked they could undermine representative democracy. Certainly, they can help swing election outcomes when they get involved.

Raising these massive amounts of campaign funds requires both wealthy groups and wealthy individuals. Campaign fundraising in both presidential and many congressional campaigns depends heavily on influential contributors who solicit and bundle $50,000 to $100,000 or more in campaign contributions. This dependence upon PACs and large contributors has to some extent begun to be offset by new website and e-mail solicitations, which serve to broaden the base of these campaigns. However, business interest groups, such as Goldman Sachs, which contributed $3.4 million in 2006, and unions, such as the National Education

Association, which contributed $2.4 million, remain critical to funding national and statewide campaigns. As Kasniunas and Rozell point out, in the 2010 midterm elections defense contract Honeywell International and AT&T each contributed over $3 million while unions like the International Brotherhood of Electrical Workers and American Federation of State, County and Municipal Employees contributed nearly as much. The interest group contributions and their influence go up in each election.

According to Kasniunas and Rozell, 527 organizations or super PACs in the 2010 election after the *Citizens United* decision spent more than $65 million. Not only have the limits on spending by interest groups been eliminated, but their donors remain secret. Their involvement in elections has tended to make elections much more ideological, negative, and vitriolic. This finding is echoed by Francia, Joe, and Wilcox who say that the *Citizens United* decision fostered the growth of outside associations and groups spending on elections and a lessening of contributor accountability and transparency.

Some wealthy individuals are having a greater impact on elections since they now solicit bundled contributions like the 221 "Rangers" and 327 "Pioneers" who raised $77 million for President Bush's reelection campaign in 2004. By the 2008 campaign, Obama had 606 fundraising bundlers and John McCain had 536, some raising as much as $500,000 for their candidates.[5]

At the beginning of the 2012 presidential campaign, the Obama campaign from January to June 2011 already had 244 bundlers or mega-fundraisers, some of whom had raised at least half a million dollars each. In the second quarter of 2011, the campaign had raised more than $86 million, signaling that the cost of elections is continuing to expand. Smaller donors contributing under $200 continued to remain important as well, since $22.1 million or 53 percent of the money raised by the Obama campaign (as opposed to contributions the campaign raised going to the Democratic Party) came from these donors.[6]

In its study of campaign fundraising in six midwestern states in 2010, the Campaign Finance Institute found:

- Big money dominated and small donors were small factors in most states. (In many states, large contributors dominated and small donors accounted for only 3 to 12 percent of the total raised.)
- Public matching funds for small donors would radically change the source of campaign funds. (A matching fund system in which public funds matched the first $50 from every contributor on a five-to-one basis would bring all of the Midwestern states up to Minnesota's 57 percent funding from small donors of $250 or less.)[7]

Big money remains critical for campaigns, more than ever, which is the import of the study.

A Candidate's Image

In any campaign, a candidate's image is important. In the 2004 presidential election, George W. Bush projected the image of a successful "war president" who led the country after the terrorist attacks of September 11, 2001, and led the war on terror in Afghanistan and Iraq.

In the 2008 campaign, Barack Obama projected the image of a young, "new" candidate who stood for change. His famous slogan "Yes, we can" was meant to signify that we can end the Iraq war abroad, incorporate minorities into the political process, and solve our domestic problems at home. In contrast, an older John McCain stood for traditional values and Republican policies. The Obama campaign was a new-age campaign using social media, in contrast to the old ways of campaigning used by McCain. This reinforced Obama's youthful persona and change theme.

Successful Image Building

The 2010 campaign of Lincoln Chafee for governor of Rhode Island, cited by Tad Devine, used the theme and logo "Trust Chafee" along with the slogan "a new way forward." The Chafee campaign did this to heighten the contrast with his opponent, Frank Caprio. Caprio, in the Chafee TV ads, was portrayed as part of the local political machine and involved in "pay to play" corrupt government contracts. Chafee ran as an Independent candidate—he did not run as a Democrat or Republican. Thus, he was able to portray himself as an independent, honest, trustworthy leader. Chafee won.

These campaign examples suggest that even before the issues of the campaign are joined, a positive image for the candidate must be created. Shaping that image is the task of the candidate, the campaign manager, and public relations consultants. Allowing an opponent's portrayal of the candidate to go unanswered will surely lose the election.

In the new campaign era, a candidate's persona can be altered more than in the past when many voters knew at least local political candidates personally. In a time of public opinion polls, various characteristics of the candidate and campaign issues can be constantly followed by tracking polls so that sophisticated media advisers can manipulate the candidate's image. This has been known as far back as Joe McGinniss's book *The Selling of the President* (1968), which tells the story of Richard Nixon's successful campaign makeover.[8]

Susan MacManus points out in her chapter that women especially are stereotyped by image—such as the clothes, hair, and makeup they use—and that this has not diminished as an important attribute as some may think. But all candidates, men and women, whites and minorities, must pay careful attention to how they present themselves in public and in the media.

Image Building and the Use of Campaign Polls

Since then, campaign polls and focus groups are used to determine the most posi-tive image of candidates and which negative attack ads best discredit their oppo-nents. They are also used to research a campaign's own candidate to determine his or her own weaknesses and to plan responses to any attacks that may come from opponents. With this information, campaigns can choose the most effective media to deliver their messages forcefully, which are sharpened by polls and focus groups. These techniques, so highly developed in presidential campaigns, are now available to any candidate for state, local, and congressional office with the money to pay for the consultants and experts who know how to use them.

The changes in techniques for public opinion polling and focus groups from random digit dialing to calling from voter files, and now to online Internet surveys, do not alter the basic use of polls and focus groups. Polls and focus groups, however conducted, are used to determine the views of potential voters on issues and the candidate's image and to test both positive and negative advertising.

Polling is no longer just a one-shot poll to provide a snapshot of opinion. Cutting-edge campaigns begin with a benchmark survey followed by focus groups to sharpen issue stands, candidate image, and the campaign message. This is fol-lowed by trend surveys and tracking or rolling samples to gauge changes in voter attitudes during the campaign. These may be supplemented by dial meter, mall testing, and more focus groups to fine-tune final campaign ads.[9]

Of course, campaign polling provides useful information to candidates, media, and public officials whether obtained by phone interviews, Internet surveys, or focus groups as Candice Nelson points out in her chapter. Unfortunately, it also has the potential to undermine the campaign process by creating a false persona for a candidate, an untrue stand of issues, or a inaccurate portrayal of one's oppo-nent. Democracy only works if the voters have accurate information to make a decision on the best person to be elected.

Delivering the Message With New Technology

Publicity and communicating through the media are used to recruit volunteers, obtain campaign donors, and win votes. The best campaigns have a single unified theme. "Free media" are not really free because they have to be exploited by profes-sional public relations staffers and highly paid political consultants, but they are cheaper than many other ways of delivering the message. Consultants call them "earned media" because the candidate has to take action and controversial stands using the proper public relations techniques to "earn" media coverage. To the tra-ditional tools of free media and paid advertising, social media (sometimes called "new media") have been added to the campaign tool kit as described by Michael Turk in his chapter. Few, if any, campaigns are solely won by press conferences and staged campaign events covered by the media. There are other methods by which a good campaign delivers its message. The traditional method is paid advertising. Other methods include personal campaigning by the candidate, precinct work by campaign supporters, direct mail and phone campaigns, creative use of the Internet, and social media.

The use of Internet websites has greatly increased in the twenty-first century, with even major aldermanic and school board campaigns beginning to employ them over the last decade. Internet mailings, websites, YouTube videos, and text messaging have been increasingly used at campaigns on all levels because it is now cheap and easy to use what were previously expensive and exotic technologies.

On the Internet

For a number of campaign cycles now, candidates have been using websites as a means to communicate with voters—to help them win elections. As Michael Turk wrote for his chapter, between 2000 and 2010, the percentage of adult Americans using the Internet to get political information during elections grew from 18 to 73 percent. Obviously, the Internet cannot be ignored by any modern campaign. Beyond previous Internet tools, new or social media on platforms such as Facebook, Twitter, and YouTube have played an ever larger role in campaigns. Cutting-edge campaigns are now working to maximize cell phone and tablets like the iPad 2 to deliver campaign messages. But some key adjustments are now necessary to utilize them effectively. Campaign websites must be developed with the smaller mobile device screens and download times in mind. Campaign e-mail blasts have to be recrafted without larger graphics and lengthy text. Since both Facebook and Twitter target the mobile audience, campaign photographs from events are often loaded directly onto the campaign's Facebook page. Finally, candidate campaigns and political parties are investing in customized applications for mobile devices.[10]

In its various forms, the Internet on computers, laptops, or mobile devices can be used to recruit and coordinate volunteers, provide background campaign information to media reporters and bloggers, raise significant sums of money, reach important opinion and community leaders, and, of course, convince voters to vote for your candidate. Direct mail fundraising costs forty cents for every dollar raised, while Internet appeals cost less than a penny for every dollar a campaign receives in contributions.

The techniques of Internet campaigning have been developed furthest by presidential campaigns. In the primary elections in 2000 Democratic candidate Bill Bradley used the Internet to rally scattered volunteers to meetings, inspire them to open home headquarters, and organize in their local communities. Bradley also raised money successfully on the Internet, as did Republican candidate John McCain who was the most successful candidate up to then in Internet fundraising.

McCain raised more than $1 million in less than forty-eight hours in the 2000 election.[11] Successful Internet campaign efforts in that year have forced all presidential candidates since then to have extensive Internet sites listing their press releases, campaign platforms, and speeches. They have also used them to recruit volunteers and, most important, raise money.

By the 2004 Democratic primary elections, Howard Dean almost won the nomination through his enormously successful Internet fundraising. He raised $7.5 million in the period from April to June 2003, $1.5 million more than John Kerry in the same period. Two-thirds of his contributions were from the Internet.[12] What was even more impressive, and later widely copied, was his mobilization of volunteers through "Meetups" in communities throughout the primary states. By 2008, blogging, social networking, YouTube, and Twitter had been added to the mix.

The 2008 Barack Obama campaign broke all fundraising records, in large part through the Internet, and congressional candidates continued to set new records in 2010. Obama raised a total of $76 million in 2008. During the critical primaries, he received $10.3 million through Internet contributions in the second quarter of 2007 and recruited an astounding 258,000 contributors during the first six months of 2007.[13]

Virtually all congressional candidates now have websites, as do all seated congressmen. Among the latest techniques are videos posted on sites such as YouTube and Facebook. The most famous YouTube videos thus far are the defeated senator George Allen's "macaca" comment, Barack Obama's "Obama Girl," and Hillary and Bill Clinton's "Sopranos" ad.[14] In the 2008 presidential campaign, CNN sponsored the first presidential debate at which Democratic candidates at the Citadel in Charleston, South Carolina, answered questions submitted by video on YouTube. The videotaped questions were selected from 3,000 entries.

In addition to websites and e-videos, many state and local candidates coordinate their volunteers by e-mail lists that allow the campaign staff to send an e-mail letter to all volunteers at once at no cost. Messages can now be received instantly on mobile phones either as emails or as text messages. Campaigns use e-mail and tweets in addition to the candidate's webpage to which constituents, supporters, and potential supporters can be referred.

Like all other communication methods, it takes money and expertise to set up campaign websites, Internet operations, and social media operations. As Turk points out, "Campaign offices will be supplemented with powerful mobile apps that make supporters an office into themselves." These applications will be used to empower fundraising volunteers to contact potential donors instantly. Precinct workers will be able to report petition signatures gathered, neighbors registered to vote, or voters canvassed for support instantly to secure campaign websites.

Of course, e-mails, text messages, and websites will have to be updated as often as several times a day. More and more campaign funds will be spent advertising on the Internet as that is where more and more voters will be. As Atiya Kai Stokes-Brown points out in her chapter, minority candidates are increasingly using new media to reach their constituents as well. Nearly all campaigns have had to add these new communication technologies to their campaign tool kits with all the costs and expertise they require.

Perils of Internet Technology

There is also danger in the use of Internet technology. As Philip Howard describes it, "Political campaigns in the United States are increasingly manipulative, as managers find new ways to distribute propaganda, mine data, mark political interests, and mislead people unfamiliar with computing technologies."[15] Yet there is also a democratizing potential to the Internet. It costs less to use than expensive mass media advertising. It can mobilize large numbers of citizens to participate in the election. It allows hundreds—or thousands—of small financial contributors to become more significant to a campaign than a few wealthy individuals or powerful interest groups freeing elected officials to represent "the people" rather than special interest groups. Anyone can support a candidate by e-mail, on Facebook, or on a blog; send a text message; or use a chat room to build the buzz for a candidate and the momentum of a campaign. The danger is that Internet technology can be used to misinform voters in ways that are hard to counter.

Press Coverage

All political campaigns from president to school board member still depend heavily on press coverage. Several disturbing trends have occurred in the mass media since the famous Kennedy–Nixon debates of 1960. As Graf and Mayer say in their chapter on press coverage, "Sound bites that played on the news for 60 seconds in 1968, have now been reduced to seven seconds in the modern era." Thus, politicians' comments are often reduced to extreme, colorful, short sound bites such as when Barack Obama and Hillary Clinton went at it in the South Carolina primary debate in 2008. Obama stated that he was a community organizer while "you were on the corporate board of Wal-Mart." Clinton retorted that while she was fighting Republicans, "you were representing your contributor Rezko in his slum landlord business."[16] Rezko was under indictment at this time. The point is that issues that are immensely important and complex are reduced to simple slogans or character attacks. So, for instance, some politicians pledge they will support "no new taxes," which may not allow for decisions that have to be made in future conditions that may require them. Slogans and character attacks made by politicians can box them into a corner before they take office.

Try an experiment for yourself. Think about any major foreign policy such as wars overseas or any domestic issue such as tax policies in the United States. Time yourself on your watch or stopwatch and try to convey what you know about the subject or what you believe in seven seconds, speaking aloud without notes. This effort will convince you how much our discussion of issues has truncated from the several-hour debates between Lincoln and Douglas before the Civil War and how unlikely we are to make good decisions about candidates or policies based on seven-second sound bites.

The second mass media trend that is troubling is the new rhythm of media coverage. With cable TV and the Internet, the news cycle is 24/7. Ever since the Clinton campaigns of the 1990s invented the war room, major political campaigns have had instant response teams ready to respond to the actions, rumors, events, and charges by the other side almost as soon as they occur. No reflection, no discussion, only a quick counterthrust. The truth is likely to be the victim under these pressures. As Graf and Mayer note, "Stories are reported rapidly, often without fact-checking, as more media compete in the marketplace. Not only does it have implications for what the press does, but it puts campaigns in a position where they have to be reactive."

Finally, the evolution of the media—especially cable TV, Internet websites, blogs, Internet ads, and directed e-mail blasts—has increased the opportunity for "narrowcasting" in addition to "broadcasting." This means that now campaigns can buy cable TV ads only for the viewers in a particular district or neighborhood and only on shows covering sports or news, or liberal or conservative talk shows. This allows campaigns to tailor their messages for particular groups rather than the general public. Other than the fear of being caught by their opponents or the mass media, campaigns can take more extreme positions on issues and even different positions for different voter audiences in order to win votes and get elected. This undermines the ability of voters to know candidates' real stand on issues.

As press and media coverage of campaigns evolves to only "headline news coverage" as we get more of our news coverage on mobile devices such as smartphones and tablets, the news coverage inevitably becomes more superficial. Like the amount you can say in a seven-second sound bite, the amount of detail you can provide on a smartphone screen is very limited. Along with that, the attention to scandals and the constant surveillance of candidates increase "the emphasis on personality, appearance, and character, and further lessens the importance of parties, platforms and issues."[17] This is a threat to our democracy.

Campaigns will continue to invest much of their money and staff time in mass media press coverage and the Internet, but these only imperfectly serve us, the voters. Sound bites and headline news coverage do not provide adequate information for us to choose the best candidate or the best public policies. Narrowcasting rather than broadcasting limits debate and biases the information voters receive.

The new rhythm of 24/7 media and the need for candidates' immediate responses to smears and misinformation do not encourage reasoned debate. Press coverage is still essential in elections, but the collapse of newspapers and the changes in press coverage of campaigns place limits on what is possible and what is good for the democratic process.

Personal Voter Contact Still Matters

Candidate image can be greatly influenced by media. Yet from the precinct to the state to the national level, voter contact still matters—a lot. Staffing a field operation with trained workers able to carry out petition and voter registration drives, a door-to-door canvass, and poll watching on Election Day is still the secret to winning most state and local elections. And it is a major component of national campaigns, including presidential campaigns. Precinct work provides a much more personal and less expensive way to reach voters, register them, deliver a campaign message, and get them to vote. It is still the best way to carry out Abe Lincoln's electioneering advice to canvas the district, identify your voters, and get them to the polls. It is also key for effective get-out-the-vote at the state and national level.

In high-tech, candidate-centered, modern campaigns, sometimes money, professional political consultants, and paid advertising along with specialized direct mail and phone campaigns can defeat precinct work campaigns. It is harder and harder in an economy that demands that everyone work, often at more than one job, to find enough people to volunteer to cover all the precincts and reach all the voters in statewide, congressional, and presidential campaigns. But in the larger districts, it will not be sufficient. It also has to be adapted to changes such as the fact that states such as Oregon, Florida, and Washington have a substantial percentage of their voters—in some cases more than half—vote before Election Day. This is a problem for all campaigns to adapt their precinct work and marketing strategies to influence the earlier voters. With redistricting, the calculus of getting voters out in newly formed congressional districts provides a new challenge to campaigns as Jeffrey Crouch discusses in his chapter.

In modern campaigns, precinct work can take on new forms and be combined with the Internet. For instance, in the 2004 campaign there was a massive attempt by MoveOn to register John Kerry student supporters in their dorms and on campus and then to mobilize them to vote. The information and instructions were sent by e-mail to all MoveOn student volunteers. They were told how to register other students to vote and how to obtain absentee ballots from their home precinct or in the precinct where the school dorm was located. Equally important to getting more students to vote for MoveOn candidates was sending e-mails reminding students to register, to vote, and to go door-to-door in the dorms to get their fellow student voters to the polls. Similar techniques are being adapted to local and state elections where the Internet and shoe leather combine to register voters, find favorable voters who will vote for your candidate, and get them to the polls on Election Day. And this effect, as Richard Semiatin writes, is that "candidate organizations, not national parties, are becoming the primary delivery vehicle of identifying citizens, targeting them, and getting them out to vote."

Voter Mobilization in Action

Of course, precinct work is only one form of voter mobilization. In the high-tech new campaigns of the twenty-first century, microtargeting, direct mail, phone campaigns, Internet advertising, and e-mail voting reminders are all part of the process for recruiting volunteers, identifying supporters, and getting them to vote on Election Day. By 2006, both the Republicans and the Democrats had developed sophisticated seventy-two-hour plans using political parties, interest groups, and volunteers to deliver "their" voters to the polls. Blogs, e-mails, and websites are pressed into service creating a "virtual community" and an online campaign to supplement the traditional precinct worker ground wars reaching voters. Yet, as Semiatin reports, precinct work is still the most powerful technique yielding one vote for every fourteen contacts in comparison to, say, phone bank calls, which yield one vote for every thirty-five calls. But all mobilization methods are critical in close campaigns.

Some modern voter mobilization techniques pose disturbing problems for our democracy. Consumer and lifestyle orientation in addition to demographic information and voter profiles from electronic databases could be used to microtarget voters in ways that undermine a citizen's right to privacy. Political parties and campaigns are gaining access to information that is private and using that information for political purposes. What if the information fell into the hands of an individual who would misuse that against voters? While microtargeting and data collection have not yet reached the intrusive level of "Big Brother," the brave new political world has the potential for campaign workers and political officials gaining too much private information about individuals.

From Party-Centered to Candidate-Centered to Interest Group Election Campaigns

For at least the last fifty years, elections have been changing from party-centered to candidate-centered. Candidates have had to raise more of their own money, define the issues on which they are running, and deliver their message to the voters with less and less help from the political parties. As Tari Renner points out, political parties remain important as central service providers. But as Kasniunas and Rozell add, interest groups both in their traditional forms and as 527 committees and SuperPacs are having an ever greater impact on campaign fundraising, issue advocacy, endorsements, and voter mobilizations. Their campaign contributions through political action committees are critical to all major campaigns. Sometimes their separate political ads such as those by the Swift Boat Veterans for Truth against John Kerry in 2004 have directly affected election outcomes. It is too much to declare that all political campaigns have become interest group centered. However when candidates are supported by parties and interest groups, they usually win. This "alliance," formal or not, has the propensity to skew the democratic process. Interest group support may represent the tipping point about who controls the dialogue in an election contest—and that can be dangerous.

Interest groups are invaluable in articulating the concerns of their members and in mobilizing voters on Election Day. Yet, interest group–controlled campaigns are also a threat to democracy. As James Madison warned in *Federalist Paper* Number 10, interest groups, which he called factions, promote the self-interest and ideological passions of some citizens over the rights of other citizens and the public interest. Interest group mobilization is good because it organizes individuals and gives a voice to their concerns. It amplifies their voices so that they are heard in government decision making. But interest groups also pose a threat.

While interest articulation is important, society also requires interest aggregation. While interest groups or movements like the Tea Party can further polarize political decision making in government, there is a need for the party-in-government function to organize different interests and factions and to bring about compromise in lawmaking. This is best done by political parties, which first of all bring together different interests and force groups to compromise in order to create a single political platform that will be supported by a majority of voters. Interest groups do not play this critical function. As candidate-centered, interest group–based campaigns become stronger, political parties may become too weak to play their role successfully. Current campaign funding laws have the effect of further limiting political parties while U.S. Supreme Court decisions open the gates wider for interest group fundraising. Thus, while there is a great advantage to involving interest groups in political campaigns, there are also dangers that they will polarize the country, elect more extreme ideologies, and skew campaign results.

Not only are campaign techniques changing, but the electorate is changing in fundamental ways. In 2008, nearly one in four voters was a racial minority. Whites still made up 76 percent of the 131 million people who voted, but blacks were 12 percent, Latinos 7 percent, and Asians 2.5 percent.[18] In the 2010 election 6.6 million Latinos voted, again representing 7 percent of the voters, but they are predicted to cast as many as 12 million ballots in 2012.[19] They continue to grow more rapidly than any other segment of society.

This has important political implications, for while 52 percent of white voters, identify as Republican and only 39 percent identify as Democratic, minorities remain steadfastly Democratic. Eighty-six percent of African Americans and 64 percent of Latino voters are Democrats or continue to identify as Democrats.[20]

The big story is the population changes that will occur. For example, Chicago, which was previously largely populated with white ethnic groups and African Americans, looks very different today. The Latino population has been growing steadily in the city and is a growing political force. While Latinos are only 29 percent of Chicago's population now, 41 percent of the Chicago children under eighteen years of age are Latino.[21] As they become eligible to vote, Latinos are going to become a major political force, not only in Chicago but in the suburbs and the country at large. Under these population changes, we have no choice but to develop multiracial and multicultural campaigns.

While it is heartening that more women and minorities are being elected to office, with more than 9,000 African Americans, 5,739 Latinos, and 2,000 Asians now holding some of the 540,000 elected positions, the simple change of gender or race of those holding public office does not automatically guarantee better government (see Chapter 13). Despite having an African American president, we have not yet reached nonracial or deracialized politics. Nor does "symbolic representation" of different racial representatives guarantee a political incorporation that creates policies in minorities' best interests. Minorities and women have been as guilty of public corruption as white men.

Winning Elections and the Democratic Process

Campaigns for elected office are exciting, demanding, and rewarding if they are well run. They are essential to democracy. New campaign techniques, for the most part, simply modernize the basic campaign strategies articulated by Abraham Lincoln. The new campaigns and new campaign technologies have the potential to allow "the little guy" to participate more effectively and to better inform the electorate. However, they also have a dark side: the possibility of manipulation, disinformation, and overly unfair negative tactics that defeat good candidates and create greater voter apathy and antipathy. They have the potential of invading our privacy to microtarget us as potential supporters of a candidate for whom we would not otherwise vote.

The ideal model of election communication is a debate in which the voters can hear all the candidates at the same time and weigh carefully the strengths and weaknesses of the candidates themselves and their stands on issues. New laws can achieve public financing of elections, require greater transparency, and provide better privacy protections. All of these contribute to the debate standard in which candidates are better able to communicate to voters and disclose their financial contributors, and are less able to use microtargeting to manipulate voters.

In the end, however, modern campaign techniques will not be controlled by new laws alone. Nor can the potential evils of new political campaigns be curbed by protests by political scientists and editorial writers. These new cutting-edge campaigns with their modern technology can be made to serve and not to subvert democracy only if the public uses the now additional available information and Internet possibilities to elect the best possible candidates. Voters must reject candidates who misuse new technology to spread disinformation about themselves or their opponents.

If the democratic ideal remains a public debate, then all candidates must have the opportunity to present themselves and their message as unfiltered as possible to the public. With public financing, full campaign contribution disclosure, and guaranteed voter privacy, candidates will have an equal chance to present their case to the voters without undue microtargeting and media manipulation. With greater candidate information presented by cable television and the Internet, careful campaign scrutiny by political reporters and bloggers, and neutral voter information pamphlets published by the government, voters will have the opportunity to cast informed votes that best reflect their beliefs and best promote the public interest. All of these changes need to occur if we are to have fair elections in the twenty-first century.

New cutting-edge political campaigns using advanced technology and new methods have the prospect of either promoting or undermining democracy. To make sure that democracy is promoted, we will need new campaign laws to be sure. Most of all, we need an aware and informed electorate that will elect those candidates who use the new techniques to increase democracy and to defeat those who would subvert it.

Notes

1. Dennis Johnson, *Campaigning in the Twenty-First Century* (New York: Routledge, 2011), 45–46.
2. Johnson, *Campaigning in the Twenty-First Century*, 44.
3. Johnson, *Campaigning in the Twenty-First Century*, 45.
4. Marc Ambinder, "Obama Finalizes Reelection Plans," (*National Journal*, March 29, 2011).
5. Robert Boatright, "Fundraising—Present and Future," in *Campaigns on the Cutting Edge*, edited by Richard Semiatin (Washington, DC: CQ Press, 2008), 17–18.
6. Campaign Finance Institute Report, "Three of This Year's Top Four Presidential Fundraisers So Far Are Relying on Small Donors" (July 19, 2011).
7. Campaign Finance Institute Report, "Small Donors in Six Midwestern States" (July 2, 2011).
8. Joe McGinniss, *The Selling of the President 1968* (New York: Simon and Schuster, 1969).
9. Johnson, *Campaigning in the Twenty-First Century*, 67; and Dennis Johnson, *No Place for Amateurs: How Political Consultants Are Reshaping American Democracy*, 2nd ed. (New York: Routledge, 2007), Chapter 5.

10. Steve Pearson and Ford O'Connell, "Down Home Digital" (*Campaigns and Elections,* June 2011), 49. See also Averill Peasin, "Consultant to Consultant," a paid insert in the same issue.

11. Campaign Finance Institute, *Small Donors and Online Giving: A Study of Donors to the 2004 Presidential Campaigns* (Washington, DC: Campaign Finance Institute, 2006).

12. Chris Taylor, "How Dean Is Winning the Web" (*Time*, July 14, 2003).

13. Reporter's Blog, "Obama Rakes in Record-Breaking $32.5 Million" (*PBS News Hour,* July 5, 2007). Accessed on September 2, 2011, from pbsorg.com.

14. Richard Auxier and Alex Tyson, "Uploading Democracy: Candidates Field YouTube Questions" (Pew Research Publications, July 24, 2007).

15. Philip N. Howard, *New Media Campaigns and the Managed Citizen* (New York: Cambridge University Press, 2006), p. 3.

16. Kathy Kiely, "Clinton, Obama Step Up Attacks at South Carolina Debate" (*USA Today*, January 21, 2008). Accessed on September 2, 2011, from usatoday.com.

17. Joseph Graf and Jeremy D. Mayer, Chapter 9, p. 150.

18. Mark Hugo Lopez and Paul Taylor, "Dissecting the 2008 Electorate: Most Diverse in U.S. History" (Pew Research Center, April 30, 2009). Accessed on November 19, 2011, from http://pewresearch.org/pubs/1209/racial-ethnicvoters-presidential-election.

19. Rick Person, "Latino Vote Projected to Hit Record in 2012" (*Chicago Tribune,* June 23, 2011).

20. "GOP Makes Big Gains Among White Voters" (Pew Research Center, July 22, 2011). Accessed on November 19, 2011, from http://pewresearch.org/pubs/2067/2012-elecd-torate-partisan-affliations-gop-gains-whitevoters.

21. "2010 Census Update" (Latino Policy Forum, August 8, 2011).

Index

Absentee voter mobilization, 93
A/B testing, 55–56
Accessories, 201
Accomplishment and vision ads, 34–35, 43–45
Acxiom Corporation, 94
Advertising. *See* New media; Paid media; Social media
AFL-CIO, 123, 134
African Americans, 178–181, 199
    See also Minority candidates; Minority populations; Redistricting
Alaska fundraising, 26 (n17)
All, David, 113
Allen, George, 57, 149, 232
American Conservative Union Conservative Political Action Committee, 130
American Crossroads, 123, 132, 133, 164, 227
American Federation of State, County and Municipal Employees, 127, 228
American Federation of Teachers, 130
American Solutions for Winning the Future, 126
Americans United for Safe Streets, 34, 42–43
Anger points, 77
Angle, Sharron, 20, 70
Anonymous campaign reports, 151–152
Armstrong, Jerome, 113
AT&T, 127, 228
Atypical workers as journalists, 144
Audio, importance of, 32
Authenticity, in fundraising, 24–25

"Back From the Future" (ad), 148–149
Baker v. Carr (1962), 179
Balz, Dan, 74–75
Bayh, Birch, 89
BCRA. *See* Bipartisan Campaign Reform Act
"Big as Texas" (ad), 41–42

Biographical ads, 34, 41–42
Bipartisan Campaign Reform Act (BCRA):
    campaign ads, 32
    campaign finance, 110
    campaign finance reform, 159–160
    impact of, initial, 160–161, 161 (table)
    impact of, on 2008 and 2010 elections, 163–164
    Roberts Court rulings on, 162–164
Blacks, 178–181, 199
    See also Minority candidates; Minority populations; Redistricting
Blaemire, Bob, 69, 73, 78 (n23)
Blaemire Communications, 69, 78 (n23)
Blended surveys, 74
Blogs and bloggers:
    campaign press coverage and, 145
    fundraising and, 19
    interest groups and, 129, 130
    minority candidates and, 216–217
    Tea Party and, 148
Botox, 200
Boundaries, political and geographic, 183
Boxer, Barbara, 79 (n28)
Bradley, Bill, 231
Bradley, Tom, 216
Broadband access to Internet, 72, 145
Brown, Scott, 14, 19–20, 23, 24–25
Bundling, 13–14, 227–228
Bush, George W.:
    fundraising, 11, 13–14, 16–17, 228
    image, 229
    MoveOn.org and, 148
    new media, 49, 50, 51
    polling and microtargeting, 77
    press coverage, 145–146
    voter mobilization, 83, 88–89, 89–90

Cable television, 37–38, 61–62, 114, 142–143
Cain, Herman, 221
California redistricting, 182
Campaign events, 14–15
Campaign Finance Institute, 228
Campaign finance reform, 157–172
   about, 8–9, 157–158
   Bipartisan Campaign Reform Act, 159–160
   Bipartisan Campaign Reform Act, impact
      on 2008 and 2010 elections, 163–164
   Bipartisan Campaign Reform Act, initial
      impact of, 160–161, 161 (table)
   Bipartisan Campaign Reform Act, Roberts
      Court rulings on, 162–164
   campaign finance deregulation, effects on
      campaign activities, 164–166
   disclosure, 164–165, 167–168
   evolution and framework of, 158–159
   Fair Elections Now Act and, 169–170, 171
   fundraising practices, change in, 164–165
   individual citizen donations, 157–158
   interest groups, 164
   legislative reform prospects, about, 166–167
   legislative reform prospects, long-term,
      168–172
   legislative reform prospects, near-term,
      167–168
   market-oriented alternatives for campaign
      finance, 171
   national party committees and, 165–166
   state-level initiatives, 171–172
Campaign press coverage, 138–153
   about, 8, 138–139, 233–235
   anonymous campaign reports, 151–152
   bloggers, 145
   challenges, 152–153
   citizen, 150–152
   citizen groups as campaign reporters,
      147–149
   digital divide, 144–145
   expectations set by media, 142
   lessons from the 2000-2008 campaigns,
      146–147
   mainstream media, decline of,
      142–144
   mobile news technology and
      campaigns, 152
   newspapers, 139–141

   opponent surveillance, 149–150
   origins and development, 139–142
   politics at the speed of light, 145–147
   radio, 141
   social media, 151
   television, 141–142
Campaign surveillance, 149–150
Campaign websites, 56, 62, 90, 214
Camp Obama, 90, 96
Candidates:
   image of, 229–230
   recruiting and training, 123–124
   See also Minority candidates; Women and
      campaigns; *specific candidates*
Cao, Anh "Joseph" Quang, 217, 223 (n17)
Caprio, Frank, 45–46, 229
Carpenter, Bob, 68, 71
Castle, Mike, 20
Catalist, 73, 78 (n23), 112, 113
CATI. *See* Computer-assisted telephone
     interviews
CBS News, 146
Cell phones, 66–69, 71, 78 (n12), 128–129
   See also Smartphones
Census, 9, 117, 177, 178, 189 (n4)
   See also Redistricting
Chafee, Linc, 30, 35, 45–46, 229
Chicago, minorities in, 238
Chu, Judy May, 212, 220
Cinema verité technique in campaign ads, 32
Citizen groups as campaign reporters,
     147–149
Citizen Legislature and Political Freedom
     Act, 171
Citizens:
   campaign donations by, 157–158
   campaign press coverage by, 150–152
   campaigns tailored to, 4
   diversity of, 92
   new media and, 56–57
   redistricting, involvement in, 187–188
   role of, 56–57
Citizens Against Government Waste, 131
Citizens for Reform, 159
Citizens United v. FEC (2010):
   campaign finance, 110–111, 162–163,
     174 (n20)
   fundraising, 20–21

interest groups, 122, 132–133, 134
  paid media, 39
Civil rights revolution and redistricting,
  179–180
Clarke, Hansen, 215, 219
Clinton, Bill, 14, 142, 151–152
Clinton, Hillary:
  clothing, 200
  fundraising, 14, 23
  laugh, 202
  polling, 65
  press coverage, 233
  tears, 195
"Clinton Chronicles, The" (video),
  151–152
Clothing of women candidates, 200–201
Club for Growth, 21, 218
Coakley, Martha, 19, 20
Commissions, redistricting, 182, 187
Common Cause, 128
Communications, maximizing effectiveness
  of, 55–56
Communications Workers of America
  Committee on Political Education
  (CWA-COPE), 126
Communities of interest, 183
Compactness, in redistricting, 183
Computer-assisted telephone interviews
  (CATI), 66, 67
Computers in redistricting, 181, 187
Comte, Auguste, 177
Conference calls, for focus groups, 76
Congressional campaigns, cost of, 227
Connolly, Gerry, 34, 42–43
Consultants, media, 30–31, 31 (box)
Contiguity, in redistricting, 183
Corker, Bob, 171
Cost per acquisition (CPA), 53
Cost per donor (CPD), 53
CPA. *See* Cost per acquisition
CPD. *See* Cost per donor
Cracking districts, 179
Creative Direct, 85
Crist, Charlie, 105
CRM. *See* Customer Relationship
  Management
Crowdsourcing, 36
Crying/tears, 195, 202

Customer Relationship Management
  (CRM), 7, 87
Cutler, Eliot, 29, 31, 35, 36, 43–45
CWA-COPE. *See* Communications
  Workers of America Committee on
  Political Education

Daily Kos (website), 147–148
"Daisy" (ad), 35
Davis v. FEC (2008), 162
DCCC. *See* Democratic Congressional
  Campaign Committee
Dean, Howard:
  fundraising, 11, 17, 18, 19, 21, 232
  party leadership and strategies, 107
  social and new media, 49, 50
  voter mobilization, 91
Debates, first televised presidential, 48, 141,
  149–150
Deeds, Creigh, 57
Definitely Maybe (movie), 209 (n12)
Democracy Is Strengthened by Casting Light
  On Spending in Elections (DISCLOSE)
  Act, 167, 168
Democratic Congressional Campaign Com-
  mittee (DCCC), 107 (table), 161 (table)
Democratic National Committee (DNC):
  leaders, 107, 196–197
  online operations, 115
  receipts, 107 (table), 161 (table)
  structure, 105
  women in, 196–197
Democratic Party:
  fundraising, 19
  ideological purists, 104
  redistricting, 181, 186, 190 (n21)
  Red to Blue program, 108, 110, 111
  *See also specific candidates and party
    organizations*
Democratic Senatorial Campaign Committee
  (DSCC), 107 (table), 161 (table)
Demographic change, 116, 219–220
  See also Redistricting
Deracialization, 212–213
Des Moines Register, 65, 71
de Vellis, Philip, 56–57
Digital divide, 144–145
Direct mail, 15–16, 61, 112–113

"Dirty Dozen" hit list, 124
DISCLOSE Act. *See* Democracy Is
    Strengthened by Casting Light On
    Spending in Elections Act
Disclosure, in campaign finance reform,
    164–165, 167–168
DNC. *See* Democratic National Committee
Doolittle, John, 171
Door-to-door voter mobilization, 86–87
Dornan, Robert, 17
Dowd, Matthew, 88
Drudge, Matt, 145
DSCC. *See* Democratic Senatorial Campaign
    Committee
Dukakis, Michael, 76
Durbin, Dick, 169

Early voter mobilization, 93
Editing of campaign ads, 36
Edwards, John, 141, 150, 199
Elections (2012), 183–186, 190 (n21)
Electronic Frontier Foundation (EFF), 94
E-mail:
    in fundraising, 17, 18
    interest group, 128, 137 (n4)
    minority candidates, 217
    Obama, campaign against, 147
    polling, 73
    use of, 232
    voter mobilization, 96
Emanuel, Rahm, 107, 108
EMILY's list, 123, 125, 127, 196, 218
Endorsements, 124
Equal population, in redistricting, 182
Exley, Zack, 54
Expectations set by media, 142
Expenditures, independent, 39–40, 132–133,
    162–164, 173 (n4)
Expressions, facial, 202
Eye contact, 202
Eyewear of women candidates, 201

Facebook:
    about, 58
    apps, future, 62
    audience, 62
    fundraising and, 22
    interest group use of, 129–130

minority candidate use of, 214–215
    See also Social media
Facial expressions, 202
Fair Elections Now Act (FENA),
    169–170, 171
Falwell, Jerry, 151–152
Family as props in ads, 204
Federal Election Campaign Act Amendments
    of 1974, 82, 158
*Federal Election Commission v. Wisconsin Right
    to Life, Inc.* (2007), 134, 162
Females. *See* Women and campaigns
FENA. *See* Fair Elections Now Act
Ferraro, Geraldine, 203
Filming of campaign ads, 35–36
Fimian, Keith, 42–43
Fiorina, Carly, 22, 37, 79 (n28), 196
501(c) groups, 173 (n4)
527 groups, 133, 173 (n4)
Florida redistricting, 185
Focus groups, 34, 75–76
Ford, Harold, Jr., 220–221
Foursquare, 91
FreedomWorks, 89
    See also Tea Party
Free Republic (website), 147–148
Friends and acquaintances, fundraising with,
    12–13
Frost, Martin, 193
Fundraising, 11–25
    about, 5, 11–12, 227–228
    authenticity in, 24–25
    blogging and, 19
    bundling, 13–14, 227–228
    campaign events, 14–15
    campaign finance reform and, 164–165
    Citizens United v. FEC and, 20–21
    direct mail, 15–16
    elections (2010), 19–22
    e-mail alerts, 128
    friends and acquaintances, 12–13
    innovations in the 2000s, 16–19
    interest group, 20–21, 125–127, 135, 218
    Internet, 17–20, 52–53, 217–218, 231–232
    minority candidates, 217–218
    niche, finding, 24
    Obama fundraising machine, replicability
        of, 18–19

online, 52–53
phone banks, 15–16
political action committee, 16
practices, traditional, 12–16
small donor, 170
social media and, 21–22, 59, 60
speed in, 19–20, 23
stealth and timing in, 23
trends and implications for future elections, 22–25
"Future" (ad), 43–45

Gans, Curtis, 93
Geographic boundaries and redistricting, 183
Geographic information system (GIS) software, 181
Georgia redistricting, 186
Gerrymandering, 178
    See also Redistricting
Gestures, hand, 202
Get-out-the-vote (GOTV) efforts. See Voter mobilization
Gibson, Charles, 142
Gingrich, Newt, 126, 130
GIS. See Geographic information system software
Glasses, 201
Goldwater, Barry, 35
Google, 40
Google Network Blasts, 113
Gore, Al, 145–146
GOTV (get-out-the-vote) efforts.
    See Voter mobilization
Goyal, Jay, 219
"Grande Como Texas" (ad), 41–42
Grayson, Alan, 123
Greenpeace, 128
Grijalva, Raúl, 212

Hacking districts, 179
Haegele, Greg, 135
Hairstyle and color of women candidates, 199
Haley, Nikki, 217
Hand gestures, 202
Handshakes, 203
Harris, Katherine, 199–200
Harris Interactive, 71–72
Hashtags, 58
Help America Vote Act (HAVA), 68–69, 70 (n22)

Hemlines of women candidates, 200–201
Herrera Beutler, Jaime, 212, 213–214
High-definition video, 35–36
Hill, Rick, 159
Hill committees, 105
    See also specific committees
Hip-hop radio stations, 85
Hispanics, 70, 188
    See also Minority candidates; Minority populations; Redistricting
Hit lists, 124–125
Hochul, Kathy, 127, 186
Honeywell International, 127, 228
Horton, Willie, 76
House Majority PAC, 164
Hugging, 203
Hulshof, Kenny, 114–115

Identification (ID) calls, 85–86
Ideological purists and pragmatists, 104–105
Illinois redistricting, 186
Image, candidate's, 229–230
Independent expenditures, 39–40, 132–133, 162–164, 173 (n4)
Integration of campaigns, 3–4, 61–62
Interactive voice response (IVR) surveys, 73–74
Interest groups, 121–136
    about, 7, 8, 121–122, 236–238
    blogging, 130
    blogs, 129
    bundling, 14
    campaign finance reform, 164
    candidates, recruiting and training, 123–124
    Citizens United v. FEC, impact of, 122, 132–133, 134
    e-mail alerts, 128, 137 (n4)
    endorsements, 124
    527 groups, 133, 173 (n4)
    fundraising, 20–21, 125–127, 135, 218
    future of, 133–134
    hit lists, 124–125
    issue advocacy and independent expenditures, 130–131, 132–133
    mobile technology and, 128–129
    new technologies and, 135–136
    paid media, 39

Interest groups (cont.)
  podcasts, 129
  pop-ups, 127
  social networking sites, 123, 129–130, 135
  Tea Party as, 121–122, 131–132
  techniques, modern, 125–131
  traditional approaches, 122–125
  webcasts, 129
  websites, 126–127, 136
International Brotherhood of Electrical
  Workers, 127, 228
Internet:
  advertising, 37
  broadband access to, 72, 145
  campaign press coverage, impact on,
    152–153
  fundraising, 17–20, 52–53, 217–218,
    231–232
  impact of, 48–49, 231–233
  minority candidates and, 214
  perils of, 233
  rise of, 49–51
  women voters and, 207
  See also New media
iPad application, Democratic National
  Committee, 115
iPhone technology and voter mobilization, 96
Issue ads, 34, 42–43, 131, 159, 160
IVR surveys. *See* Interactive voice response
  surveys

Johnson, Haynes, 74–75
Johnson, Lyndon, 35
Journalism and journalists, 140–141,
  143, 144
JUSTPAC, 39

Kay, Tim, 114
Kennedy, Anthony, 162
Kennedy, John, 48, 82, 141, 149–150
Kerry, John:
  fundraising, 11, 13, 14
  new media, 48, 54
  polling and microtargeting, 77
  press coverage, 146–147
  Swift Boat Veterans for Truth and,
    146–147, 237
  voter mobilization, 90, 235

Kilbride, Tom, 39
Kimbia, 59
Kissing, 203–204
Knowledge Networks, 72

Labor unions, 125, 174 (n20)
Latinos, 70, 188
  See also Minority candidates; Minority
    populations; Redistricting
Laughing, by women candidates, 202
LCV. *See* League of Conservation Voters
League of Conservation Voters (LCV), 124
League of United Latin American
  Citizens, 128
Lee, Chris, 186
Levin Amendment funds, 159–160, 173 (n9)
Lincoln, Abraham, 226, 238
List matching, 54
Local campaigns, cost of, 226
Lowden, Sue, 20

Madison, James, 227, 237
Mail voter mobilization, 93
Majority-minority districts, 180, 188, 222 (n4)
Makeup, 199–200
McCain, John:
  fundraising, 52–53, 228, 231–232
  image, 229
  new media, 52–53, 56
  Palin and, 203, 204
  press coverage, 142
  voter mobilization, 91
McCall, Carl, 216, 223 (n23)
McConnell v. Federal Election Commission
  (2003), 160, 162
McDonnell, Bob, 85
McDonnell, Jeanine, 85
McInnis, Scott, 131
Media. *See* New media; Paid media; Social
  media
Media consultants, 3–4, 30–31, 31 (box)
Meetups, 49, 50, 90–91, 232
Mellman, Mark, 70, 71
Mellman Group, The, 70, 79 (n28)
Message development research, 32–34
Message testing, 55–56, 74–75, 76
Metrics, web tool, 51
Michigan redistricting, 185

Microtargeting:
   campaign communication and, 116
   custom messaging and, 112–113
   direct mail and, 112–113
   of minorities, 218–219
   polling and, 77
   traditional media and, 114
   voter mobilization and, 87, 88–89,
      218–219
Migration patterns and redistricting,
   183–184
Miller, Joe, 21, 26 (n17)
Minority candidates, 211–222
   about, 9–10, 211–213
   blogs, political, 216–217
   campaign activities, 213–218
   campaign websites, 214
   challenges in future elections, 219–221
   demographic changes and, 219–220
   e-mail, 217
   fundraising, 217–218
   Internet and, 214
   microtargeting, 218–219
   racial messages, 220–221
   social media and, 214–216, 221
   statistics, 211–212
   texting, 217
   traditional media, 213–214
   voter mobilization, 218–219
Minority populations, 116, 117, 218–219,
   237–238
   See also Redistricting
Minority representation, in redistricting,
   182–183
Minority rights and redistricting, 178–181
Missouri Democratic Party, 114–115
Missouri voting data, 83, 97 (n8)
Mobile payment solutions, 60
Mobility, 3, 59–60, 128–129, 152
Mobilization of voters. See Voter
   mobilization
Mondale, Walter, 203
Moore, Gwendolynne, 218
Morton, John, 143
MoveOn.org, 91, 98 (n28), 148–149, 235
Multivariate testing, 55–56
Murkowski, Lisa, 21, 26 (n17)
Murphy, Scott, 113

Murray, Patty, 109
Music in campaign ads, 32

Narrowcasting, 151–152, 234
National Association of Realtors, 125–126
National Health Interview Survey, 66–67
National party organizations:
   campaign finance deregulation and,
      165–166
   direct mail and microtargeting, 112–113
   leadership and strategies, 107–110
   media, traditional and new, 114–115
   online operations, 115
   party leaders, styles, and vision, 107–108
   party leadership and tactics, effectiveness on
      outcomes, 108
   strategy, importance of, 109–110
   structure, 105–106
   technologies, traditional and new, 111–115
   voter mobilization, 113–114
   See also Political parties
National Republican Congressional Committee
   (NRCC), 86, 107 (table), 161 (table), 165
National Republican Senatorial Committee
   (NRSC), 107 (table), 161 (table)
National Rifle Association (NRA), 126, 127, 152
National Women's Political Caucus (NWPC), 124
Necklines of women candidates, 200–201
Negative ads, 35, 45–46, 203
Neighborhood Team Leaders, 91–92, 96
Nelson, Terry, 83
New Hampshire, paid media in, 37–38
New media:
   about, 6, 230–233
   communications, maximizing effectiveness
      of, 55–56
   defined, 51
   direct mail, personalized, 61
   harnessing, 53–55
   integration of, 61–62
   online future, 60–62
   political parties and, 114–115
   rise of, 49–51
   voter role and, 56–57
   websites, campaign, 56, 62
   See also Social media
Newspapers, 139–141, 142, 143
New York redistricting, 186

"Next" (ad), 42–43
Niche markets, reaching, 24, 37–38
Nixon, Jay, 114–115
Nixon, Richard, 48, 141, 149–150
Nonverbal behavior, 202–203
North, Oliver, 17
North Carolina redistricting, 185–186
NRA. *See* National Rifle Association
NRCC. *See* National Republican
    Congressional Committee
NRSC. *See* National Republican Senatorial
    Committee
NWPC. *See* National Women's Political
    Caucus

Obama, Barack:
    campaign information distribution, 38
    e-mail campaign against, 147
    fundraising, 11, 17–18, 170, 217, 228, 232
    image, 229
    message testing, 55
    microtargeting, 218–219
    narrowcasting, 152
    new media, 49, 53, 54–55, 56–57, 214, 217
    paid media, 46 (n3)
    polling, 65, 74–75
    press coverage, 233
    social media, 52, 151, 215, 216
    traditional media, 114
    voter mobilization, 4, 7, 85, 87, 90, 91–92,
        96, 218–219
    women in campaign, 195
O'Donnell, Christine, 20
Online focus groups, 76
Online fundraising, 17–18, 52–53, 217–218,
    231–232
Online surveys, 71–73
Opponent surveillance, 149–150
Opt-in component of online polling, 72
Oropeza, Jenny, 220

PACs. *See* Political action committees
Paid media, 28–46
    about, 6, 28–29
    accomplishment and vision ads, 34–35,
        43–45
    advertising, cutting-edge changes in, 35–38
    audio, importance of, 32

biographical ads, 34, 41–42
campaign ads, writing, 31–32
case studies, 41–46
digital technology, 35–36
future of, 38
independent expenditures for, 39–40
interest groups and, 39
Internet and advertising, 37
issue ads, 34, 42–43
media consultants, role of, 30–31, 31 (box)
message development research, 32–34
negative ads, 35, 45–46
niche markets, reaching, 37–38
projective research, 33
quantitative and qualitative research, 33–34
smartphones, 38
television advertising, 29–30
video, importance of, 32
Palin, Sarah:
    campaign events, 14–15
    clothing, 200
    e-mails, release of, 138–139
    eyewear, 201
    McCain and, 203, 204
    press coverage, 141
    Saturday Night Live portrayal of, 195
    social media, 52
Panel back surveys, 33, 46 (n11)
Parties. *See* Political parties
Pataki, George, 223 (n23)
Patrick, Deval, 217–218, 219
Paul, Rand, 32, 75, 89
Paul, Ron, 18, 19
Payment solutions, mobile, 60
"Pay to Play" (ad), 45–46
Pennsylvania redistricting, 185
Perry, Rick, 117
Personalized direct mail, 61
Personal Precinct program, 49
Peterson, Dale, 37
Phone banks, 15–16
Phone conference calls, for focus groups, 76
Phone surveys:
    cell phone users, 66–69, 71, 78 (n12)
    future of, 69–71
    interactive voice response surveys, 73–74
    practices and problems, 66–69
    random digit dialing, 66, 68, 69, 71

Reid Senate campaign case study, 69–71
   voter files, 68–69
Photo ID, 95
Physical appearance of women candidates,
   198–201
Podcasts, 129
Political action committees (PACs), 16, 125,
   130–131, 132, 163–164, 173 (n4)
Political advertising, paid. *See* Paid media
Political boundaries and redistricting, 183
Political parties, 103–118
   about, 7–8, 103
   campaign finance changes, 110–111
   demographic change and, 115
   direct mail and microtargeting, 112–113
   future challenges, 115–116
   ideological polarization and, 104
   ideological purists and pragmatists,
      104–105
   media, traditional and new, 114–115
   national party organizations, leadership and
      strategies of, 107–110
   national party organizations, structure of,
      105–106
   national party organizations, traditional and
      new technologies, 111–115
   newspapers and, 140–141
   online operations, 115
   receipts, 107 (table), 161 (table)
   redistricting and, 116
   Service Party Model, 106, 107 (table)
   voter mobilization, 82, 113–114
Politico, 143–144
Polling, 65–78
   about, 6–7, 65–66, 230
   blended surveys, 74
   focus groups, 75–76
   image building and, 230
   interactive voice response surveys, 73–74
   as message development research, 33–34
   for message testing, 74–75, 76
   microtargeting and, 77
   online surveys, 71–73
   phone surveys, 66–71, 73–74, 78 (n12)
Pop-ups, 127
Potter, Trevor, 165–166
Pragmatists, ideological, 104–105
Precincts, underperforming, 84

Presidential campaigns, 65, 92, 157, 227
   See also specific candidates
Presidential debates, first televised, 48, 141,
   149–150
Press coverage. *See* Campaign press coverage
Projective research, 33
Prosumerism, 135–136
Public financing options, changes in, 168–172
Purists, ideological, 104–105

QR codes, 60, 61
Qualitative research, 34
Quantitative research, 33–34
Queen Bees, 197, 208 (n10)

Racial messages, and minority candidates,
   220–221
Radio, 85, 141
Ram, Kesha, 216
Random digit dialing (RDD), 66, 68, 69, 71
Rap radio stations, 85
Rather, Dan, 146
RDD. *See* Random digit dialing
Real ID Act (2005), 94
Reapportionment, 178
   See also Redistricting
Receipts, party, 107 (table), 161 (table)
Redistricting, 177–188
   about, 9, 177–178
   civil rights revolution and, 179–180
   Democratic Party and, 186, 190 (n21)
   elections (2012) and, 183–186
   equal population in, 182
   hacking, cracking, stacking, and tacking
      districts, 179
   implementation techniques, modern, 181
   Latinos, growing population of, 188
   migration patterns and, 183–184
   minority rights and, 178–181
   political parties and, 115
   political reasons for, 180–181
   principles of, 182–183
   Republican Party and, 184–186, 187,
      190 (n21)
   responsibility for, 182
   split control of, 186, 190 (n21)
   technology and, 187–188
   trends, current and future, 186–188

Red to Blue program, 108, 110, 111
Reid, Harry, 69–71, 81
Republican National Committee (RNC):
  leaders, 107–108
  media consultants and, 31 (box)
  online operations, 115
  receipts, 107 (table), 161 (table)
  structure, 105
  Team Leader program, 50
Republican Party:
  ideological purists, 104–105
  minority populations and, 116, 117
  polling, 65
  redistricting, 180, 184–186, 187, 190 (n21)
  STOMP program, 86, 113
  Young Guns program, 109–110, 111
  See also Tea Party; *specific candidates and
    party organizations*
Research, message development, 32–34
Restore Our Future, 165
Richardson, Laura, 220
RightChange, 130
RNC. *See* Republican National Committee
Roberts Court, 162–164
Robocalls, 73–74
Romney, Mitt, 15, 65, 141, 165
Rubio, Marco, 215
Ruffini, Patrick, 87, 91
Russell, Bill, 69, 73

Samaha, Omar, 43
Samaha, Reema, 43
Sandoval, Brian, 216
Saturday Night Live, 195
Schumer, Charles, 167, 168
Scott, Tim, 218
Security moms, 76
Selzer, Ann, 71
Service Party Model, 106, 107 (table)
Seventy-two-hour program, 86, 113
Sewell, Terri, 212, 218
Shaiko, Ronald, 105, 110
Shami, Farouk, 34, 41–42
Shaw v. Reno (1993), 180, 188
Sidarth, S. R., 149
Sierra Club, 126, 128, 135, 157
Smartphones, 38, 60, 96
  See also Cell phones

Social media:
  campaign press coverage, 151
  defined, 51–52
  fundraising and, 21–22, 59, 60
  impact of, 52
  interest groups and, 123, 129–130, 135
  minority candidates and, 214–216, 221
  mobile voters and, 59–60
  rise of, 58–59
  voter mobilization and, 90–91
  women voters and, 207
  See also New media
Soft money, 158–159
Software, in redistricting, 181
Sound bites, 139, 152, 153, 233–234
SpeechNow.org v. FEC (2010), 163
Square (mobile payment solutions
    provider), 60
Stacking districts, 179
State campaigns, cost of, 226
State legislature redistricting responsibility, 182
State-level initiatives for campaign finance
    reform, 171–172
Steele, Michael, 107–108
Stewart, Jon, 138–139
STOMP program. *See* Strategic Task Force to
    Organize and Mobilize People program
Strategic Task Force to Organize and Mobilize
    People (STOMP) program, 86, 113
Sullivan, Andrew, 145
Super PACs, 132, 163–164, 173 (n4)
Supreme Court, 162–164, 166–167
  See also specific cases
Surveillance, campaign, 149–150
Surveys:
  blended, 74
  interactive voice response, 73–74
  National Health Interview Survey, 66–67
  online, 71–73
  panel back, 33, 46 (n11)
  phone, 66–71, 73–74, 78 (n12)
  See also Polling
Swift Boat Veterans for Truth, 146–147, 237

Tablets, 38
Tacking districts, 179
"Taliban Dan" (ad), 123
Team Leader program, 50

Tea Party:
  blogs and, 148
  ideological purists and pragmatists, 105
  as interest group, 121–122, 131–132
  polling, 65
  voter mobilization, 89
  See also Republican Party
Tea Party Patriots, 130
Tears/crying, 195, 202
Telemarketing, 15–16
Telephone surveys. *See* Phone surveys
Television:
  cable, 37–38, 61–62, 114, 142–143
  decline of, 142–143
  minority candidate ads, 213–214
  new media and, 53–54
  paid media, 29–30
  presidential debates, first, 48, 141,
    149–150
  press coverage, origins and development of,
    141–142
  women candidates and, 198
  women voters and, 207
Testing, message, 55–56, 74–75, 76
Texas:
  minority population, 117
  redistricting, 184–185, 189 (n4)
Texting, 217
Thompson, Fred, 56, 152
Thornburg v. Gingles (1986), 180
Thurmond, Strom, 118 (n2)
Toomey, Patrick, 21, 55
Trackers, 57, 149
Tran, Van, 216–217
Trippi, Joe, 50, 57, 90
Tuck, Dick, 149–150
Tucker, Karen, 112
Turnout mail, 84–85
Twitter, 22, 58, 215
  See also Social media

Underperforming precincts, 84
Unions, labor, 125, 174 (n20)

Van Hollen, Chris, 108, 167, 168
Video:
  in campaign surveillance, 149
  famous examples of, 232

  in fundraising, 17, 18
  high-definition, 35–36
  importance of, 32
  power of, 56–57
  viral, 114–115
  of women candidates, 198
  See also New media
Viral videos, 114–115
Virginia Tech massacre, 42–43
Virtual zip codes, 96
Voice, 202–203
Volunteers, and new media, 53, 54–55
"Vote Different" (web video), 56–57
Voter files, 68–69
Voter mobilization, 81–97
  about, 4, 7, 81–82, 235–236
  citizen diversity and, 92
  cost of, 94–95
  door-to-door, 86–87
  early, absentee, and mail voting, 93
  future of, 95–97
  identification calls, 85–86
  information supply *versus* privacy
    concerns, 94
  minority, 218–219
  MoveOn.org ad for, 148–149
  online operations, 115
  photo ID and, 95
  political parties and, 82, 113–114
  presidential campaigns as party
    organizations, 92
  radio, 85
  relationships, building, 91–92
  social media and, 90–91
  technology and, 89–90
  traditional model, 82–87
  traditional model, merging with new
    variables, 88–89
  traditional voter contact, reinvigorating,
    93–94
  turnout mail, 84–85
  in twenty-first century, 87–90
  voter registration, 84
  voter registration lists, 84
  voting data, 83
  women, 204, 205 (figure), 206–207
Voter modeling, 112, 113
Voter registration, 84

Voter registration lists, 84
Voters. *See* Citizens
VoteVets.org, 133
Voting data, 83
Voting Rights Act, 180, 183, 222 (n4)

Wamp, Zach, 171
Wasserman Schultz, Debbie, 196–197
Webcasts, 129
Websites:
   campaign, 56, 62, 90, 214
   citizen group, 147–148
   interest group, 126–127, 136
Webster, Dan, 123
Web tool metrics, 51
Weiner, Anthony, 186
Wellstone, Paul, 17
Wesberry v. Sanders (1964), 182
West, Allen, 213, 215–216
Winston, David, 68, 76, 78 (n12)
Women and campaigns, 193–208
   about, 9, 193–194
   "brains *versus* beauty" battle, 198–204
   family as props in ads, 204
   future of, 207–208
   kisses, hugs, and handshakes, 203–204

nonverbal behavior, 202–203
physical appearance, 198–201
voter mobilization of women, 204, 205
   (figure), 206–207
voter turnout of women, 204, 205
   (figure), 206
women and media presence, 196–197
women as campaign consultants, 195–196
women candidates, increase in, 196, 208 (n5)
women candidates, perennial questions
   concerning, 194–195
women in campaigns, growing presence of,
   195–197
women judged differently than men, 198
women voters, 197
Wright, Isaac, 114–115
W Spann LLC, 165

Yang, Fred, 68, 73, 74, 76
Yellowtail, Bill, 159
"Yes We Can" (video), 57
Young Guns program, 109–110, 111
YouTube, 90, 195, 215–216, 232
   See also Social media; Video

Zip codes, virtual, 96

⑤SAGE research**methods**
The Essential Online Tool for Researchers

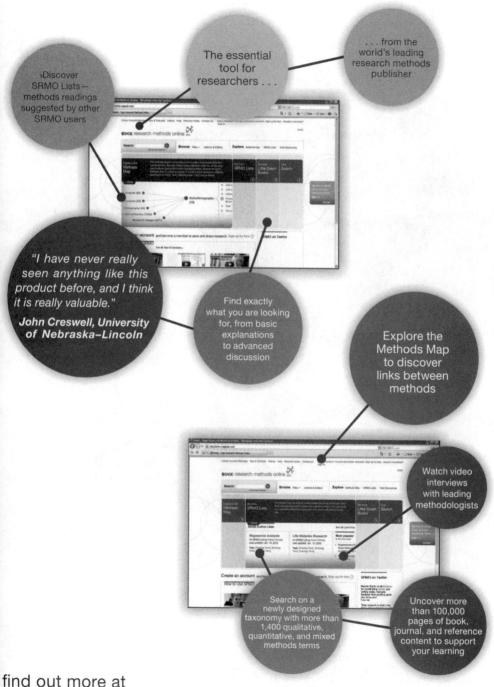

...from the world's leading research methods publisher

The essential tool for researchers . . .

Discover SRMO Lists— methods readings suggested by other SRMO users

"I have never really seen anything like this product before, and I think it is really valuable."

John Creswell, University of Nebraska–Lincoln

Find exactly what you are looking for, from basic explanations to advanced discussion

Explore the Methods Map to discover links between methods

Watch video interviews with leading methodologists

Search on a newly designed taxonomy with more than 1,400 qualitative, quantitative, and mixed methods terms

Uncover more than 100,000 pages of book, journal, and reference content to support your learning

find out more at
srmo.sagepub.com